D0743858

MANCHURIAN RAILWAYS
and the
OPENING OF CHINA

A publication of the Northeast Asia Seminar

Rediscovering Russia in Asia
Siberia and the Russian Far East
Edited by Stephen Kotkin and David Wolff

Mongolia in the Twentieth Century
Landlocked Cosmopolitan
Edited by Stephen Kotkin and Bruce A. Elleman

Korea at the Center
Dynamics of Regionalism in Northeast Asia
Edited by Charles K. Armstrong, Gilbert Rozman,
Samuel S. Kim, and Stephen Kotkin

**Manchurian Railways and
the Opening of China**
An International History
Edited by Bruce A. Elleman and Stephen Kotkin

MANCHURIAN RAILWAYS

and the

OPENING OF CHINA

An International History

Edited by

Bruce A. Elleman and Stephen Kotkin

M.E.Sharpe

Armonk, New York
London, England

Library of Congress Cataloging-in-Publication Data

Manchurian railways and the opening of China : an international history / [edited] by Bruce A.
Elleman and Stephen Kotkin.
    p. cm.
Includes bibliographical references and index.
    ISBN 978-0-7656-2514-4 (cloth : alk. paper) — ISBN 978-0-7656-2515-1 (pbk. : alk. paper)
    1. Railroads—China—Manchuria—History—20th century. 2. Manchuria (China)—History—
20th century. 3. China—Economic conditions—20th century. I. Elleman, Bruce A., 1959- II.
Kotkin, Stephen.
  HE3289.M3M36 2009
  385.0951'8—dc22
                                              2009020607

For Serge Kassatkin (1917–2007), UC Berkeley Professor:
Harbin émigré, expert on M[...]
and beloved [...]

Contents

About the Editors and Contributors

Chang Jui-te is Professor of History at Chinese Culture University and Adjunct Researcher at the Institute of Modern History, Academia Sinica, Taipei. His main publications include *Ping-Han tielu yu Hanbei di jingji fazhan, 1905–1937* (*The Peking-Hankow Railroad and Economic Development in north China, 1905–1937* (Taipei: Academia Sinica, 1987); *Zhongguo jindai tielu shiye guanli di yanjiu: zhengzhi cengmian di fenxi, 1876–1937* (*Railroads in Modern China: Political Aspects of Railroad Administration, 1876–1937*) (Taipei: Academia Sinica, 1991); and *Kangzhan shiqi di guojun renshi* (*Anatomy of the Nationalist Army, 1937–1945*) (Taipei: Academia Sinica, 1993).

Bruce A. Elleman is a Research Professor in the Maritime History Department, Center for Naval Warfare Studies, at the US Naval War College, and author of *Diplomacy and Deception: The Secret History of Sino-Soviet Diplomatic Relations, 1917–1927* (M.E. Sharpe, 1997); *Modern Chinese Warfare, 1795–1989* (Routledge, 2001, translated into Chinese); *Japanese-American Civilian Prisoner Exchanges and Detention Camps, 1941–45* (London: Routledge, 2006); and *Moscow and the Emergence of Communist Power in China, 1925–30: The Nanchang Uprising and the Birth of the Red Army* (London: Routledge, 2009).

Elisabeth Köll is an Associate Professor in the Entrepreneurial Management unit at the Harvard Business School. She is author of *From Cotton Mill to Business Enterprise: The Emergence of Regional Enterprises in Modern China* (Harvard University Asia Center, 2003) and various articles. Her current book project involves a multi-faceted analysis of how railroads as new technology and infrastructure contributed to China's economic and social transformation from 1895 to the present.

Stephen Kotkin is Rosengarten Professor of Modern and Contemporary History at Princeton University, where he is also a Professor of International Affairs in the Woodrow Wilson School for policy, and has authored, co-authored, or co-edited twelve books, including most recently *Uncivil Society: 1989 and the Implosion of the Communist Establishment*, with a contribution by Jan Gross (New York: Random House, 2009).

Y. Tak Matsusaka is an Associate Professor in the History Department at Wellesley College. He is the author of *The Making of Japanese Manchuria, 1904–1932* (Harvard University Asia Center, 2001) and various articles. His current research explores the relationship between armament, imperialism, and domestic politics, with an emphasis on popular nationalism, in Meiji and Taishô Japan.

S.C.M. Paine is a Professor in the Strategy and Policy Department at the US Naval War College and author of *Imperial Rivals: China, Russia and Their Disputed Frontiers* (M.E. Sharpe, 1996) and *The Sino-Japanese War of 1894–1895: Perceptions, Power and Primacy* (Cambridge, 2002); and co-editor with Bruce A. Elleman of *Naval Blockades and Seapower: Strategies and Counter-strategies, 1805–2005* (London: Routledge, 2006), and *Naval Coalition Warfare: From the Napoleonic War to Operation Iraqi Freedom* (London: Routledge, 2008). Current research interests include a book project on Japan, Russia, the United States and the Long Chinese Civil War.

Felix Patrikeeff is Lecturer in the Department of Politics at Adelaide University, Australia, and author of *Mouldering Pearl: Hong Kong at the Crossroads* (London: George Phillip, 1989); *Russian Politics in Exile: The Northeast Asian Balance of Power, 1924–1931* (New York: Palgrave, 2002); and *Railways in the Russo-Japanese War: Transporting War*, with Harold Shukman (New York: Routledge, 2007).

Harold M. Tanner is an Associate Professor in the Department of History at the University of North Texas and author of *Strike Hard! Anti-Crime Campaigns and the Chinese Criminal Justice System* (Cornell East Asia Series, 1999); *China: A History* (Hackett Publishing, 2009); and articles on Chinese criminal justice and military history. He is currently working on two book projects concerning the Chinese civil war in Manchuria.

Zhang Shengfa is a Professor at the Institute of Russian, Eastern European and Central Asian Studies, Chinese Academy of Social Sciences. He was a visiting scholar at the Center of International Studies of Princeton University in 2003, and at the Saint-Petersburg State University in 2005–2006. He is author of *Sidalin yu lengzhan* (Stalin and the Cold War, Beijing: China Press of Social Sciences, 2000, 2007[2-ed.]; Taiwan: Shuxing Press, 2000); and coauthor of *Suweiai wenhua yu Suweiai ren* (Soviet Culture and Soviet People, HangZhou: Zhejiang People Press, 1991; Taiwan: Shuxing Press, 1991); and editor of *Sulian lishi dangan xuanbian* (Collection of Historical Archives of Soviet Union, Vols. 17, 18, 19, out of 40 Volumes, Beijing: Chinese Press of Social Literature, 2002). His recent publication is *Ershi shiji dongxifang guanxishi* (A History of East-West Relations in the Twentieth Century—forthcoming).

Acknowledgments

Our thanks to Robert Bickers, University of Bristol, UK, for permission to use the cover photograph from the Historical Photographs of China Collection, and to Helen Sanders, Taylor and Francis Books, for permission to reprint the "The Trans Siberian Railway 1891–1917" map from Martin Gilbert's *Atlas of Russian History*.

Patricia Kolb of M.E. Sharpe has maintained a strong interest in our series over many years. Along with the able Maki Parsons and Ana Erlic at M.E. Sharpe, Pat provided invaluable editorial assistance on the current volume.

Finally, the editors would like to thank their spouses, Sarah C.M. Paine (Elleman) and Soyoung Lee (Kotkin), for their support.

Preface

Stephen Kotkin

The Chinese Eastern Railway (CER), completed at the dawn of the twentieth century through what was then known as Manchuria, helped link the Far East and Central Europe. The CER did so as a strategic southerly shortcut for Russia's Trans-Siberian Railroad, which was first opened around the same time across more than 6,000 miles. The 1,700-mile CER connected Chita, in Siberia, to Vladivostok, in the Russian Far East, via Harbin, in Chinese territory. This was a region of China that had never before been accessible by train. A separate 500-mile spur off the CER, eventually known as the South Manchuria Railway (SMR), was built from Harbin southwards to the ice-free deep-water port of Lüshun (Port Arthur), envisioned as a northern Hong Kong, as well as to Dalian, on the Liaodong Peninsula. The Russian-owned railways through Chinese territory had been agreed in secret, in the wake of China's defeat in the Sino-Japanese War (1894–95), as China sought a possible counterweight to imperialist Japan and Russia sought its own imperialist gains. It turned out to be a fateful step, with consequences well beyond what anyone envisioned at the time. The introduction of Russian-controlled railroads in China helped provoke the Russo-Japanese War of 1904–5. More broadly, the Manchurian railways helped set the stage for the second Sino-Japanese War, part of World War II in the Pacific (1937–45). Small wonder, then, that the great scholar of Northeast Asia, George Lensen, dubbed these railroads "the damned inheritance."[1] For China, however, the Manchurian railroads contributed to the process of opening the country up to the world and to itself.

The international as well as national aspects of the CER and the SMR form the subject of the present volume, the latest in the Northeast Asia series that I founded with David Wolff and have continued with Bruce Elleman. The series began with *Rediscovering Russia in Asia: Siberia and the Russian Far East* (1995), followed by *Mongolia in the Twentieth Century: Landlocked Cosmopolitan* (1999), and *Korea at the Center: Dynamics of Regionalism in Northeast Asia* (2005). The present compilation differs from the previous three in that it was not based upon a scholarly conference. But it shares the longstanding series aim, which is to engage in analysis that goes beyond exclusively national frameworks, while joining the often separated study of Asia and of Russia.

Global or international history has lately flourished, but in our view it could be more regionally grounded. Manchuria long occupied a central place at the intersection of China, the Korean peninsula, Mongolia, and Russia, as well as in Japan's forays on the Asian mainland. True, Manchuria's rail lines may not be as infamous as the Burma Death Railway, which was built by slave labor during World War II in Japanese-controlled southeast Asia, but few objects in the world have been more at the vortex of intense political and military rivalries than these infrastructure projects in northern China. Luxury and romance were the stuff of the Orient Express, whose sumptuous coaches originally ran from Paris via Vienna to Istanbul. The CER was destined to carry troops and materiel.

Back and forth the Manchurian lines went. Russia lost the South Manchuria Railway (from Changchun to Lüshun) and the Liaodong peninsula to Japan as a result of the Russo-Japanese War. During a good part of Russia's civil war in the Far East theater (1918–24), the Chinese Eastern Railroad was administered by an American, the former chief engineer of the Panama Canal, as part of an Inter-Allied Commission meant to stave off a Japanese seizure. By 1923, the Chinese had assumed *de facto* control, assisted by many émigré Russians (whom the Soviet authorities dubbed the "Whites," or anti-Bolsheviks). From 1924, however, the Soviet Union and China administered the CER jointly, while Japan maintained sway over the SMR. In 1929, the Chinese seized the CER outright, but the Soviets intervened militarily to re-establish joint administration—a forcible re-possession the Japanese supported, mindful of their own claims to the SMR. That Tokyo could side with its arch enemy, Moscow, indicated the depth of China's dilemma.

Sure enough, in 1931, the Japanese army staged a violent incident in Manchuria that led the following year to the region's separation from China as Manchukuo, a Japanese-sponsored puppet state. Three years later, the Soviets sold their rights in the CER for a fraction of their worth to Manchukuo, in order to deny Japan a pretext to stage another such incident and provoke war with the USSR. War came anyway, of course, but in a manner that would prove advantageous to the Soviets. With the shattering defeat of Japan in World War II, the CER in 1945 again came under the joint control of the Soviet Union and China; the Soviets also re-occupied the Liaodong Peninsula and established joint control with China over the SMR. The CER and SMR were merged into the "Chinese Changchun Railway." Following the 1949 Communist victory in China's civil war, the Soviet Union (on 31 December 1952) transferred the Chinese Changchun Railway to the People's Republic of China. Part of the price was Mao's acceptance of Chiang Kai-shek's reluctant recognition of Outer Mongolia's independence back in 1946.[2]

China's victorious Communists inherited a railroad network roughly equal to that of the United States a century earlier, and of Russia back in 1878. Simply put, China had come late to the great railway age. Still, the latter was not very old when the first tracks of the Chinese Eastern Railroad were laid in 1898. It had been only in the 1850s, in a mania of construction, that Great Britain was internally connected by a national rail network—more than 6,000 miles of track by mid-century, joining all the country's major cities and ports. Before the turn of the twentieth century, total British track leapt to more than 21,000 miles, while the number of annual rail passengers grew from 73 million to more than 1 billion. In 1869, America's Pacific Railroad, subsequently dubbed the First Transcontinental Railroad, completed the linkage between the eastern and western seaboards. Construction had been launched in 1862, under President Lincoln, as a way to unite the states during the civil war. U.S. railway mileage, which had been 10,000 in 1850, reached nearly 200,000 in 1900. The Iron Horse was a technological marvel, never mind who was in the way. In China, however, railroad construction was resisted because of its association with foreign imposition.

To be sure, not just the CER but many rail projects of the late nineteenth and early twentieth centuries were linked to imperialism. The Cape-to-Cairo Railway was initiated in the late nineteenth century to connect contiguous African possessions of the British Empire from South Africa to Egypt. France developed a rival scheme in the late 1890s to link its African colonies west to east, and the Portuguese toyed with ideas of erecting rail lines to buttress their African claims. Much of the British south-north project, however, was actually built, although the Cape-to-Cairo line remains unfinished, lacking a major section from Sudan to Uganda. Outside Africa, the Baghdad Railway, launched under German auspices in 1903, was designed to connect the Ottoman Empire cities of Konya and Baghdad. Because German companies had already built an Anatolian Railway from Istanbul to Konya, the proposed extension would have joined Berlin and Baghdad, site of oil fields and onward linkages to ports on the Persian Gulf. Following interruption by World War I, construction was completed in 1940, long after the Ottoman Empire and Wilhelmine Germany were gone.

What imperialism started, in short, others could finish. For the Chinese, the Manchurian rails, which had been built under conditions of national humiliation, became drivers of national integration, before emerging as a key to victory in the civil war between the Nationalists and the Communists. In other words, ours is a story of competing imperialisms, followed by competing Chinese nationalisms.

In the essays contained herein, strategic aspects and diplomatic wrangling predominate, but commercial interests are kept in mind too. Each of the protagonists used the railways to sponsor economic development. Deng Xiaoping's shift toward market economics and global integration in the 1980s and 90s put Chinese railways at the forefront of the country's multidecade double-digit economic growth, including China's recent "Open Up the West" campaign. These days, the old

Manchurian lines continue to carry massive freight, including shipments of Siberian oil to China (in the absence of promised but still unbuilt eastward-flowing oil pipelines). In sum, even as they provide a means to help integrate China, the railways may be opening up to a new era of internationalism, so far, at least, much more peaceful. And yet, given the scope of China's ongoing rise, as well as Russia's demographic weakness, Japan's system gridlock, the Korean peninsula's division, volatile natural resource considerations, and lingering territorial disputes, Northeast Asia's geopolitics remain unpredictable.

Notes

1. George Alexander Lensen, *The Damned Inheritance:The Soviet Union and the Manchurian Crises, 1924–1935* (Tallahassee, FL: The Diplomatic Press, 1974).

2. Dieter Heinzig, The *Soviet Union and Communist China, 1945–1950: The Arduous Road to Alliance* (Armonk, NY: M.E. Sharpe, 2004), 146; Sergey Radchenko, "New Documents on Mongolia and the Cold War," *Cold War International History Project Bulletin*, 16 (2008): 341–98.

Maps

Map of Trans-Siberian Railway, 1891–1917

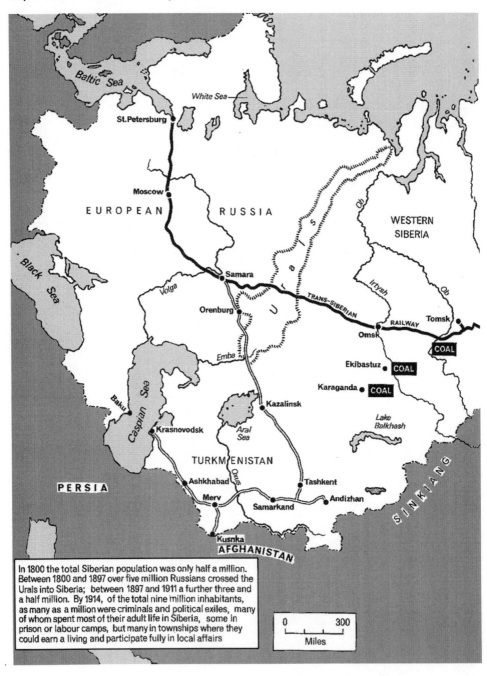

In 1800 the total Siberian population was only half a million. Between 1800 and 1897 over five million Russians crossed the Urals into Siberia; between 1897 and 1911 a further three and a half million. By 1914, of the total nine million inhabitants, as many as a million were criminals and political exiles, many of whom spent most of their adult life in Siberia, some in prison or labour camps, but many in townships where they could earn a living and participate fully in local affairs

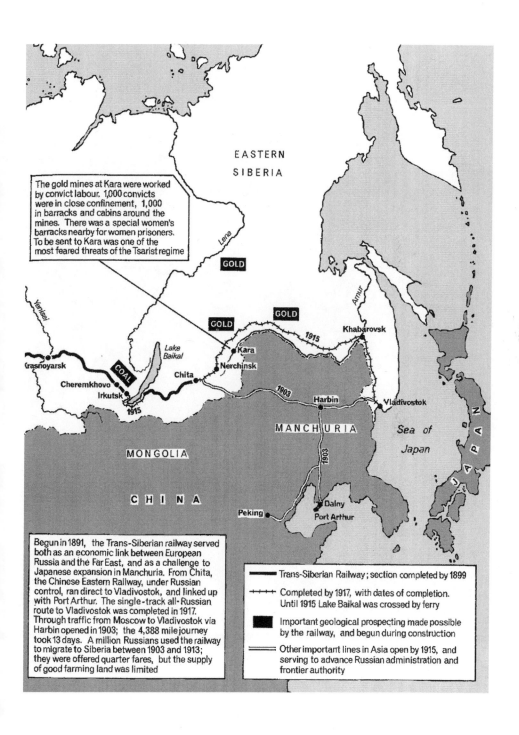

EASTERN
SIBERIA

The gold mines at Kara were worked
by convict labour. 1,000 convicts
were in close confinement, 1,000
in barracks and cabins around the
mines. There was a special women's
barracks nearby for women prisoners.
To be sent to Kara was one of the
most feared threats of the Tsarist regime

Lena

GOLD

Yenisei

GOLD

GOLD

1915

Khabarovsk

Amur

Krasnoyarsk

Lake
Baikal

Kara

COAL

Cheremkhovo

Nerchinsk

Chita

Irkutsk

1903

Harbin

Vladivostok

1915

MANCHURIA

Sea of
Japan

MONGOLIA

1903

J A P A N

C H I N A

Peking

Dalny
Port Arthur

Begun in 1891, the Trans-Siberian railway served
both as an economic link between European
Russia and the Far East, and as a challenge to
Japanese expansion in Manchuria. From Chita,
the Chinese Eastern Railway, under Russian
control, ran direct to Vladivostok, and linked up
with Port Arthur. The single-track all-Russian
route to Vladivostok was completed in 1917.
Through traffic from Moscow to Vladivostok via
Harbin opened in 1903; the 4,388 mile journey
took 13 days. A million Russians used the railway
to migrate to Siberia between 1903 and 1913;
they were offered quarter fares, but the supply
of good farming land was limited

—————— Trans-Siberian Railway; section completed by 1899

++++++ Completed by 1917, with dates of completion.
Until 1915 Lake Baikal was crossed by ferry

■ Important geological prospecting made possible
by the railway, and begun during construction

═══════ Other important lines in Asia open by 1915, and
serving to advance Russian administration and
frontier authority

Manchurian Railways

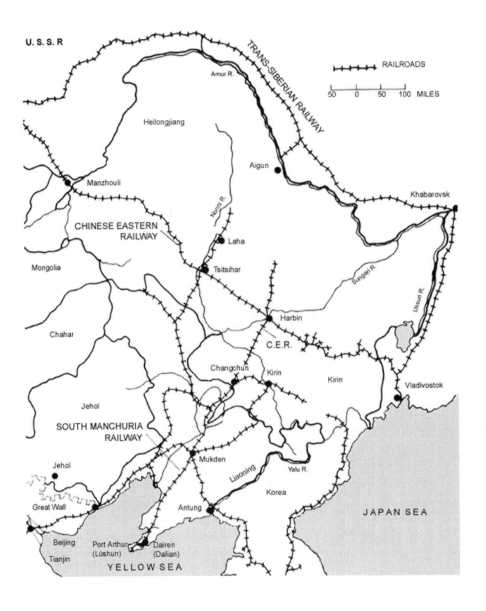

MANCHURIAN RAILWAYS

and the

OPENING OF CHINA

Introduction

Bruce A. Elleman, Elisabeth Köll, and *Y. Tak Matsusaka*

> There are in Manchuria three lots of railway lines. First, certain Chinese Government-owned railways. . . . [Second] Concerning the Chinese Eastern Railway it needs to be remembered that physically and economically it is not an independent railway unit: it is a link in the one and only direct railway route from Europe, across Siberia, to the Asiatic ports of the Pacific Ocean. [Third] Concerning the South Manchuria line it needs to be remembered that it is the link between the Trans-Siberian line and the ports and territories of China and Japan. These lines, therefore, no matter who built them or who owns them or who administers them, are not exclusively of Chinese, exclusively of Russian or exclusively of Japanese concern. They were born in and of international politics. They serve not alone the people or the purpose of any one country. They are "public carriers" in a much broader sense than that which is usually connoted by that expression. One war has already been fought because of them,--a war very expensive to the two belligerents and to the country upon whose soil it was fought.
>
> —Stanley K. Hornbeck, the Chief of the Division of Far Eastern Affairs, Department of State, commenting on the ongoing Sino-Soviet railway conflict during a 27 August 1929 address to the Williamstown Institute of Politics.[1]

Compared to railroad systems in Western Europe, Russia, the United States, India, and Japan, the Chinese railway network emerged relatively late during the nineteenth century with a mix of colonial, state-sponsored, and private lines. Chinese railway history began in 1875 with the building of a ten-mile track between Shanghai and Wusong by the British. This occurred without permission from the Chinese government, which purchased the line in 1877 and demolished it, fearing foreign control through this means of transportation.

The government's apprehension and general conservatism prevented any serious railroad development, with the exception of some short tracks for mining purposes, for most of the rest of the nineteenth century. By 1894, only 195 miles of track had been built in China proper. China's loss of the war to Japan in 1895 not only triggered efforts for promoting indigenous industrialization but also gave new impetus to railroad construction.[2] Most railroads started out as direct foreign investment in the form of companies controlled by British, Belgian, French, and German syndicates. Between 1895—when only 255 miles of railroad lines existed—and 1911, about 5,500 miles of new track were laid in China.[3]

The manifestation of foreign presence led to an increasingly nationalist reaction by the Chinese public, sparking the Railway Rights Recovery Movement in 1911, which indirectly led to the collapse of the Qing dynasty.[4] Railway construction continued unabated under the Republican government, rising to about 8,700 miles in 1927 and 13,500 miles in 1937.[5] However, China in 1937 still had only about the same amount of railway track as England had in 1871.[6]

Despite increasing trade and industrial production, improved business legislation and better access to financial capital in the early Republican period, the fragmented political situation under warlord regimes and competing political authorities meant that only 8,000 miles of new tracks were built in the twenty-five years between 1911 and 1937. Nevertheless, the expansion of the railroad network, in combination with other more traditional transportation methods, created growing cargo traffic, in particular coal, and passenger transportation, as well as stimulating trade, the introduction of more productive cropping patterns, and industrialization in new parts of the country.[7] For all of these reasons, "railway power" was one of the most important elements in China's early twentieth century development.

*   *   *

"Railway power" of the kind that took root in China in late 1890s consisted of two basic components. The military applications of rail technology formed the first and foremost component. By the time that competing Great Powers launched the first major spate of railway initiatives in China following the Sino-Japanese War (1894–95), western military organizations had accumulated a substantial body of experience in the use of track and locomotives in war.

Applied in a series of conflicts between 1859 and 1871, the new transportation technology transformed the prevailing U.S. and European assumptions of nineteenth century warfare, not only increasing the strategic and tactical mobility of ground forces, but vastly expanding the size of front-line armies that could be deployed and sustained. Railways introduced a new level of firepower on the battlefield, enabling the use of weapons once restricted to warships and fixed fortifications. Rapid and flexible deployment, moreover, offered the possibility of significant economies in overall troop strength, permitting greater strategic coverage with fewer units.

By the late nineteenth century, strategic planners had incorporated railway projects into their ledgers of military balance, assigning them no less importance in the international arms race than infantry divisions and armored warships. Staff officers well trained in railway logistics understood the configuration and capacity of a railway network, one's own as well as those of one's adversaries, as defining points of potential troop concentration, the rate of deployment to those points, as well as the maximum size of an army that could be supplied.

Military planners, accordingly, paid serious attention to the construction and counter-construction of strategic transportation systems, hardwiring battlefields, lines of march, and supply routes for future wars. A quintessential "dual-use" technology, the railway paid for itself as a commercial venture in peacetime, but was always ready for conversion into a vital military installation in the event of war.[8]

The second component of railway power stemmed from its economic uses. Late nineteenth century businessmen, politicians, and public intellectuals waxed enthusiastic about the transformative impact of the railway on the economic environment, as acknowledged in the epithet "engine of development." The translation of its effects on economic activity into a source of power, however, rested on the susceptibility of this technology to fine administrative control by a relatively small bureaucratic organization, whether public or private.

Under the right circumstances, control of a railway offered the possibility of directing the course of a regional economy. Railway management provided numerous administrative levers over economic activity, but routing decisions and the ability to set rates counted among the most effective and far-reaching. Routing decisions could determine patterns of settlement, land use, and access to a wide range of natural resources. They could also dictate, intentionally or not, which localities would prosper and which would decline.

Rail connections would reshape relations between communities and the integration of markets as well as the flows of people, knowledge, and culture. Rates could well determine what local farmers and manufacturers could profitably produce and merchants, market. They could also encourage the distribution of some goods while discouraging others, direct flows to certain areas and away from others, or selectively favor certain trade routes, market towns, and manufacturing centers.[9]

A railway agency or company could wield enormous economic power in proportion to the dependence of a region on its services. Railway companies with monopoly rights in its service territory or "catchment" area, an arrangement often demanded by builders based on the high fixed capital cost and long-term horizons entailed in railway investment as well as the purportedly destructive nature of railway competition, could enforce a high degree of dependency.

Traditional overland transport or waterways, where available, might provide some alternatives for certain categories of goods, but to the extent that modern market capitalism came to pervade the regional economy, the speed and security of rail transport offered too many advantages for other modes to remain fully viable. For example, in southern Manchuria of the early twentieth century, the freight charges for shipping soybeans from the market center of Fengtian to the seaport of Yingkou were lower for river than for rail transport. The speed of rail transport, however, decreased the turnaround time for a merchant's working capital and its security reduced the effective costs of insurance. The railway also provided regular, year-round service and permitted shippers to move their beans at times of optimum market prices.[10]

In "frontier" lands undergoing rapid settlement, such as the western United States or China's Northeast, monopoly railways wielded extraordinary power, functioning in some areas, as full-blown "development agencies."[11] To be sure, such economic power might be used wisely or unwisely and result in good or ill, but insofar as it represented a form of power, it became subject to contest and, accordingly, generated politics. Private railway companies with monopoly rights frequently found themselves at the center of political conflict, cast, for example, as the principal villains in the populist narratives of railway "barons" against the "little people." The term "baron" invokes a feudal metaphor, and indeed, many critics of unrestrained railway power saw company owners and managers as lords answerable to none, exercising proprietary rule over large territories, and squeezing their "peasants" to the limit by way of oppressive rates.[12]

Viewed in this light, railway power, with its administrative control over economic life and its capabilities as an instrument of war, would seem to have been made to order as a "tool of empire." Indeed, one group of historians has even coined the term "railway imperialism" to describe its empire-building applications.[13] Perhaps nowhere in East Asia did this term apply more aptly than in Manchuria, where foreign-dominated railways helped set the conditions for the region's political, economic, and social growth.

*   *   *

"Railway imperialism" was crucial to Manchuria. The new imperialist technology quickly made itself indispensable in colonial lands, particularly those acquired in the great scramble of the late nineteenth century, where networks of track served to transform claims demarcated on maps drawn in the capitals of Europe into realities of possession on the ground. Railways extended the power of the colonizer beyond coastal enclaves into the interior, making both military and commercial access economically feasible for the first time in many cases. Harnessed as engines of development and coupled to the new management approach of "scientific colonization," they even promised the transformation of initially disappointing acquisitions into something of value to the mother country.[14]

The lack of formal rights of territorial possession did little to hamper the capacity of this technology to create colonial realities out of diplomatic fiction. Indeed, it could do so in contravention of internationally recognized claims of sovereignty and contest, on the ground, control of territory conceded in the arena of high diplomacy.[15] Diplomats could, moreover, reconcile such encroachments with international agreements and extend legal protection to these activities so long as they proceeded under the formal guise of legitimate business enterprise.

The dynamics of railway imperialism contrast sharply with the nation-building role commonly attributed to the railway. Colorful images abound of iron rails as the bones and sinews of the nation, or in the particular case of Italy, a means of "sewing up the Italian boot."[16] Railways made a vital contribution to integrating emerging political economies. They reduced the political and cultural alienation of distance, erased natural barriers and the historic insularity they nurtured, and made possible, for the first time, the creation of a "national village."

Culture also flowed along these lines of rapid communication, becoming increasingly homogenized or hybridized as news, fashion, and common consumer goods spread throughout the network.[17] Railways greatly accelerated the process of "imagining the nation" that the print revolution and the great vernacular literary movements had started.[18] German nationalists, well aware of these possibilities, regarded railway and customs unions among the states of Central Europe as the first step toward the building of a unified Germany.[19]

The power of the railway as an imperial instrument is often obscured by the analytical categories of "formal" (colonial) and "informal" (non-colonial) empire when applied too rigidly or loaded with additional meaning, such as the equation of the latter with the "imperialism of free trade."[20] Railway imperialism, when practiced in countries like China that retained nominal sovereignty, must be considered, by definition, "informal." Yet such a classification misleads insofar as it implies equivalence between foreign railway operations and, say, the foreign management of textile mills in the treaty ports and emphasizes differences primarily in the quantity of investment. It also misleads by erecting a high wall that separates formal colonial rule from the quality of territorial control potentially exercised by monopoly railway companies. Railway power created "gray areas" of sovereignty in which territorial rule was continually contested and where the often problematic term "quasi-colonial" fits quite well. This book will attempt to explore these "gray areas" in China's northeastern provinces, otherwise known as Manchuria— simultaneously a "bridge" and a "moat" responsible for connecting Northeast China to Mongolia in the West, Siberia in the North, and Korea in the East.

Notes

1. Tokyo, Japan, Japanese Foreign Ministry Archives (Gaimusyo), File F 192.5-4-7.

2. On the role of government in promoting industrial enterprises after 1895 see Elisabeth Köll, *From Cotton Mill to Business Empire*: *The Emergence of Regional Enterprise in Modern China* (Cambridge: Harvard University Asia Center, 2003), chapter 2.

3. Ralph W. Huenemann, *The Dragon and the Iron Horse: The Economics of Railroads in China, 1876–1937* (Cambridge, MA: Harvard University Press, 1984), 76–77. However, by 1911 Chinese government lines still occupied only 5 percent of China's total track mileage, with colonial concessions owning 42 percent and financial concessions owning 45 percent of the mileage. Ibid., 78.

4. For a discussion of Chinese nationalism and railroads see, for example, Joseph Esherick, *Reform and Revolution in China:The 1911 Revolution in Hunan and Hubei* (Berkeley: University of California Press, 1976); Lee En-Han, *China's Quest for Railroad Autonomy, 1904–1911: A Study of the Chinese Railway-rights Recovery Movement* (Singapore: Singapore University Press, 1977).

5. Huenemann, 76–77. See also Cheng Lin, *The Chinese Railways: A Historical Survey* (Shanghai: China United Press, 1935), 18.

6. Simon Ville, "Transport," in *The Cambridge History of Modern Britain: Industrialisation, 1700–1860*, edited by Roderick Floud and Paul Johnson, (Cambridge: Cambridge University Press, 2004), 295–331.

7. Thomas Rawski, *Economic Growth in Prewar China* (Berkeley: University of California Press, 1989), 208–212.

8. A useful overview of the military history of railways may be found in Edwin A. Pratt, *The Rise of Rail-Power in War and Conquest, 1833–1914* (Philadelphia: J.P. Lippincott Co., 1916); an early Japanese army study of the military uses of the railway is Sanbō honbu [Army General Staff], *Tetsudō ron* (1888), reproduced in *Sanbō honbu tetsudō ronshū*, ed. Noda Masaho, Harada Katsumasa, Aoki Eiichi, Oikawa Yoshinobu (Tokyo: Nihon keizai hyōronsha, 1988).

9. For a sampling of the literature of railways and economic development, see T.R. Gourvish, *Railways and the British Economy, 1830–1914* (London: Macmillan, 1980); Alfred Dupont Chandler, *The Visible Hand: The Managerial Revolution in American Business* (Cambridge, MA: Belknap Press, 1977), 79–205; a skeptical view is offered in Robert W. Fogel, *Railroads and American Economic Growth: Essays in Econometric History* (Baltimore, MD: Johns Hopkins Press, 1964). Administrative control over economic activity is one of the central themes in Chandler, *The Visible Hand*; he regards railway management as one pioneering enterprises in this regard.

10. Minami Manshū tetsudō kabushikigaisha chōsaka (Ueda Kenzo), *Ryōga no sui'un*, Dairen: SMR, 1911. Also see Y. Tak Matsusaka, *The Making of Japanese Manchuria, 1904–1932* (Cambridge, MA: Harvard Asia Center, 2001), 127–33.

11. Such "development agencies" were crucial to the building of the Atchison, Topeka, and Santa Fe railway in the 1870s. On railways and the development of the Western United States, see Arthur Johnson and Barry Supple, *Boston Capitalists and Western Railroads* (Cambridge, MA: Harvard University Press, 1967), esp. 293–98 for the case of the Atchison.

12. On the politics of railway power, see Austin Kerr, *Railroad Politics, 1914–1920: Rates, Wages and Efficiency* (Pittsburgh: University of Pittsburgh Press, 1968); Lee Benson, *Merchants, Farmers and Railroads: Railroad Regulation and New York Politics, 1850–1887* (New York: Russell and Russell, 1969); Lloyd J. Mercer, *Railroads and Land Grant Policy: A Study in Government Intervention* (New York: Academic Press, 1982); Steven J. Ericson, *The Sound of the Whistle: Railroads and the State in Meiji Japan* (Cambridge, MA: Council on East Asian Studies, Harvard University, 1996).

13. "Tool of empire" from Daniel Headrick, *The Tools of Empire: Technology and European Imperialism in the Nineteenth Century* (New York: Oxford University Press, 1981); Clarence B. Davis and Kenneth E. Wilburn Jr., eds., *Railway Imperialism* (New York: Greenwood Press, 1991).

14. A good overview of the use of railways in empire-building may be found in Raymond Betts, *Uncertain Dimensions: Western Overseas Empires in the Twentieth Century* (Minneapolis: University of Minnesota Press, 1985), 77–90. On Japanese perceptions of the colonial uses of railways, Nagao Sakurō, *Shokuminchi tetsudō no sekai keizaiteki oyobi sekai seisakuteki kenkyū* (Tokyo: Nihon hyōronsha, 1930).

15. "In these decades of imperialism," writes Ian Nish, "railways were a means of one country expanding its territory." Ian Nish, *Origins of the Russo-Japanese War* (New York: Longman, 1985), 18.

16. Steven J. Ericson, "The Engine of Change: Railroads and Society in Meiji Japan," *KSU Economic and Business Review*, No. 21 (May 1994): 37–60, 55.

17. Ericson, *The Sound of the Whistle*, 92–94.

18. Benedict Anderson, *Imagined Communities* (New York: Verso, 1991).

19. Hajo Holborn, *A History of Modern Germany, 1840–1945* (Princeton: Princeton University Press, 1969), 20–22.

20. For an extensive discussion of the meaning of "informal imperialism" in China, see Peter Duus, "Introduction," in Peter Duus, Ramon H. Myers, and Mark R. Peattie, eds., *The Japanese Informal Empire in China, 1895–1937* (Princeton: Princeton University Press, 1989), xi–xxix; Jurgen Osterhammel, "Semi-Colonialism and Informal Empire in Twentieth Century China: Toward a Framework of Analysis," in Wolfgang Mommsen, ed., *Imperialism and After: Continuities and Discontinuities* (Boston: Allen and Unwin, 1986), 290–314.

PART I

Competing Railway Imperialisms

In Manchuria, the strategic goals of outside powers were not always attained. As Sally Paine shows, Imperial Russia's primary aim in building the Trans-Siberian Railway, and the Chinese Eastern Railway (CER) linking it to Vladivostok, was strategic. Russian leaders hoped to tip the balance of power in Northeast Asia in Russia's favor, and poured vast sums into the building of its Asian railway network. But Japan opposed Russia's strategic advance, and following its unexpected victory in the Russo-Japanese War, Japan secured possession of the southern sections of the railway line, as well as the crucial ports of Lüshun and Dalian. In the end, the Chinese Eastern Railway did not give Russia unchallenged power over Northeast Asia, but instead put enormous strains on Russia's budget, as well as becoming a major strategic liability.

Japan's windfall, at Russia and China's expense, helped shape the course of the entire twentieth century in East Asia. Y. Tak Matsusaka examines the Japanese acquisition of the southern part of Manchuria as a result of Tokyo's victory in the 1904–5 Russo-Japanese War. The division of the Chinese Eastern Railway into two parts, with Japan obtaining the 400-mile railway line connecting Port Arthur and Dalian with the interior, began the lengthy series of events that culminated with the September 1931 "Manchurian incident" and the subsequent formation of the puppet state of "Manchukuo" under Japanese tutelage. During this twenty-six-year period, Japan's principal agency of colonial transformation was the "steam locomotive" and the "iron rail" under the control of a quasi-official corporation known as the South Manchuria Railway (SMR) Company. The SMR not only provided the "bones and sinews" of Manchukuo, but helped to shape the Japanese imperial ethos, while resulting in feats of architecture, engineering, and industry. Perhaps most importantly, the SMR became a symbol of man versus nature, with an iconic Asia Express Locomotive racing across the Manchurian prairie.

Meanwhile, Soviet Russia, as Bruce A. Elleman discusses, attempted to open diplomatic relations with China, as well as to reclaim its lost rights and privileges over the Chinese Eastern Railway. Following the chaos and turmoil in Russia due to the Bolshevik seizure of power in October 1917, the management of the Chinese Eastern Railway was disputed between the new Soviet government and the warlord-dominated Republican government in Beijing. Bolshevik propaganda in 1919 promised that the CER would be returned to China without compensation. The 25 July 1919 Karakhan Manifesto annulled all of the tsarist government's former "unequal" treaties with China, but it did not replace them with new treaties. But Elleman details how the Soviet government used a series of secret agreements with Beijing, as well as support for the southern-based Communist-Nationalist United Front, to put pressure on the northern government. In the event, Moscow was able to retake majority control over the CER. But Soviet "Red imperialism" backfired. The Nationalist reunification of China set the Soviets and China on the path to conflict.

Felix Patrikeff shows how these frictions led to the 1929 Sino-Soviet War. Following the 1928 assassination of the Manchurian warlord Zhang Zuolin, his son, Zhang Xueliang, quickly became locked in a military struggle with the USSR over control of the CER. By the end of the brief hostilities the Soviet Union had managed to retain physical control over the railway, but Russia's position in northern Manchuria was weakened, economically and socially. When Japan invaded northern Manchuria in 1931, on a pretext, it was supported by a wide cross-section of people living in northern Manchuria, including many émigré Russians, who greeted Japanese troops with rousing *Banzais*. By 1935, the Soviets were forced to sell the CER to Japan. This sale allowed Japan to unify the Manchurian railways for the first time since 1905, and made Manchuria the primary base from which Japan could extend its power into China proper, beginning in 1937. That was the onset of the Second Sino-Japanese War, or World War II in Asia.

1

The Chinese Eastern Railway
from the First Sino-Japanese War
until the Russo-Japanese War

S.C.M. Paine

From 1891 to 1916, Russia constructed the Trans-Siberian Railway. Until its completion in 1916, Russia relied on a trans-Manchurian line to connect European and Asiatic Russia. This was the Chinese Eastern Railway (CER), with 1,782 miles of track linking Chita with Vladivostok, and with a spur to the south to Port Arthur. This railway system constituted an enormous public investment, in some of the most sparsely populated regions of the Russian and Chinese Empires, by a government chronically short of investment capital, and by a country with a grossly inadequate transportation grid even in the most densely settled parts of European Russia. To understand why the Russian government chose to allocate its scarce public funds in this way, this essay will examine the political, economic, and national security reasons that led to the building of the Chinese Eastern Railway.

Why Russia Built the Chinese Eastern Railway

Expanding the Russian empire was one primary reason behind the decision to build the Chinese Eastern Railway. Russia had long-standing ambitions in East Asia, as suggested by the name "Vladivostok," Russia's most important eastern port, whose name translates to "Ruler of the East." Russia's most talented public servant of the late-tsarist period, Minister of Finance Sergei Iul'evich Witte, saw Russia's eastward expansion in terms of manifest destiny and social Darwinism. Each European power was competing to take "as large a share as possible of the inheritance of the outlived oriental states, especially of the Chinese colossus. Russia, both geographically and historically, has the undisputed right to the lion's share of the expected prey" because Russians had been spreading eastward for over five hundred years. Manchuria was simply the latest phase. Witte stated in 1903: "Given our enormous frontier line with China and our exceptionally favourable situation, the absorption by Russia of a considerable portion of the Chinese Empire is only a question of time."[1]

Anticipated economic benefits were another reason. Minister of War General Aleksei Nikolaevich Kuropatkin wrote in 1900: "When Russia has in her hands a railway between the Baltic Sea and the Pacific Ocean, and when she reaches her feelers down to the Bosporus on to the Indian and Pacific Oceans, then with her inexhaustible supply of natural resources she will offer all the powers of the world awesome economic competition."[2] Tsar Nicholas II also believed that the Russian East Asia would become self-supporting.[3]

National security was the third and most immediate reason from the point of view of Russian leaders. In the period leading up to the First Sino-Japanese War (1894–95) and continuing beyond the Russo-Japanese War (1904–5), Russian railway development in Asia can be seen as a function of foreign policy. Railway building in Asia ebbed and flowed largely in response to regional and national security needs.

In 1881, China forced Russia to evacuate territories occupied in 1871 during the massive rebellions of China's Muslim subjects in Xinjiang (Sinkiang) from 1862 to 1878. When China suppressed these rebellions, it had large forces deployed in Xinjiang that could have forcibly retaken the occupied territories had Russia not backed down. Because of these large Chinese deployments and because of Russian financial problems caused by the expensive Russo-Turkish War (1877–78), Russia agreed to scrap the 1879 Treaty of Livadia giving it these territories, in order to sign the 1881 Treaty of St. Petersburg.

The key Russian negotiator for the Treaty of St. Petersburg blamed this unusual Russian setback in its dealings with China on the lack of a railway system capable of deploying troops to defend the borders. He advised the Russian foreign minister: "It is absolutely necessary to have *defensive* naval forces in Vladivostok and to consolidate our military presence along the entire Siberian frontier." He continued: "Of all the means for defense, the most effective and at the same time, the most economical—because it would be productive—is the Siberian railway! I ardently hope that we can proceed with it as rapidly as possible."[4] Later he added: "The only way to reduce these unproductive expenses for defense is, I repeat, a Siberian railway. It has become a political necessity of the first order for us."[5]

Since as early as 1857, there had been intermittent discussion among Russian officials to lay such a line. Railroads did not reach the Ural Mountains, the geographic divide between European and Asiatic Russia, until 1878 with the links to Orenburg and Ekaterinburg.[6] In 1887, Russia undertook preliminary surveys of the route from the western Siberian city of Tomsk to Irkutsk on Lake Baikal, and from the southern shores of Lake Baikal to Sretensk, a town located on the Amur River, which forms the Russo-Chinese border. Then on 29 March 1891 a special imperial rescript announced the intention to build a Trans-Siberian railway.[7]

The first major section of the Trans-Siberian Railway, from the Urals town of Cheliabinsk eastward to the Ob River, opened in 1896; the section between Vladivostok and the Amur town of Khabarovsk in 1897; the section between Krasnoyarsk and Irkutsk in 1898; the Irkutsk-Lake Baikal Line as well as the Ussuri River section in 1899; and the section between the eastern shore of Lake Baikal to Sretensk in 1900. Due to the extremely rough terrain, the section around the southern end of Lake Baikal was completed only in 1904; before that time ferries linked the railway line.[8]

In other words, by 1904 the Russians had completed railway lines connecting European Russia to the Chinese border south of Lake Baikal and connecting Vladivostok via Khabarovsk to the Chinese border in the east. This left a major gap in between. Until 1896, the route for the final section connecting Lake Baikal to Vladivostok remained unresolved. It was in this period that a major foreign relations crisis, the Sino-Japanese War, precipitated a decision to build the Chinese Eastern Railway.

The First Sino-Japanese War and the Chinese Eastern Railway

The First Sino-Japanese War overturned the long-standing balance of power in East Asia to make Japan the dominant regional power at Chinese expense. China had unsuccessfully attempted to maintain Korea's tributary status and limit Japan's increasing influence there. But China's rapid defeat, resulting in the 1895 Treaty of Shimonoseki, forced China not only to abandon claims of suzerainty over Korea, but also to cede Taiwan, the Pescadore Islands, and the Liaodong Peninsula in southern Manchuria, to Japan. Russia, however, successfully intervened to stop the cession of Liaodong, with the support of France and Germany. In the Triple Intervention, Japan was forced to give up the Liaodong Peninsula and its strategically important harbor of Lüshun (Port Arthur), located within easy striking distance of Beijing.[9]

During the war, Russian officials repeatedly discussed the possibility of Russia's absorbing part of Korea and northern Manchuria.[10] The government policy announced in the spring of 1895 was "[o]fficially to inform the European powers, and likewise China, that we consider it necessary, for the protection of our interests, to insist that Japan renounce the annexation of the southern portion of Manchuria, without seeking any annexations on our part."[11] Despite this official denial of Russian territorial ambitions in East Asia, the tsar had already secretly recommended taking an ice-free port in eastern Korea as well as territory along a proposed railway line through Manchuria.[12]

From the Russian point of view, Japan's victory in the Sino-Japanese War marked the beginning of a new era in Russo-Chinese relations.[13] Should the Japanese establish themselves in either Korea or Manchuria, the Russians feared that the next objective would be to expel the Russians from eastern Siberia. During the Sino-Japanese War, security concerns became widespread in the Russian press. Once the terms of the Treaty of Shimonoseki became known, such security concerns received front-page coverage with special emphasis given to the Japanese occupation of the strategic Liaodong Peninsula. There were renewed calls for the Russian acquisition of an ice-free port in East Asia as a terminus for the Trans-Siberian Railway. Not only the Russian press, but Russia's leaders also concluded that Japan now posed a serious security threat whose antidote was the expansion of Russia's East Asian railway system.[14] Above all, Russia wanted closely to circumscribe Japanese activities on the mainland and to limit its expansion up the Korean Peninsula.

During the war, Russian engineers realized how technically difficult the Amur section of the Trans-Siberian Railway would be to build. They immediately looked into an alternative route cutting straight across Manchuria from the east side of Lake Baikal to Vladivostok. Without securing Chinese permission, by August 1895, the Russian government had sent a surveying mission and by January 1896, Russia had drawn up the plans for a railway concession. After China's defeat in the war, Russia preferred a straight line through Manchuria for reasons of foreign policy as well as geography—it wanted to preempt any Manchurian ambitions of Japan or any other country.[15] Military leaders argued that the significantly shorter line (shorter by 1,300 miles) running straight through Manchuria would both be much easier to defend than a long meandering line following the course of the Amur River and would create a buffer zone protecting the river transport from being cut.[16]

While the Russian government revised its East Asian strategy to take into account China's growing weakness, it simultaneously engaged in a massive industrialization program at home under the direction of Finance Minister Witte, who was also the architect of the Trans-Siberian Railway and in many ways of the entire Russian East Asian policy in the 1890s. During his tenure as minister, the Ministry of Finance eclipsed the Ministry of Foreign Affairs for formulating Russia's East Asian policy.[17] In Witte's mind the economic development of Russia; the maintenance of Russia's great power status; the construction of the Trans-Siberian Railway; and Russia's East Asian policy were all inextricably linked. He believed that successful Russian industrial development required the integration of Siberia into European Russia in order to dominate Asian territories and markets still untouched by the other powers. He hoped that a railway link to Vladivostok via northern Manchuria would open lucrative Chinese markets, guarantee Russian dominance in Manchuria, and prevent access by other powers.[18] Witte dreamed of a Manchuria where the

Russian Empire would be "recognized not as a colony of the West but as a 'mother country' equal in status with the other great powers."[19]

At the time of the Triple Intervention after the Sino-Japanese War, Chinese newspapers had rumored that, in return for Russian help in expelling Japan from the Liaodong Peninsula and in return for the loan to China of 6 July 1895, Russia had extracted Chinese permission to build a Manchurian railway ostensibly to protect both countries from any future Japanese aggression.[20] By the spring of 1896 the Russian envoy to Beijing had already approached the Chinese about building the railway.[21] The Chinese rejected the proposal despite Russia's threat to ally with Japan if China did not cooperate. Russia, in turn, rejected China's preferred plan to build a Manchurian railway of its own within six years.

During the coronation of Nicholas II, Witte resumed the negotiations with the attending Chinese dignitary, Li Hongzhang. Witte offered a defensive alliance with China against Japan and a three-million-ruble bribe to Li, in exchange for permission to build what became known as the Chinese Eastern Railway.[22] The offer of a defensive alliance proved increasingly attractive to China.

The Creation of the Sino-Russian Alliance

After China's defeat by Japan, Li Hongzhang and other prominent officials concluded that China must ally with Russia as a counterweight to Japan.[23] In return for Russia's guarantee of help in the event of further Japanese aggression, China granted Russia a railway concession cutting through Manchuria, which, according to the treaty of alliance, implied no territorial designs by Russia or in any way diminished Chinese sovereign rights over the territory in question. On 3 June 1896, China and Russia signed the secret treaty of alliance, providing for the construction of the Chinese Eastern Railway and a fifteen-year alliance for China, whereby both countries agreed to support each other in the event of a Japanese attack on Russia, China, or Korea, and promised not to make a separate peace with Japan.[24] According to the Russian envoy to Beijing: "In concluding the contract of 1896, given the weakness of China at that time, we had in mind nothing other than the annexation in due course, if not of all, then at any rate of the northern part of Manchuria."[25]

The railway contract was later negotiated in Berlin and signed on 8 September 1896.[26] It provided for a 900-mile-long railway concession connecting Vladivostok with Chita, a city located about four hundred miles to the east of Lake Baikal.[27] Because Li Hongzhang would not agree to a railroad owned or constructed by the Russian government, Witte agreed to put the railroad under the control of a nominally independent joint stock company called the Chinese Eastern Railway.

However, by manipulating the company's stock sales in Russia, in contravention to the agreement with Li, the Russian Ministry of Finance (which meant Count Witte) actually ran the concession. This was accomplished by a public sale of the railway shares, announced in the official Russian government newspaper only on the morning of the sale, thus precluding the participation of independent investors. At that time, the Russian government bought outright just 25 percent of the shares, but it acquired an option, held by the Russo-Chinese Bank, to buy the rest. By 1902, after the Boxer Uprising, the Russian government had exercised this option to acquire a majority stake, bringing its outright control to 53 percent.[28] According to Witte, as another "subterfuge," the railway security guard was made up of "'temporarily retired' soldiers from the border guards and retired soldiers."[29]

The twelve-article railway contract[30] stipulated a track gauge following Russian specifications, making the railway incompatible with the other railway lines in China. The railway gauge integrated northern Manchuria into the Russian transportation system, while isolating it from the Chinese railway system. Russia received preferential tariff rates—less by a third compared to those stipulated for the maritime trade dominated by the Western Europeans. Although China retained the right to buy back the railway thirty-six years after its completion or to take control automatically after the passage of eighty years, Witte considered the financial terms of redemption for the railway to be so difficult that Russia would run the railway for the full eighty-year term of the lease.[31]

The treaty did provide for Chinese legal control over the railway zone, but the lands and even income of the railway were exempt from Chinese taxation.[32] After the Boxer Uprising, the Russians unilaterally revised the statutes governing jurisdiction over the railway zone. In an edict dated 2 August 1901, the tsar in effect declared extraterritoriality over the zone, when he put all Russian citizens under Russian legal jurisdiction. The only exception would be cases where the accused was not a Russian subject.[33]

The *Statutes of the Chinese Eastern Railway,* signed in St. Petersburg on 16 December 1896, had repeated the contents of the original railway contract. But the document also gave Russia such additional privileges as the right to build and maintain mining, industrial, and commercial enterprises, as well as telegraph lines along the track, while further limiting the Chinese jurisdiction over the railway zone itself.

Years later the commander of Russian troops on the Amur prior to World War I wrote: "It is a well known fact that the private C.E.R. Company represents a plain fiction, inasmuch as it exists exclusively at the [Russian] state's expense." He continued: "The Chinese Eastern Railway Administration represents, in the full sense of the word, a *colonial government* with all the functions inherent in it. The manager of the railway administers at the same time the territory of the zone together with its population through all branches and in all respects; he is even endowed with the power of diplomatic relations, for which there is a special department in the structure of the administration."[34]

The Construction of the Chinese Eastern Railway

With the construction of the Chinese Eastern Railway, Russian security interests no longer extended just to the Amur River, but several hundred miles southward into Manchuria. This made any possibility of foreign occupation of the Liaodong Peninsula or other areas in northern China particularly threatening. Protection of the railway line required a sizable naval force in East Asia, but Vladivostok's harbor was inadequate as a naval base because, even with the introduction of icebreakers, it remained frozen for an average of fifty-two days per year.[35] So Russian leaders wished to secure an ice-free port, particularly after Germany made clear its determination to take Jiaozhou harbor, and the city of Qingdao (Tsingtao), in the North China province of Shandong.

In 1897, Russia failed to secure Chinese permission to build a southern Manchurian railway line to either an ice-free Manchurian or ice-free Korean port. Even worse from the Russian point of view, China attempted to counterbalance the growing Russian influence in Manchuria by permitting Britain to build a line from Jilin (Kirin), Manchuria to Shanhaiguan (whose name literally means the pass between the mountains and the sea), near where the Great Wall meets the sea. This initial attempt by China to counterbalance Russia with Britain failed to stop further Russian expansion because, at that time, Russia and Britain were delimiting their respective spheres of influence in China. In an agreement signed on 28 April 1899, Britain said it would forego any railway concessions north of the Great Wall while Russia said it would not seek any railway concessions in the Yangzi River Basin.[36] Although this agreement curtailed Britain, Russian's most important European rival, Russia had not come to terms with Japan.

In December 1897, Russia informed the Chinese that it had seized the Liaodong Peninsula ports of Lüshun and Dalian, under the ruse that the measure was temporary in order to protect China from Germany, which had just seized Jiaozhou Bay.[37] In fact, Russia and Germany had reached a prior accommodation to support each other in the seizure of the Liaodong Peninsula and Jiaozhou Bay.[38] According to the annual report for 1897 of the Russian Foreign Ministry, the Chinese were so desperate to secure Russian help against Germany that they agreed for the time being to open all ports to Russian ships and granted them the use of all port facilities and arsenals.[39] Far from trying to dislodge the Germans from Jiaozhou, the Russians planned to use the German occupation as a pretext for their impending seizure of Lüshun.[40]

In January 1898, Russia began forcibly evicting Chinese living in the vicinity of the Liaodong Peninsula and killing those who resisted.[41] On 4 March 1898, Russia formally requested a concession encompassing the ports Lüshun and Dalian on the grounds that the single port of Vladivostok prevented Russia from providing China with year-round protection in keeping with their treaty of alliance. The note warned that the Russian government would interpret a Chinese failure to respond favorably in four days as proof that China did "not want to resolve the matter in friendship, after which the Imperial Government in turn will make the appropriate decision."[42] Only in the eleventh hour did the Chinese agree to negotiate.[43]

Had the Chinese refused to sign the lease agreement, Russia planned that very day to launch an attack by sea in order to occupy Lüshun.[44] Eleven days before the actual lease was signed, the Russian military had already cleared the area of Chinese military forces.[45] As Witte noted, had China refused to yield, Russia "could easily have occupied the territory, for the Chinese had no troops there and the fortress at Port Arthur [Lüshun] was a mere toy."[46] Well-placed bribes—according to Witte, he paid 500,000 rubles to Li Hongzhang and a 250,000 ruble bribe to Li's subordinate—combined with decisions by the other powers not to block Russia or Germany, but to follow suit and carve out their own concessions, left China with little room for maneuver.[47]

On 27 March 1898, China and Russia concluded a twenty-one-year lease agreement for Lüshun, China's most important northern naval base.[48] When Russia declared Lüshun to be a closed naval port, the British protested so vehemently that Russia then promised to build a large commercial port at the nearby town of Dalian, which would be open to foreign ships.[49] The lease agreement excluded Chinese military forces from the leased territory and put it under exclusive Russian military jurisdiction. Similarly, supreme civil administration would be in Russian hands. Although Chinese subjects could continue to live in the area, any who committed crimes would be expelled and put in custody of Chinese authorities. In a neutral zone buffering the concession from Chinese territory, the Chinese retained full control of civil administration, but could deploy troops only with Russian consent.[50]

The Liaodong concession, like the Chinese Eastern Railway before it, still did not satisfy Russian national security concerns. Russia negotiated another agreement to link the Liaodong concession by rail to the Chinese Eastern Railway at its mid-point at Harbin (Ha-er-bin in Mandarin). The 6 July 1898 agreement established the Southern Manchurian Branch of the Chinese Eastern Railway, a branch traversing another 500 miles of Chinese territory, where Russia gained additional coal mining and timber rights.[51]

Thus, within two years of the Russo-Chinese alliance, Russia had taken the very territory from China that the alliance was supposed to protect. This Russian incursion into southern Manchuria, a far more densely populated area than the region traversed by the Chinese Eastern Railway, caused a wave of Chinese resentment.[52] It also led to the fall of Li Hongzhang from power. Unlike the Chinese Eastern Railway, the Southern Manchurian Railway cut through prime agricultural lands and cut off traditional trade routes.[53]

According to Witte, Li had warned of a severe popular backlash if Russia sought concessions south of the Chinese Eastern Railway.[54] Russia's appropriation of farmland to build the railway system and requirement that Chinese residents pay Russian taxes fueled tensions. The annual report for 1898 of the Russian Ministry of Foreign Affairs hailed the Russian acquisition of the concessions for the South Manchuria Railway, Dalian, and Lüshun, falsely stating: "Russia achieved all these results without resorting to coercion, without infringing on the sovereign rights of our neighbor, but by exclusively using our long-established friendly relations with the Celestial Kingdom, which completely appreciated the importance of her compromises made for the sake of her own interests."[55]

In terms of square miles, each of the two Russian railway concessions in Manchuria was individually far larger than any other foreign concession ever appropriated from China. The Chinese Eastern Railway cut a three to four hundred-mile-deep swath through the heart of Manchuria along the hypotenuse of the big northward arc of the Amur River. Upon completion it comprised 1,073 miles of track. The second largest concession was Russia's South Manchuria Railway with 709 miles of track. A distant third was the French-owned Yunnan Railway with 289 miles. Meanwhile, Britain, the most successful commercial power in China operated the 22-mile-long Canton-Kowloon Railway.[56]

In a supplementary agreement signed in St. Petersburg on 7 May 1898, China agreed not to grant any third powers concessions within the neutral zone surrounding the Liaodong concession, nor at any ports to the east or west of the zone.[57] This stipulation excluding all other powers created an exclusive Russian sphere of interest. Russia then constructed the Chinese Eastern and South Manchurian Railways from 1897 to 1904.[58]

The Impact of the Boxer Uprising, 1900

During the 1900 Boxer Uprising, the Russian government gained greater rights and privileges throughout Manchuria. At the turn of the century, Russia was poised to establish a permanent and exclusive sphere of interest in Manchuria and eventually to annex part, if not all, of the region. This took place much sooner and more rapidly than the Russian government had planned. Chinese hostility against foreigners of all stripes came to a head in 1900 with the outbreak of the Boxer Uprising, a viscerally anti-foreign movement that rejected the presence not only of foreigners in China, but also their technology and especially their railways.[59] Most accounts of the uprising focus on the Boxer siege of the foreign legations in Beijing and the relatively small foreign expeditionary forces sent to rescue them. The bigger story was the full-scale Russian invasion and occupation of the three provinces comprising Manchuria.

Once hostilities broke out and the British threatened to send troops into Beijing to protect the foreign legations besieged since 4 June 1900, the Boxers received the official support of the Empress Dowager herself. Over the summer, the government executed five ministers for their sympathetic attitudes toward foreigners including the negotiator for the 1896 contract for the Chinese Eastern Railway as well as the supplementary lease agreement for the Liaodong Peninsula.[60] At first the Russians did not feel threatened by the Boxer movement, since they regarded it as a response to foreign missionary and commercial activities, neither of which particularly concerned them. Therefore, Russia did not join with Britain, America, Germany, France, and Italy in the original protest of 27 January 1900 demanding the suppression of the movement.[61]

When the unrest spread to Manchuria, however, Russian attitudes changed. The Boxers' military strategy in Manchuria entailed cutting railway lines to stop hostile troop movements. Posted imperial edits ordered coordinated attacks on the Russian population and the Boxers soon occupied most of the stations of the South Manchuria Railway. Russians in the border town of Blagoveshchensk, on the Russian bank of the Amur River, panicked and drove several thousand Chinese residents to their deaths in the river. These were descendants of the original Chinese population whose rights of domicile on the northern bank of the Amur had been guaranteed by the 1858 Treaty of Aigun.[62]

Back in St. Petersburg, on 11 July 1900, Witte informed the Chinese minister that Russia planned to send troops, but would withdraw them as soon as the unrest had subsided.[63] Russia deployed six army corps, or about 100,000 troops, and occupied all of Manchuria including the international treaty port of Yingkou (Newchwang) within three months.[64] The occupation of Yingkou was of particular concern to Britain, which collected the international customs there for the Chinese government, and to Japan, which sent much of its trade to China via Yingkou. Russia unilaterally assumed the British responsibility of collecting customs, without carrying out the corresponding obligation of transferring these funds to the Chinese. Since these revenues were raised largely on Japanese and British trade, with Russian trade accounting for less than one percent of the total, the other powers strenuously objected and demanded an immediate Russian troop withdrawal.[65]

The Boxer Uprising in Manchuria caused enormous damage to the Chinese Eastern and South Manchuria Railways. On the eve of the unrest, Russia had spent about one billion rubles—half on investments and half on operating costs, laid 850 miles of track, and had 208 locomotives and 5,400 cars in operation.[66] These three years of expenditures represented nearly three-quarters of the total government budget for one year,[67] and one-third of total foreign investment in China.[68] The uprising destroyed or damaged two-thirds of this new railway system, meaning a staggering financial loss for the Russian government.[69] Witte estimated damages of at least 50 million rubles.[70] The costs of deploying over 100,000 Russian troops in Manchuria were also sizeable, totaling over 56 million rubles in 1900 and 18 million more in 1901.[71]

With Russian administration of Manchuria in place and with the powers united in their desire to extract a large indemnity from China, Russia proceeded with plans to cut a separate deal behind the backs of the others, who were trying to coordinate a joint financial settlement with China.[72] In return for a troop withdrawal, Russia demanded: 1) a large indemnity to cover railway damages; 2) Russian control over Manchurian administration; 3) exclusion of foreign concessions from Manchuria, Mongolia, and North China, as well as exclusion of Chinese railway development in Manchuria and Mongolia; 4) replacement of England with Russia for the collection of Manchurian customs; 5) Russian control of the Yingkou-Shanhaiguan section of the Yingkou-Tianjin Railway (a railway financed by British loans);[73] 6) additional tax preferences for the overland railway trade; and 7) expansion of the Liaodong concession to include Jinzhou. The Chinese negotiator argued that such terms would transform Manchuria into a Russian protectorate much in the manner that Bukhara or India were for Britain, setting a dangerous precedent for the other powers.[74] China soon leaked these treaty drafts to the other foreign powers, which renewed their demands that Russia withdraw.[75]

Although Russia stuck to its hard line in Manchuria,[76] on 7 September 1901, it did join the other powers to sign the Final Protocol regarding the Boxer Uprising.[77] This protocol's most significant provision specified an indemnity of 67.5 million pounds sterling, with an interest rate of 4 percent to be repaid over forty years.[78] Russia accounted for the largest share of this indemnity, nearly one third.[79] Russian heavy-handedness led directly to the Anglo-Japanese Alliance of 30 January 1902 that threatened to bring Britain on the side of Japan should events in East Asia spiral out of control.[80] To avoid this eventuality, on 8 April 1902 Russia first signed a troop withdraw agreement with China, but then actually met the troop withdrawal deadline for only the first of three stages.[81]

By August 1903, the hardliners came to the fore in Russia, when Nicholas II fired the main proponent of withdrawal, Sergei Witte, and subsequently greatly expanded the authority of a major advocate for annexing Manchuria, Admiral Evgenii Ivanovich Alekseev.[82] Alekseev was put in charge of both the military forces and the diplomatic relations of a newly created Viceroyalty of the Far East, composed of the Amur region and the Liaodong concession. Japan was horrified and further negotiations between Russia and China were called off.[83]

Dividing the Chinese Eastern Railway after the Russo-Japanese War, 1904–5

Russia's flamboyant policies in Manchuria not only provoked the condemnation of the Western nations, but, more importantly, these policies directly threatened Japanese national security and aspirations to become a regional power. Russian occupation of the Liaodong Peninsula in 1898, on the heels of forcing Japan to give it up in 1896, enraged the Japanese. After the Russian invasion of Manchuria in 1900, Japan refused to discuss the neutralization of Korea until Russian troops evacuated Manchuria. Anti-Russian sentiment in Japan grew rapidly.[84] The Japanese were concerned not simply by Russia's invasion of Manchuria during the Boxer Uprising and its unwillingness to withdraw thereafter, but more importantly by its continuing attempts to move into Korea, as indicated by the development of Russian timber concessions along the Yalu and Tiumen Rivers, which constitute the boundary between Manchuria and Korea.[85] From the Russian point of view, control of this territory was highly desirable since the Tiumen area was not far from the militarily vulnerable city of Vladivostok, while the mouth of the Yalu lay on the sea approaches to Lüshun.[86] Moreover, the Yalu River was of singular strategic importance since it was the only river in northern or eastern Manchuria to run south. The Tiumen, Ussuri, and Sungari Rivers all run north.[87]

The Russians refused seriously to consider repeated Japanese requests, starting in 1896, to defuse tensions by delimiting spheres of influence in northeastern Asia.[88] Russia did not want to close off the possibility of taking the Korean Peninsula, whose southern location was strategic because it sat astride both the sea lane between Vladivostok and Lüshun as well as the sea lane between Japan and the Asian mainland, while Pusan was the terminus for a Japanese-built railway to Seoul.[89] In 1903, the Japanese government offered to exchange its recognition of a Russian sphere of influence in Manchuria, for Russian recognition of Japan's sphere of influence in Korea.[90] As war loomed on the horizon in December 1903, General Kuropatkin warned Nicholas that Russia's East Asian railway lines were not ready to support a war with Japan.[91] It did not seem to occur to Nicholas or Kuropatkin that the Japanese might decide to act before the completion of these lines.

On 8 February 1904, Japan started the Russo-Japanese War by making a surprise attack on the Russian fleet in Lüshun (better known as the siege of Port Arthur). When the hostilities began, much of the extensive damage to the Manchurian railway system incurred during the Boxer Rebellion remained unrepaired, the Trans-Siberian Railway remained to be double-tracked, and the link around Lake Baikal remained unfinished; "Lake" is in some ways is a misnomer because Lake Baikal approximates the size of Switzerland. Despite the enormous public expense, the Trans-Siberian, Chinese Eastern, and South Manchuria Railways were not even well constructed. Travel between Moscow and Vladivostok was supposed to take one week, but under optimal conditions it took over a month, and during half the year it took a month and a half.[92]

This meant that at the onset of hostilities, Russia could transport only 20,000 to 40,000 men per month to the front. Thereafter, it took a year and a half to increase the number of trains per day from four to twenty pairs.[93] By this point, the decisive battles had already been fought.[94] By the Battle of Mukden, the final battle of the war, the train system could transport 100,000 men per month. If at the beginning of the hostilities, this carrying capacity had been available, Japan would have lost the war because Russia could have taken advantage of its vast superiority in manpower; without a fully functioning railway system through Russia, however, Japan successfully leveraged its initial superiority in numbers in the theater to win its early victories.

In fact, the inadequacies of the railway line constituted the crucial bottleneck between Russia's vast military reserves in European Russia and the East Asian theater where the troops were needed. To quote a French colonel who wrote a two-volume analysis right after the war: "Never has a railway had, perhaps never will a railway have, such decisive importance in a war."[95] As a result of an inadequate Manchurian railway system, Russia would lose the southern third of the Chinese Eastern Railway system.

With revolution spreading through the Russian Empire, with Japanese forces stretched to their limit, and with both sides verging on financial exhaustion, Russia and Japan agreed to accept the U.S. offer of mediation.[96] Japan could not continue hostilities since its army had been decimated by the war and unlike Russia, it did not have any—let alone Russia's numerous—fresh regiments.[97] Had Russia not been beset by domestic turmoil, which was secretly financed by Japan, it could have brought the war to a successful conclusion.

In the peace treaty signed in Portsmouth, New Hampshire, on 5 September 1905, Russia recognized Japan's sphere of influence in Korea, and ceded to Japan the South Manchuria Railway as well as its warm-water ports of Lüshun and Dalian.[98] Gone were Russian hopes of controlling all future railway development throughout Manchuria. Japan had secured the Liaodong concession lost to the Triple Intervention in the Sino-Japanese War and, in lieu of an indemnity, it received the partially-developed Russian concessions and a railway line north to Changchun as well as the accompanying coal mines, including Manchuria's most important coal mine at Fushun. In addition, Russia ceded the southern half of Sakhalin Island to Japan. Troop levels in the railway zones were strictly limited.[99] Thereafter, the Korean government unilaterally annulled all treaties and conventions concluded with Russia.[100] China then opened sixteen towns in Manchuria to foreign commerce in order to satisfy Japanese demands and also to counteract Russian attempts at domination.[101] Thus, the foreign presence, which Russia had tried so hard to exclude from Manchuria, would be permitted right up to Russia's borders.

For Russia, its debacle in East Asia had proven enormously costly in terms of lives, funds, national security, and prestige. All told, 400,000 Russian soldiers had either been killed or wounded.[102] The war cost Russia 6.6 billion rubles, of which 3.9 billion went to pay interest on foreign and domestic loans. Less than half a billion rubles were paid from cash reserves or budget revenue.[103] The war left Russia more heavily indebted than ever. With a Japanese sphere of influence in southern Manchuria, Russia felt compelled to build the tortuous Amur section of the Trans-Siberian Railway—the section that the Chinese Eastern Railway was supposed to render unnecessary and thereby save millions.[104] It completed this section in 1916.[105]

Defeat also greatly complicated Russian national security. Henceforth, Russia would have to be prepared to fight a two-front war, one in Europe and one in Asia.[106] As time went on, this proved ever more costly and consequently, more burdensome to Russia's economy. The damage to Russian prestige was enormous. Not only had Russia not won a single major battle, but also it had suffered defeat at the hands of a previously minor Asian country—or so the Russians thought.[107] It had become apparent that an Asian country had industrialized more effectively than Russia.[108]

By the Portsmouth Peace, Russia also lost potentially the most valuable part of its concessions in Manchuria, since future profits were supposed to be generated by the spread of trade from southern Manchuria northward and westward into Russia. Now this trade would be diverted eastward to Japan.[109] Ultimately, the loss of the war crippled further attempts by Russia to dominate Manchurian commerce and dashed dreams of eventually assuming a preponderant position in China. The Chinese Eastern and South Manchuria railway system, which had come into existence in response to one war, the First Sino-Japanese War, was truncated by another war, the Russo-Japanese War.

The Economic and Strategic Rationale for the Chinese Eastern Railway

The tsarist Ministry of Finance was forced to commit to "extraordinary expenditures" in East Asia. For Russia the investment was substantial since, in those years, total annual expenditures of the imperial government ranged from one to two billion rubles.[110] From 1897 to 1902 the average annual deficit of the Russian government in East Asia was on the order of 171 million rubles. Meanwhile the entire government budget for 1903 was only 1.3 billion rubles of which 22 percent was allocated for interest and loan payments, 36 percent for the military, and only 42 percent or 542 million rubles for everything else. Thus, expenditures in East Asia took an enormous bite out of these 542 million rubles in discretionary funds—about one third.

The total expenses for the Viceroyalty of the Far East and the Chinese Eastern Railway for 1897 through 1902 exceeded one billion rubles. Tariffs and freightage only covered about ten percent of the railway costs, while the interest and principal payments for the loans amounted to 289 million rubles in 1903 alone.[111] Government freight on the Chinese Eastern Railway accounted for ten times the receipts of private freight, whereas on railways in European Russia the reverse was the case.[112] As a result, the railway perennially operated at a deficit.[113]

Despite these enormous government subsidies, the Russian shipping costs by railway were not even close to being economically competitive: at the turn of the century, shipping costs by train from Bremen, Germany, to Dalian were 220 marks per long ton, while the rates by sea were but 22 to 23 marks. Even with preferential tariffs, therefore, the railways were unable to compete with the sea traffic.[114] By 1904, private investment in Manchuria totaled less than 15 million rubles, while the state had spent almost 500 million on the Chinese Eastern Railway, the South Manchuria Railway, and the Liaodong Peninsula concession, paying nearly three times the cost per mile for track compared to railway construction costs in European Russia.[115]

Similarly, Russia's administrative expenses for the Russian East Asia exceeded its revenues from the area by a factor of two or three.[116] Russian trade always operated at an enormous deficit with China and was never able to compete with the Western European trade in East Asia.[117] Even in Manchuria, the focus of most Russian investments in China, Britain, the United States, and Japan dominated commerce.[118] With the exception of Russian vodka and tobacco exports, Russian firms could not compete with the other foreign goods retailed by local Chinese, and Japan and other foreign countries provided the materials to build Lüshun, Dalian, and much of the Manchurian railway system.[119]

Even though the opening of the Chinese Eastern Railway led to a jump in Russian exports to China, from 0.8 million rubles in 1902 to 13.7 million in 1903, the corresponding import figures were 12.4 million rubles and 22.9, respectively. The Russians continued to buy twice as much as they sold in China through the beginning of the First World War in 1914.[120]

Likewise in banking, Russian citizens preferred doing business with Western European banks over their own government's heavily subsidized Russo-Chinese Bank. Less than one-fifth of its deposits were private, while the rest were mostly connected with the Russian government or Chinese Eastern Railway, and still the bank required cash infusions from France and Belgium to stay afloat.[121]

The Russian government relied on state planning via the Chinese Eastern Railway Company to fill the role played by the private sector in other European concession areas.[122] Yet Russian state planning and massive public investments failed to create vibrant commercial centers out of Lüshun and Dalian. According to a British journalist writing in 1904: "From a spectator's point of view Port Arthur [Lüshun] is a miserable hole."[123] His description of Dalian is no more favorable: "But even in its present embryo state Dalny [Dalian] is one of the marvels of the present age. For surely nowhere else in the world had a Government built a city and port of such dimensions on absolutely barren soil, hundreds of miles from its own borders, without a penny's worth of trade already in existence to justify the expense." He continued: "Dalny is, in fact, a 'boom' town without any reason for a 'boom,' but different in this respect, that the mushroom growth is the work of a Government which is determined to build itself a metropolis complete in every detail."[124]

Once the Japanese took over Dalian as part of the settlement of the Russo-Japanese War, they transformed it into an important center of commerce, while Vladivostok remained a commercial backwater for the duration of the Romanov Dynasty. Even more embarrassing, although in 1914 the Chinese Eastern Railway continued to operate at a loss, running deficits of over 50 million rubles between 1909 and 1914, the South Manchuria Railway, ceded to Japan after the Russo-Japanese War, was already earning considerable profits in 1907 of 3.6 million *yen,* which reached 14.3 million *yen* in 1912, or a double digit rate of return to capital. Unlike the Russians, the Japanese charged low rates to attract business.[125]

Conclusions

As this chapter has sought to show, the goal behind Russia's penetration of East Asia was not mainly political or economic but was primarily strategic. Russian leaders intended the Trans-Siberian Railway and Manchurian lines to tip the balance of power in Northeast Asia in Russia's favor by permitting rapid troop deployments as well as the militarization of the Russian side of the border. This militarization took place after the Boxer Uprising, with Russian troop levels in East Asia increasing by 400 percent between 1893 and 1903.[126] Russian leaders believed that these changes should prevent a repetition of the unfavorable balance of power of the 1880s, when China had compelled Russia to return territory.

Bungled diplomacy with Japan followed by an incompetent military strategy and an equally incompetent execution of that flawed strategy during the Russo-Japanese War, however, again cost Russia territory, this time territory with expensive railway investments.[127] In the end, the Chinese Eastern Railway proved to be an ineffective strategy for either cost-effective border defense or for the development of commerce. Foreign Minister Aleksandr Petrovich Izvol'skii (Iswolsky) remarked in his memoirs that the development of the Chinese Eastern Railway was "of a purely artificial character" since Russia did not need the land as an outlet for its population, while the railway put enormous demands on Russia's scarce cash reserves.[128]

When Roman Romanovich Rosen, the former Russian minister to Japan, considered whether "the colossal expenditure incurred in . . . Manchuria could be justified to the neglect of infinitely more pressing needs which remained unsatisfied in Russia proper," he concluded that Russia could not justify "spending hundreds of millions in providing a foreign country with railways, while the most crying unsatisfied need of our own country was precisely the glaring insufficiency of our railway mileage, not to mention the almost total absence of good country roads, a deficiency which was most seriously hampering the economic development of our rural population; that is to say, of about 80 percent of the Russian people."[129] However, as the next chapter will show, once the Chinese Eastern Railway was built, and especially after the southern portion was ceded to Japan in 1905, its existence had an enormous impact on Manchuria's development and eventual annexation by Japan in 1931 as the puppet state of "Manchukuo."

Notes

1. Sergei Iul'evich Witte, *The Memoirs of Count Witte,* Abraham Yarmolinsky, trans. and ed. (Garden City: Doubleday, Page and Co., 1921), 122 [Hereafter Witte and Yarmolinsky.]; B.A. Romanov *Russia in Manchuria (1892–1906),* Susan Wilbur Jones, trans. (Ann Arbor: American Council of Learned Societies, 1952), 60].

2. Dietrich Geyer, *Russian Imperialism,* Bruce Little, trans. (New Haven: Yale University Press, 1987), 12.

3. *Dnevnik A. N. Kuropatkina* (Diary of A. N. Kuropatkin) (Moscow: Nizhpoligraf, 1923), 98.

4. Italics in the original. Charles and Barbara Jelavich, eds. *Russia in the Far East 1876–1880* (Leiden: E.J. Brill, 1959), 122.

5. Jelavich, eds., 131.

6. Donald W. Treadgold, *The Great Siberian Migration* (Princeton: Princeton University Press, 1957), 107–8; G.V. Glinka, ed. *Aziatskaia Rossiia* (Asiatic Russia), Vol. 2 (1914. Reprint. Cambridge, MA: Oriental Research Partners, 1974), 513–4; Romanov, *Russia in Manchuria,* 38–9.

7. Romanov, *Russia in Manchuria,* 5.

8. Treadgold, 131; Ian Nish, *The Origins of the Russo-Japanese War* (London: Longman, 1985), 16; J.N. Westwood, *A History of Russian Railways* (London: George Allen and Unwin, Ltd., 1964), 106–16, 302–3; Glinka, *Aziatskaia Rossiia,* Vol. 2, 524.

9. See S.C.M. Paine, "The triple intervention and the termination of the First Sino-Japanese War," in Bruce A. Elleman and S.C.M. Paine, eds., *Naval Coalition Warfare: From the Napoleonic War to Operation Iraqi Freedom* (London: Routledge, 2008), 75–85.

10. A.L. Popov and S.R. Dimant, eds. "Pervye shagi russkogo imperializma na Dal'nem Vostoke (1888–1903)" (The first steps of Russian imperialism in the Far East [1888–1903]) *Krasnyi arkhiv* 52 (1932), 62–108; Romanov, *Russia in Manchuria,* 52–3.

11. Popov and Dimant, 83.

12. Bakhmeteff Archives, Columbia University, NY, Witte Collection, [Hereafter BA], box 11, file 22, part 3, no. 1; Popov and Dimant, 75–6.

13. BA, box 11, file 27, no. 1, 114–5 Archive of Russian Foreign Policy, Ministry of Foreign Affairs, Moscow, Russia (Hereafter ARFP), *f. Kitaiskii stol* (China Desk), *d.* 120, 1903, no. 2, *l.* 6.

14. S.C.M. Paine, *The Sino-Japanese War of 1894–1895: Perceptions, Power and Primacy* (New York: Cambridge University Press, 2003), 282–4.

15. R.K.I. Quested, *"Matey" Imperialists?* (Hong Kong: University of Hong Kong Press, 1982), 21; Popov and Dimant, 83; Glinka, *Aziatskaia Rossiia,* Vol. 2, 526; Romanov, *Russia in Manchuria,* 62–3; ARFP, f. 133 kantseliariia (chancellery), op. 470, d. 85, l. 108.

16. Central State Military History Archive, Military Scientific Archive of the USSR, Moscow, *f.* 447, no. 69, 4–8. The underlining is from the original.

17. David MacLaren McDonald, *United Government and Foreign Policy in Russia, 1900–1914* (Cambridge, MA: Harvard University Press, 1992), 9–30; B.H. Sumner, *Tsardom and Imperialism in the Far East and Middle East, 1880–1914* (1940; reprint, Hamden, CT: Archon Books, 1968), 8.

18. Popov and Dimant, 93–100.

19. Geyer, 147.

20. Andrew Malozemoff, Andrew, *Russia Far Eastern Policy 1881–1904* (1958. Reprint. New York: Octagon Books, 1977), 77; Shuhsi Hsu, *China and Her Political Entity* (New York: Oxford University Press, 1926), 200.

21. Romanov, *Russia in Manchuria,* 75.

22. Irwin Jay Schulman, "China's Response to Imperialism, 1895–1900," (Ph.D. diss. Columbia University, 1967), 148; Malozemoff, 77–80.

23. Palace Museum Archives, Taipei, Taiwan, *Chou ban yi wu shi mo* (The complete account of barbarian management) *Guangxu* 21 nian, 5–6 *yue,* 152, 223–5 *ye;* George Alexander Lensen, *Balance of Intrigue,* Vol. 2 (Tallahassee, FL: University Presses of Florida, 1982), 488–9.

24. Romanov, *Russia in Manchuria,* 84; Witte and Yarmolinsky, 90; BA, box 11, file 22, part 3, no. 6.

25. ARFP, *f. Kitaiskii stol, on.* 491, 1908, *d.* 129, *l.* 713–4.

26. Arthur W. Hummel, ed. *Eminent Chinese of the Ch'ing Period (1644–1912)* (1943. Reprint. Taipei: Ch'eng Wen Publishing Co., 1970), 312.

27. Chao Wei, "Foreign Railroad Interests in Manchuria" (Ph.D. diss. St. John's University, 1970), 2–3.

28. ARFP, *f. otchet MID, op.* 475 *za* 1896, 191–2; Quested, *"Matey" Imperialists?,* 21–2; Malozemoff, 82; Romanov, *Russia in Manchuria,* 84, 86–7.

29. Sergei Iul'evich Witte, *The Memoirs of Count Witte,* Sidney Harcave, trans. and ed. (Armonk, NY: M.E. Sharpe, Inc., 1990), 181. [Hereafter Witte and Harcave.]

30. John V.A. MacMurray, comp. *Treaties and Agreements with and concerning China 1894–1919,* Vol. 1 (New York: Oxford University Press, 1921), 74–7. Note especially articles 3, 5, 10, and 12. For the Chinese version, see *Qing ji wai jiao shi liao,* 122 *quan,* 13b–17b *ye.*

31. BA, box 11, file 22, part 3, no. 6. For an additional copy, see BA, box 11, file 22, part 4.

32. MacMurray, Vol. 1, 76. Articles 5 and 6.

33. Ibid., Vol. 1, 88–90.

34. Cited in Peter S.H. Tang, *Russian and Soviet Policy in Manchuria and Outer Mongolia 1911–1930* (Durham, NC: Duke University Press, 1959), 53. Italics are Tang's.

35. Malozemoff, 77.

36. Romanov, *Russia in Manchuria,* 124–6, 140–1, 146–7, 151–67; MacMurray, Vol. 1, 204; A. Popov, "Anglo-russkoe soglashenie o razdele Kitaia (1899 g.)," (The Anglo-Russian agreement on the division of China (1899)), *Krasnyi arkhiv* 25 (1927), 111–34; ARFP, *f. otchet MID, op.* 475 *za* 1898, 90–1.

37. Popov and Dimant: 103–7; Witte and Yarmolinsky, 98–102; BA, box 11, file 22, part 3, no. 9.

38. Lensen, *Balance of Intrigue,* Vol. 2, 740–7.

39. ARFP, *f. otchet MID, op.* 475 *za* 1897, 191–217.

40. ARFP, *f. Kitaiskii stol, op.* 491, *d.* 115, 1898, *l.* 24; 9 March 1898, *l.* 25.

41. *Qing ji wai jiao shi liao,* 129 *quan,* 2a, 5a–6a, 8a, 10b, 12a, 17b–18a *ye; Chou ban yi wu shi mo,* archives, *Guangxu* 24 *nian,* 1–2 *yue,* 2, 30, 95 *ye.*

42. Emphasis as in the original. *ARFP,* f. Kitaiskii stol, op. 491, d. 115, 1898 g., l. 31-4; Huang Yan and Wang Taofu, eds. *Qing ji wai jiao shi liao* (Historical materials on international relations from the Qing period) (1932, Reprint; Peking: Shu mu wen xian chu ban she, 1987), 130 *quan,* 12b–13a *ye.*

43. ARFP, *f. Kitaiskii stol, op.* 491, *d.* 115, 1898, l. 43–4.

44. Iurii Iakovlevich Solovev, *Dvadtsat' piat' let moei diplomaticheskoi slyzhboi (1893–1918)* (Twenty-five years of my diplomatic service [1893–1918]) (Moscow: Gosudarstvennoe izdatel'stvo, 1928), 59.

45. Nish, 43.

46. Witte and Harcave, 277.

47. Ibid., 277.

48. John Albert White, *The Diplomacy of the Russo-Japanese War* (Princeton: Princeton University Press, 1964), 21.

49. Witte and Harcave, 278.

50. MacMurray, Vol. 1, 119–21. Articles 1, 3, 4, 5, 6; BA, box 11, file 22, part 2, no. 29; *Qing ji wai jiao shi liao,* 132 *quan,* 16b–19a *ye.*

51. MacMurray, Vol. 1, 154–6.

52. Palace Museum Archives, Taipei, Taiwan, *Chou ban yi wu shi mo,* archives [Hereafter *Chou ban yi wu shi mo,* archives], *Guangxu* 24 *nian,* 1–2 *yue,* 118 *ye. Guangxu* 24 *nian,* 3–4 *yue,* 87-8 *ye; Guangxu* 24 *nian,* 8 *yue,* 38 *ye.*

53. Quested, *"Matey" Imperialists?,* 35, 38–40.

54. Witte and Harcave, 237.

55. ARFP, *f. otchet MID, op.* 475 *za* 1898, 194.

56. Quested, *"Matey" Imperialists?,* 106. Chi-ming Hou, *Foreign Investment and Economic Development in China 1840–1937* (Cambridge, MA: Harvard University Press, 1965), 65; William L. Langer, *The Diplomacy of Imperialism 1890–1902,* 2nd ed. (New York: Alfred A. Knopf, 1956), 487–8.

57. MacMurray, Vol. 1, 128. Article 5; BA, box 11, file 22, part 2, no. 29.

58. Glinka, *Aziatskaia Rossiia,* Vol. 2, 526.

59. Immanuel Chung-yueh Hsu, *The Rise of Modern China,* 3rd. ed. (Hong Kong: Oxford University Press, 1983), 391; Joseph W. Esherick, *The Origins of the Boxer Uprising* (Berkeley: University of California Press, 1987), xiv–xvi, 327–8.

60. Lensen, *Balance of Intrigue,* Vol. 2, 795. Chester C. Tan, *The Boxer Catastrophe* (New York: Columbia University Press, 1967), 70–1, 75, 93–5, 106, 112; Nish 70; Esherick, xiv.

61. Malozemoff, 124–9; Tan, 112; Nish, 71–2, 76.

62. S.C.M. Paine, *Imperial Rivals: China, Russia, and Their Disputed Frontier* (Armonk, NY: M.E. Sharpe, 1996), 212–5.

63. Malozemoff, 130–1, 138–9; Tan, 157–9.

64. Quested, *"Matey" Imperialists?,* 49–50. Another source put the number of troops at 170,000, emphasizing that "Manchuria was thus occupied by the greatest military force ever sent from Europe to the Far East." Geyer, 206. Malozemoff put the figure at 177,000. Malozemoff, 166; Shuhsi Hsu, 239, 243; *Annuaire diplomatique de l'Empire de Russie,* 1901 (St. Petersburg: Imprimerie de F. Bellizard, 1901), 439.

65. Japanese Foreign Ministry Archives, (Gaimushō gaikō shiryōkan), Tokyo Japan [Hereafter JFM], 2.1.2–14, Vol. 1, 201; Nish, 32, 113–4, 148; George Alexander Lensen, ed. *Korea and Manchuria between Russia and Japan 1895–1904* (Tallahassee, FL: The Diplomatic Press, 1966), 131, 136, 139–40; Romanov, *Russia in Manchuria,* 208–9; I. Erukhimovich, ed., "Nakanune russko-iaponskoi voiny," (On the eve of the Russo-Japanese War) *Krasnyi arkhiv,* 63 (1934): 3–54.

66. Ralph Edward Glatfelter, "Russia in China: The Russian Reaction to the Boxer Rebellion," (Ph.D. diss. Indiana University, 1975), 56; M.I. Sladkovskii, *History of Economic Relations between Russia and China,* M. Roublev, trans. (Jerusalem: Israel Publications for Scientific Translations, 1966), 120.

67. Romanov, *Russia in Manchuria,* 32–3; Malozemoff, 188–9; Westwood, *Railways,* 114.

68. Mark Mancall, "Russia and China: the Structure of Contact," in *Russia and Asi,* ed. Wayne S. Vucinich, Hoover Institution Publications 107 (Stanford: Hoover Institution Press, 1972), 327–8.

69. Geyer, 206; George Alexander Lensen, *The Russo-Chinese War* (Tallahassee, FL: The Diplomatic Press, 1967), 5; Aleksei Nikolaevich Kuropatkin, *The Russian Army and the Japanese War*, A.B. Lindsay, trans., W.D. Swinton, ed., Vol. 1 (New York: E. P. Dutton and Company, 1909), 154–5.

70. JFM, 2.1.2–9, Vol. 1, 25.

71. William C. Fuller, *Civil-Military Conflict in Imperial Russia 1881–1914* (Princeton: Princeton University Press, 1985), 56.

72. Lensen, *Korea and Manchuria,* 130–155; Romanov, *Russia in Manchuria,* 200.

73. Nish, 53, 86, 88.

74. Tan, 173–5; Huang Yan and Wang Taofu, eds., *Xi xun da shi ji* (Record of important events regarding the inspection of the West) [Hereafter *Xi xun da shi ji*] in *Qing ji wai jiao shi liao* (Historical materials on international relations from the Qing period), Vol. 5. (1932. Reprint. Peking: Shu mu wen xian chu ban she, 1987), 4 *quan,* 15a–16b *ye;* Huang Yan and Wang Taofu, eds. *Qing ji wai jiao shi liao* (Historical materials on international relations from the Qing period) (1932, Reprint; Peking: Shu mu wan xian chu ban she, 1987), 145 *quan,* 17b–20b *ye.*

75. Nish, 140; Lensen, *Korea and Manchuria,* 136–55, 167; ARFP, *f. otchet MID, op. 475 za 1901,* 80–1; Romanov, *Russia in Manchuria,* 209–12; *Qing ji wai jiao shi liao,* 145 *quan,* 7b–9a *ye; Xi xun da shi ji,* 5 *quan,* 13b–14b, 29a–b *ye;* JFM, 2.1.2–9, Vol. 1, 86–94; JFM, 2.1.2–9, Vol. 2, 27–9; JFM, 2.1.2–9, Vol. 2, 65–70, *passim.*

76. Tan, 181–7; *Xi xun da shi ji,* 6 *quan,* 21a–b *ye.*

77. MacMurray, Vol. 1, 278–85.

78. Ibid., 278–308.

79. ARFP, *f. otchet MID, op. 475 za 1902,* 77–8; MacMurray, Vol. 1, 311.

80. MacMurray, Vol. 1, 324–5; Nish, 129–30.

81. MacMurray, Vol. 1, 327. For the Chinese text, see *Qing ji wai jiao shi liao,* 158 *quan,* 11b–15a *ye;* Bei yang da chen, Chinese Foreign Ministry, Guangxu 29/5/13, no. 0049; Shengjing military governor, Chinese Foreign Ministry, Guangxu 29/4/9 and 28/9/13, no. 0049; *Qing ji wai jiao shi liao,* 170 *quan,* 6b, 11a–b *ye;* Lee, 138; Nish 147–8.

82. Shuhsi Hsu, 261; Malozemoff, 224, 226; M. Pokrovskii, ed., "Dnevnik A.N. Kuropatkina" (The diary of A.N. Kuropatkin) *Krasnyi arkhiv* 2 (1922): 18.

83. Vladimir Iosifivich Gurko, *Features and Figures of the Past,* J.E. Wallace Sterling, et. al, eds. Laura Matveev, trans. (Stanford: Stanford University Press, 1939), 270, 274, 278, 281–2; ARFP, *f. otchet MID, op. 475 za 1903,* 89–91; BA, box 11, file 25, nos. 27–33; JFM, 2.1.2–14, Vol. 4, 1700–1; JFM, 2.1.2–14, Vol. 4, 1726; Lensen, *Korea and Manchuria,* 214–6, 228–30.

84. Erukhimovich, 8–9, 15, 17, 19, 22, 28; Lensen, *Korea and Manchuria,* 160–97; Nish, 29, 32, 44, 48, 67, 95–6, 105–6, 194–5.

85. Gurko, 266, 268; Malozemoff, 177; Romanov, *Russia in Manchuria,* 267–70.

86. White, 33.

87. Owen Lattimore, *Inner Asian Frontiers of China* (New York: American Geographical Society, 1940), 108.

88. Japan, Foreign Office, *Correspondence Regarding the Negotiations between Japan and Russia (1903–1904)*, Presented to the Imperial Diet, March 1904, 1–2; BA, box 10, file 21, no. 3, 3; Popov and Dimant, 11; I. Erukhimovich, 48, 50–1, 53–4; BA, box 11, file 23, part 2, no. 5, 6; White, appendix I, 349–58; Geyer, 207.

89. White, 33.

90. Japan, Foreign Office, *Correspondence Regarding the Negotiations,* 3–4, 28–33; Nish 183–4; *Qing ji wai jiao shi liao,* 180 *quan,* 19b–20b *ye.*

91. Kuropatkin, *Dnevnik,* (Diary), 95–6; Nish, 138–9.

92. Steven G. Marks, *Road to Power* (Ithaca: Cornell University Press, 1991), xii, 170, 175, 177, 194, 196–7, 200–1, 206, 218.

93. Vladimir Nikolaevich Kokovtsov, *Out of My Past: The Memoirs of Count Kokovtsov,* ed. H.H. Fisher, trans. Laura Matveev, (Stanford: Stanford University Press, 1935), 25; Marks, 201–3. Kuropatkin considered inadequate railway capacity to be a major factor accounting for Russia's poor military showing. Kuropatkin, *Russian Army,* Vol. 1, 134.

94. Bruce W. Menning, Bruce W. *Bayonets before Bullets* (Bloomington: Indiana University Press, 1992), 195.

95. E.L.V. Cordonnier, *The Japanese in Manchuria 1904,* trans. Capt. C.F. Atkinson Vol. 1 (London: Hugh Rees, 1912), 38.

96. Hugh Seton-Watson, *The Russian Empire 1801–1917* (Oxford: The Clarendon Press, 1967), 591–7; Hosea Ballou Morse, *International Relations of the Chinese Empire,* Vol. 3 (Shanghai: Kelly and Walsh, Ltd., 1918), 427.

97. Peter Gatrell, *Government, Industry and Rearmament in Russia, 1900–1914: The Last Argument of Tsarism* (Cambridge: Cambridge University Press, 1994), 70.

98. MacMurray, Vol. 1, 523.

99. Ibid., 522–6.

100. JFM, 2.1.2–15, Vol. 1; White, 124–5; Romanov, *Russia in Manchuria,* 95.

101. MacMurray, Vol. 1, 549–53; *Xi xun da shi ji,* 6 *quan,* 9b–10b *ye;* White, 364–68.

102. William C. Fuller, *Strategy and Power in Russia 1600–1914* (New York: The Free Press, 1992), 406.

103. Romanov, *Russia in Manchuria,* 323. Fuller cites lower figures: 2.5 billion rubles to fund the war coupled with a loss of a quarter of a billion rubles in naval assets. Fuller, *Strategy and Power,* 406; Fuller, *Civil-Military Conflict,* 160. Gurko cites the figures of the representative in France of the Ministry of Finance, Artur Germanovich Rafalovich, who tabulated that the war cost for Russia as 2.3 billion rubles. Gurko, 529, 680.

104. Westwood, *Railways,* 115.

105. Paine, *Imperial Rivals,* 274.

106. White, 170; Kuropatkin, Vol. 1, 269.

107. Fuller, *Strategy and Power,* 394, 403, 405, 408; Dominic C.B. Lieven, *Russia and the Origins of the First World War* (New York: St. Martin's Press, 1983), 19–21; Fuller, *Civil-Military Conflict,* 133.

108. Albert J. Beveridge, *The Russian Advance* (New York: Harper and Brothers, 1904), 147–8.

109. Ernest Batson Price, *The Russo-Japanese Treaties of 1907–1916* (1933, Reprint; New York: AMS Press, 1971), 26.

110. Paul R. Gregory, *Russian National Income 1885–1913* (Cambridge: Cambridge University Press, 1982), 252; Kuropakin, *Russian Army*, Vol. 1, 188–9.

111. Malozemoff, 188–9. Romanov's figures indicate an annual average deficit for these years of nearly 200 million rubles. This figure represents the combined outlays for the Chinese Eastern Railway and the Viceroyalty of the Far East. Romanov, 32–3; Geyer, 209. Other estimates put the total costs of Russian schemes to develop Manchuria at 480 million rubles by 1903. Quested, *"Matey'" Imperialists?*, 155.

112. Malozemoff, 191.

113. From the second half of 1903 to 1914, this deficit totaled 178.6 million rubles. Sladkovskii, *History of Economic Relations,* 121.

114. Benno Aleksandrovich De Siebert and George Abel Schreiner, eds., *Entente Diplomacy and the World* (New York: Knickerbocker Press, 1921), 20; Malozemoff, 191, 193.

115. Geyer, 210–1; Gurko, 259. Gurko writes that the cost per *verst* of track was 150,000 rubles for the Chinese Eastern Railway, as opposed to 60,000 rubles in European Russia. Ibid.

116. G.V. Glinka, ed., *Atlas Aziatskoi Rossii* (Atlas of Asiatic Russia). St. Petersburg: Izdanie Pereselencheskogo upravleniia, 1914), no. 65.

117. M.I. Sladkovskii, *Istoriia torgovo-ekonomicheshikh otnoshenii narodov Rossii s Kitaem* (The history of trade and economic relations between the peoples of Russia and China) (Moscow: Izdatel'stvo "Nauka," 1974), 214–5, 265, 270, 272, 275, 337; Sumner, 18–9; N. N. Krotkov, *Russkaia manufaktura i eia konkurenty na kitaiskom rynke* (Russian manufactures and their competition on the Chinese market) Ministerstva torgovli i promyshlenosti, otdel torgovli (Ministry of Trade and Production, Department of Trade) (St. Petersburg: Tipografiia V.F. Kirshbauma, 1914), 32–3.

118. Lensen, *Korea and Manchuria,* 189; Krotkov, 68–9.

119. Geyer, 209.

120. Quested, *"Matey" Imperialists?*, 216.

121. Rosemary Quested, *The Russo-Chinese Bank* (Birmingham: Department of Russian Language and Literature, University of Birmingham: 1977), 30–1, 37, 47, 53, 62–3.

122. Witte to Lamzdorf, 30 October 1898 (11 November 1898), BA, box 11, file 22, part 2, no. 48.

123. H.J. Whigham, *Manchuria and Korea,* (London: Isbister and Co., Ltd., 1904), 4.

124. Whigham, 8. Another British observer writing the same year is more favorable about Lüshun, but concurs on Dalian. B.L. Putnam Weale, *Manchu and Muscovite* (London: Macmillan and Co., Ltd., 1904), 74–8, 85; Weale 149.

125. Quested, *"Matey'" Imperialists?*, 231; Ramon H. Myers, "Japanese Imperialism in Manchuria: The South Manchurian Railway Company, 1906–1933," in *The Japanese Informal Empire in China, 1895–1937,* eds. Peter Duus, Ramon H.

Myers and Mark R. Peattie (Princeton: Princeton University Press, 1989), 110, 112–6, 126; Geyer, 324; Kungtu Sun and Ralph W. Huenemann, *The Economic Development of Manchuria in the First Half of the Twentieth Century* (Cambridge, MA: Harvard University Press, 1969), 67; Canfield F. Smith, *Vladivostok under Red and White Rule* (Seattle: University of Washington Press, 1975), 4.

126. BA, box 11, file 27, part 2, 26.

127. Denis Warner and Peggy Warner, *The Tide at Sunrise* (London: Angus and Robertson, 1974).

128. Iswolsky, 121.

129. Rosen, Roman Romanovich. *Forty Years of Diplomacy*, Vol. 1 (New York: Alfred A. Knopf, 1922), 202–3.

2
Japan's South Manchuria Railway Company in Northeast China, 1906–34

Y. Tak Matsusaka

The Japanese seizure of Northeast China, a region foreigners once commonly called "Manchuria," may be understood as a series of events that began with the eruption of armed conflict in September 1931. At the same time, it must also be viewed as a protracted process of incremental encroachment and colonial reconstruction that originated decades earlier with Japan's acquisition of a bridgehead on the Liaodong Peninsula along with a 400-mile railway line connecting Liaodong to the interior. Japan's endeavors in Northeast China during the quarter-century spanning the Russo-Japanese War and the Manchurian Incident provided foundations and scaffolding for the subsequent construction of the puppet state of Manchukuo. Steam locomotive and iron rail served as the principal instruments of colonial transformation, harnessed to Japanese imperial designs by an extraordinary quasi-official corporation known as the South Manchuria Railway company (SMR). This chapter offers a brief look at the history of the SMR and the dynamics of a process that well-deserves characterization as "conquest by railway."[1]

The South Manchuria Railway Company: An Overview

Railway imperialism in various forms, with and without the political and legal superstructure of a colonial state, enjoyed widespread practice throughout the subject world in the late nineteenth and early twentieth centuries. Japan's South Manchuria Railway Company stands, perhaps, as the most ambitious and successful project of its kind. The Japanese government founded the SMR in 1906 in order to operate the portion of the Russian railway network in Northeast China ceded to Japan in the Treaty of Portsmouth at the end of the Russo-Japanese War. Although organized under Japanese law as a private, joint-stock corporation, a state charter, which mandated the government's position as majority shareholder and its concomitant power to appoint or approve all top management officials, gave it quasi-official status. Its legal standing as a private entity proved useful as diplomatic "camouflage," but beyond such duplicity, its actual operation as a profit-oriented business enterprise capable of mobilizing private investment provided the financial underpinnings of the Japanese venture in the region. The company's charter initially set its authorized capital at 200 million yen, a level subsequently doubled in 1918. Whether assessed in terms of authorized or paid-up capital, the SMR ranked as the largest joint-stock corporation in the Japanese empire before the 1930s.[2]

The trunk line of the SMR originated in the deep-water, ice-free port of Dairen (Dalian) situated in the Kwantung (Guandong) Leased Territory, a 1,300-square-mile tract on the tip of the Liaodong Peninsula also ceded to Japan by Russia in the Treaty of Portsmouth. From a secure anchor in Kwantung, over which Japan exercised effective colonial rule, the trunk ran 438 miles north to the city of Changchun deep in the Manchurian interior. There, the Japanese railway made a connection, problematic because of both gauge differences and restrictive traffic policies, to the southern branch of the Russian-owned Chinese Eastern Railway (CER). This Russian segment from Changchun joined, at the junction city of Harbin, the main trunk of the CER that ran across northern Manchuria and connected the Chita branch of the Trans-Siberian to Russia's Pacific port of Vladivostok.

The loss of the Dairen-Changchun segment of the CER's southern branch to Japan represented a major blow to Russian imperial scheme. This not only placed great strategic as well as commercial value on Kwantung's harbors, but counted on high-volume export traffic bound for Dairen to subsidize the operating costs of the less remunerative east-west trunk. From a purely business perspective, Japan fared better in the division of the railway system.[3]

In 1911, the SMR completed construction of a branch line from Fengtian (Mukden, later named Shenyang), the regional Chinese administrative and commercial center, to Andong on the Yalu River border with Japanese-ruled Korea where it connected to the colonial Korean railway system. The Korean trunk line, in turn, afforded access to the port of Pusan, a relatively narrow body of water away from the Japanese homeland ports of Shimonoseki and Moji. Many policymakers, along with colonial interest groups in Korea, hoped that the Pusan-Andong-Fengtian route would eventually supplant the access route from Dairen.[4]

The SMR, along with its estranged-parent CER, were among the few foreign railways in China wholly-owned by the concession-holding power. Most other foreign railway concessions entailed nominal Chinese ownership and financing through foreign loans commonly linked to managerial or supervisory rights accruing to the lending power for the duration of the loan. These "loan concessions" might appear relatively benign, and in some cases, they resulted from Chinese requests for foreign help. In many others, however, foreign powers pressured reluctant Chinese authorities into undertaking both the railway construction projects and the loans to finance them.[5]

Japan's coercive diplomacy managed to secure for the SMR's Andong-Mukden branch the same terms applied to the Dairen-Changchun trunk, but Chinese negotiators refused to yield to any further demands of this sort. All of the SMR's subsequent network expansion took place through loan concessions, secured through a combination of coercion and bribes in the form of padded construction loans. Japanese diplomats interpreted treaty provisions governing the SMR as guaranteeing the company an effective rail monopoly in southern Manchuria, but neither the Chinese nor other powers shared this interpretation, asserting their own rights to railway development in the region. Protecting the company from "destructive competition" thus became a major preoccupation of the foreign ministry's bureau responsible for China.[6]

The financially self-sufficient operation, maintenance, and expansion of the railway line formed the core of the company's mission, but its activities moved into a wide range of fields from the start, largely in response to the lack of an adequate industrial and commercial infrastructure in the territory. In order to run the railway efficiently, the SMR had little choice but to establish an entire complex of support and ancillary operations. These included harbor works, connecting steamship services, construction and engineering facilities, coal mines, electric power plants, warehouses, housing for employees, and hotels for travelers, along with a network of financial and commercial institutions indispensable to generating railway traffic.

Some of these ancillary operations acquired importance in their own right. Of special note was the Fushun Colliery, connected by a short spur to the SMR trunk, another Russian property turned over to Japan and one of the richest and most productive coal mines in East Asia. Fushun coal provided the SMR's locomotives and steamships, as well as electrical power plants, with a cheap and easily accessible source of fuel, and in the case of gas-generating plants, raw material. It also represented an increasingly important export commodity in its own right and, accordingly, a major source of railway traffic.

The SMR quickly established itself as one of the most formidable competitors in the East Asian coal market. Part of the company's strength lay in the unusually rich and accessible seams at Fushun and in the extensive mechanization of operations. But, it also exploited the advantages of vertical integration in production and distribution, which allowed for very flexible business strategies.[7]

By World War I, cheap Fushun coal found new uses as fuel for energy-intensive manufacturing ventures, as well as a raw material for coal-based chemicals.[8] Such steps led the SMR into an increasingly wide range of projects, some of them on the cutting edge of industrial technology in the Japanese empire. Diversification on the part of railway companies was, in itself, not exceptional, although rarely assuming the scope and scale seen in the SMR. Such ramified developments are often driven by the need to secure and develop sources of traffic, by the new economic opportunities created by the railway itself, and by the continuous effort to employ its capital assets as fully as possible. The elaboration of the company's railway workshops into comprehensive engineering and machine-building operations that began producing locomotives during World War I offers a good example of the latter.[9] The SMR's extensive research and development apparatus, which included economic research units and agricultural stations, as well as industrial and geological laboratories, actively facilitated such diversification.

This research apparatus proved particularly valuable in the SMR's most striking venture in industrialization, the Anshan Iron Works. The fortuitous location of a vast but low-grade ore field near the SMR's Anshan station inspired the project, and the efforts of company scientists to develop "reduction roasting" techniques that facilitated the exploitation of low-grade ore, made it commercially feasible. The SMR's integrated operations in coal mining, machine building, and transportation lent further support to what seemed a risky venture at first. So too, did a long investment horizon made possible by deep pockets continually refilled by steady railway revenues. The gamble appeared to be paying off by the mid-1920s when the Anshan Iron Works began producing just under 20 percent of the iron used in Japanese steel production.[10]

The wide extent, as well as the heavy-industrial direction of its diversification, made the SMR unique among foreign railways in China. The Japanese railway project, however, also enjoyed an exceptional endowment of special rights inherited from the Russians. In addition to direct ownership, a particularly significant privilege lay in the company's administrative control over a narrow strip of land along its right of way known as the Railway Zone.[11] At station stops, the Zone expanded into substantial nodes of real estate accommodating "railway towns."

The South Manchuria Railway Zone might be regarded as analogous in some respects to the Panama Canal Zone, although much more modest at only 105 square miles in extent. Nonetheless it served a vital function as a colonial sheath enfolding the SMR, an urbanized corridor, policed and administered by the Japanese, penetrating deep into the Manchurian heartland. The SMR directly managed Zone settlements, conceived as models of urban planning, where it operated schools, hospitals, public utilities, and housing projects.[12]

Another element in the special portfolio of rights attached to the SMR, shared by the Russian CER, was the right to station fifteen guards per mile of railway. These terms enabled the Japanese army to deploy six battalions of so-called Railway Guards along the SMR's right of way in peacetime.[13] A division-strength force stationed in Kwantung, whose commander served simultaneously as the governor-general of the Leased Territory, substantially augmented Japan's regional military presence. In 1919, the Tokyo government separated military from civil authority in Kwantung, creating the notorious military unit known as the Kwantung Army.[14]

Railway Imperialism and the South Manchuria Railway

Contemporary observers, both friendly and hostile, tended to emphasize the extraordinary features of the SMR in their characterizations of its activities in Manchuria, particularly its management of the Railway Zone and its ventures in industrial diversification.[15] Descriptions often tended to downplay the nature of the company as a railway enterprise. Doubtless, Zone administration and heavy industrialization contributed to the company's overall strengths and to the unusual quality of the Japanese presence in Manchuria. As intriguing as these exotic features might be, however, the SMR's effectiveness as an agent of colonial power lay primarily in its seemingly prosaic nature as a monopoly railway company. It may be useful, therefore, to consider briefly how the SMR's railway operations produced and sustained what may be regarded as the company's three, principal colonial functions of military installation, instrument of territorial integration, and economic development agency.

The strategic applications of railway technology lay at the foundations of Japanese power in Manchuria. The SMR functioned, first and foremost, as a covert military installation left in place, in the manner of a Trojan Horse, after the evacuation of Japanese occupation troops in 1907. Anticipating a second war against Russia, Japan's strategic planners sought to maintain a military railway network that would give them a decisive advantage in deploying massive forces in the Manchurian heartland before the enemy could fully mobilize. The army's plan called for landing troops in Korea and Kwantung, concentrating forces at a point on the SMR trunk north of Fengtian, then advancing along the rail corridor to capture the junction at Harbin before Russia's main force reached the region by way of the Trans-Siberian and CER. Given the limits of the carrying capacity of the initially single-tracked Russian railway system, enemy troops arriving in relatively small increments would be subject to attack by superior Japanese forces and prevented from accumulating troop strength sufficient for a counterattack.

In order to ensure the success of this strategy, the army demanded stringent construction specifications regarding carrying capacity and speed for the SMR trunk.[16] By 1911, the army had defined its target as the ability to deploy one million men in one hundred days.[17] With growing confidence in the years that followed, army planners elaborated their strategies, calling for the development of a "first strike" capability against the Russians in northern Manchuria by building "interceptor" lines from the SMR trunk toward the segment of CER west of Harbin.[18]

Confident in the effectiveness of their schemes against the modern armies of Russia and, subsequently, the Soviet Union, Japanese strategists almost took for granted their ability to overwhelm any military challenges from a weaker China. Chinese forces, moreover, lacked independent railway access to the territory except for a single line connecting Beijing to Fengtian. To their further disadvantage, the Beijing-Fengtian line ran through a choke point at Shanhaiguan, bracketed by mountains on one side and the sea on the other, making it vulnerable to armed interdiction, as evidenced by a series of incidents between 1911 and 1931.[19] For all intents and purposes, the Chinese conducted military and police operations in the Three Eastern Provinces, as they described the region, at the pleasure of Japanese authorities. Only through the SMR and with the company's express permission could Chinese forces gain access beyond Fengtian junction. This arrangement rendered any operations deemed inimical to Japanese interests all but impossible. Even if Chinese troops managed to avoid the use of the SMR for transport, they could only cross the SMR and the Railway Zone with Japanese assent, a condition that proved quite effective in a passive but decisive intervention in the civil war between Chinese factions in Manchuria in 1925.[20]

The SMR's network, in effect, "hardwired" the territory for war and occupation, reducing the southern part of the territory to a Japanese military protectorate. This circumstance alone contributed much to the SMR's second major function as an instrument of territorial integration. Zones of military control defined by strategic railways went a long way toward transforming Russian and Japanese diplomatic claims to spheres of interest in the region into operative spheres of influence that divided Manchuria into northern and southern sections.[21] The centrality of railways to all dimensions of social, political, and economic life in frontier regions such as Manchuria further enhanced the importance of the catchment basins, or "railway valleys," defined by these transportation systems in recasting regional geography.

Although it might be possible to identify some ecological, economic, demographic, or historical grounds for distinguishing northern from southern sections of Manchuria, the primary logic of parsing the territory in this way lay in the configuration of Russian and Japanese railways. This manner of partition, in fact, overwrote the historical division between Manchuria and Mongolia, as well as more recently established Chinese administrative subdivisions. Harbin and Jilin, cities of the same province, for example, found themselves situated in different railway spheres of influence. Further artifice made possible by railway technology served to distinguish the two spheres. Russia's prohibitive southbound rates on the Harbin to Changchun branch of the CER offers a case in point. These rates effectively increased the southbound distance between Harbin and Changchun as measured in cost or, metaphorically, raised an economic mountain range between Russian and Japanese Manchuria.[22]

The location of Manchuria's external railway connections served to enhance the reality of functional spheres of influence and simultaneously facilitated the gradual alienation of the territory from China south of the Great Wall. Five railway portals controlled access to Manchuria: two under Russian control at Manzhouli and Pogranichnaya, two under the Japanese at Dairen and Andong, and a single gateway at Shanhaiguan held by China. In addition, the SMR controlled all rail access to northern Manchuria from points south, further alienating the Russian sphere from China. Foreign powers not only controlled four out of five railway portals, but through those access points they sought to tie Manchuria to their own territory by means of rate incentives and reduced tariffs. The notion of integrating colonial Korea and southern Manchuria by such means enjoyed widespread support among both military and civilian policymakers, as well as colonial interest groups.[23] Customs and railway unions had served as instruments of nation-building in Central Europe. In Manchuria, they functioned as instruments of partition and imperial integration.

The layout of foreign railway networks in Manchuria also defined new axes of integration and development within the territory. The SMR trunk formed a north-south axis from which tributary feeders reached deep into its eastern and western flanks. In time, invasive runners would stretch north toward the domain of the CER. This trunk and tributary system overwrote older patterns of regional integration centered on the Liao and Sungari River valleys, the overland route from Fengtian to Jilin, and the Inner Mongolian trade route from Qiqihar to Tianjin. In southern Manchuria, all roads led to Dairen, the emerging imperial center of the region.[24]

The transformation of Dairen, from fishing village to what might euphemistically be called the "Hong Kong of the north," points to one of the more prominent outcomes of the SMR operating as a regional development agency, its third colonial function. Company managers engaged in the deliberate, administrative manipulation of the development process. Informed by painstaking research and long-term forecasts, they made use of differential railway tariffs, expansionist construction programs, and targeted investment policies in their efforts to engineer economic change in the catchment area. Such activity, in many respects, would seem to anticipate state planning closely associated with Japanese policy in Manchukuo in the 1930s.

In particular, the SMR stimulated the rapid growth of a regional commercial economy centered on the export of soybeans and soy products. It also encouraged new settlement and cultivation, resulting in more than a doubling of the population before 1931.[25] The company's rate policies, along with direct initiatives in agricultural research, promoted land reclamation, crop improvement and diversification, the spread of new techniques, and the introduction of new breeds to expand animal husbandry.[26] Fine-tuned control over the movement of goods and people throughout the region also had significant corollaries in public health. During an outbreak of plague in 1910, for example, the SMR imposed a selective quarantine on certain categories of passengers in an effort to contain the epidemic.[27]

Urbanization and industrialization in the Railway Zone, the result of extensive investment not only in subsidiary business ventures but in a wide range of infrastructural projects and public works, including education, sanitation, and disease control. It should be noted, though, that the company's far-ranging investments outside the field of railway operations as such ultimately rested on railway earnings. In this respect, SMR reinvested income from freight and passenger tariffs into a variety of projects in the same way that a developmental state might redirect tax revenues into targeted areas of infrastructure and production. Chinese provincial governments and the Japanese railway company, in effect, competed for control of the surpluses produced by Manchuria's soybean economy in order to underwrite rival economic policies.[28]

At the same time, as much as this aggressive program might appear to anticipate state planning of the 1930s, it is important to recall that such economic activism was not unique to SMR, but could be found in other long-haul "frontier" or "pioneer" railways such as those found in the Western United States. The early emergence of "plan rationality"[29] in Japanese Manchuria reflected, in large part, the proclivity of monopoly railway companies to "manage" their economic service areas.

Profits and Policy in the Management of the South Manchuria Railway

The multidimensional power of the SMR in Northeast China highlights the effectiveness of the railway as a instrument of territorial control. At the same time, Japanese efforts to harness railway power introduced significant complications in the formulation and execution of imperial policy. Effective and efficient management of railways, particularly in an environment such as Manchuria in the early twentieth century, demanded high levels of technological and institutional support. The SMR's need to transplant a complex of ancillary facilities in order to sustain its operations has been noted. Railway construction and maintenance was also notoriously costly, and had the SMR not been able to pay its own capital and operating costs, the project would have been prohibitively expensive for a relatively poor Japan. Not surprisingly, architects of this venture embraced profitable operation as a fundamental component of the company's initial policy mandate.[30] Sound business management, however, entailed some unforeseen ramifications for other aspects of the SMR's mission.

The need to defend the company's business interests against purportedly "destructive" competition, for example, led even moderate diplomats to oppose foreign and Chinese railway building initiatives in the vicinity of the SMR with an inflexibility at odds with their own inclinations in China policy.[31] During the 1920s, the SMR's traffic acquisition strategies, favoring the northward expansion of feeder railways, began encroaching on the Soviet Union's inherited railway sphere in northern Manchuria. This competitive orientation simultaneously undermined the foreign ministry's efforts to maintain the *status quo*, while giving unintended support for a more belligerent army policy of challenging Soviet power.[32]

The SMR's business interests could, in this way, push policy in a more aggressive direction than many in Tokyo might have wanted, but it could also slow down and even obstruct essential policy measures. The SMR could not meet the army's stringent specifications until long after the prospects of a second war against Russia had faded from serious consideration, since it was limited to a pace of development consistent with the company's mandate for profitable management, which demanded a reasonable correspondence between investment in carrying capacity and actual traffic volume. Faced with a problem of costly construction without offsetting revenue projections, the company also dragged its feet on completing the railway link to Korea, which was vital for both strategic and colonial integration schemes.[33]

Economic policymakers in Japan often found development initiatives driven by the SMR's business interests less than welcome, violating what they regarded as the proper division of labor between periphery and metropole. Low-cost Fushun coal offered serious competition against Japanese domestic producers in the Asian coal market. In the 1920s, the problem of competition extended to the output of the Anshan Iron Works and other industrial projects of the SMR.[34]

The company's business interests also impinged significantly on the crucial policy goal of facilitating Japanese immigration. The SMR's hiring practices favored low-wage Chinese workers over Japanese, which reduced one of the few sources of gainful employment available to prospective immigrants from Japan.[35] Although sometimes exaggerated, complaints that the company's development efforts did little to benefit Japanese while providing generous opportunities for local Chinese workers, farmers, and landowners, were not entirely unfounded.[36] As a territorial railway company, declarations of corporate patriotism notwithstanding, the SMR's business interests lay more in creating a flourishing service region in southern Manchuria than in promoting the prosperity of the homeland.[37]

As a further complication in the management of policy, the business interests of the SMR played a major part in defining a complex of relationships with local communities and government authorities. Railway power must be understood as a larger phenomenon not limited to imperialist contexts. Territorial railways enjoying monopoly rights in the United States, for example, have frequently developed uneasy relationships with the communities they served because of their perceived stranglehold on the economic life of the region. The dynamics of Sino-Japanese interaction and conflict in Northeast China, then, must be understood not only in terms of the politics of imperialism, but of the broader patterns of railway politics that gave rise, for example to fights between the Grangers and the railway "barons" in the United States. Competition between provincial governments, on the one hand, and the SMR, on the other, over wealth produced by the local economy, has been already noted. Ample reason, quite apart from rising nationalist consciousness, not least among them high freight charges, also existed for local Chinese business interests to attempt to break the SMR's monopoly by investing in competitive railway projects.[38] It might be noted, too, that Japanese small-business proprietors in the Railway Zone found themselves among the most vociferous critics of the overweening power of the SMR.[39]

The business interests of the SMR could deflect and sometimes distort policy, and, in some situations, they might even define divergent directions. Efforts to enforce official policy against those business interests proved difficult, so long as the project as a whole depended on the company's profitability. At the same time, it must be recognized that the logic of business management helped to stabilize Japan's long-term engagement in Manchuria and contributed a measure of consistency and coherence to Japanese activity in the region that it might have lacked otherwise. Political elites in Japan were deeply divided over foreign policy throughout the early twentieth century, and mechanisms for resolving differences remained weak. Rival agencies often pursued conflicting agendas. The directions and emphases in foreign policy also shifted dramatically over time.[40]

The Japanese project in Manchuria exemplified these characteristics of inconstancy and endemic policy conflict. The SMR itself lay within multiple military and civilian jurisdictions, and competing policymakers held substantially different views of the railway venture. To some, the SMR represented something of a white elephant that could not be abandoned because of its symbolic significance as a prize of the Russo-Japanese War, whereas others regarded it as an asset vital to the nation's survival. Moderates tended to view the company as a simple commercial enterprise, while the more ambitiously imperialist regarded it as modern-day, Japanese version of the East India Company. In this context of a poorly coordinated, conflict-ridden, and changeable body of policy, the business operations of the SMR offered a source of stability and coherent direction based on the one point of general consensus, that the company would be managed on sound business principles.[41]

If the SMR's business logic could stabilize as well as deflect Japan's policy in Manchuria, it could also inspire. It should be remembered that the SMR took form, not as the result of an autonomously-formulated Japanese scheme of railway imperialism in Manchuria, but through the takeover of part of a larger project designed by the Russians. The central question facing policymakers in the immediate aftermath of the Russo-Japanese War lay not in defining Japanese aims and methods in Manchuria from scratch, but in deciding what to do with this inherited railway. The early formulation of policy entailed, for the most part, an adaptation of Japanese purposes to Russian designs. In this respect, the railway should be understood not as a subservient instrument of Japanese policy but, rather, as a scaffolding of opportunities that policymakers employed in the construction of their various schemes.

Not surprisingly, this process of adapting ends to available means compounded the tendency toward policy contention and instability. Moreover, the construction of policy around the opportunities presented by the railway resulted, on the whole, in a more audacious course of action than the conservative mainstream of policymakers in late 1905 would have favored. Senior members of the Japanese cabinet had been quite prepared, for example, to sell a fifty-percent share in the railway to the American magnate E.H. Harriman shortly after the conclusion of the Portsmouth treaty.[42] Over the long run, the colonial opportunities inherent in railway operations, more than the persistence or political clout of those advocating an aggressively expansionist program, appeared to have weighed in favor of an approach to Manchuria that, in time, came to toe the threshold of outright control.

The vast horizons of possibility opened by the railway gave rise to specific policy initiatives as well. Of particular note was the scheme of developing heavy industry in Manchuria. Historians have commonly regarded the heavy industrialization of a peripheral territory, quite unusual in the history of modern imperialism, as an identifying peculiarity of Japanese policy in Manchukuo of the 1930s. Yet, not only did this idea, shaped by the lessons of World War I, emerge as a novel centerpiece of Japanese military thinking about wartime economic self-sufficiency during the 1920s, but the direct inspiration lay in the SMR's successful diversification, by the beginning of the decade, into iron and steel as well as coal-based industries. Long before the army had seriously entertained the notion of strategic autarky, officials working for the SMR had inaugurated a program of heavy industrialization based on business rather than strategic logic.[43]

The Decline of Railway Imperialism

Sketched in broad strokes, the history of the SMR between 1905 and 1931 presents a picture of steady institutional growth and expanding Japanese power in Manchuria, even if the logic of business—more than coherent visions of empire—shaped this trajectory. At the same time, signs of serious difficulties appeared early on that, in time, gradually undermined the effectiveness of railway imperialism and the confidence of Japanese imperialists in this approach. The power of the SMR as an instrument of territorial control rested heavily on its monopoly over rail transportation. To be sure, monopoly rights found official justification on business grounds. Even private railway builders in non-imperialist contexts often received exclusive rights based on the argument that protection against potentially destructive competition provided a guarantee indispensable to attracting the huge capital investment necessary to build them. Japanese diplomacy, beginning with the Treaty of Portsmouth, thus worked tirelessly to prevent "destructive competition" most egregiously represented by "parallel construction."

Those who sought to challenge Japanese power in Manchuria clearly understood the importance of the SMR's monopoly. From 1905 on, the attempt to build competing railway lines took center stage in their efforts. One early initiative, launched by Chinese regional officials, surfaced in 1907 in an attempt to extend to the north a branch of the Beijing-Fengtian Railway that would run parallel to the SMR on its western flank. A second in 1909, with American backing, sought to build a north-south line further west of the SMR, which planners believed would be sufficiently separated from the Japanese rail trunk to forestall any reasonable objection based on charges of "parallel construction."

Japanese diplomacy, nonetheless, succeeded in thwarting both initiatives, as well as the U.S. scheme under Secretary of State Knox in 1910 to neutralize foreign railways in Manchuria by placing them under international management. In the process, claims to monopoly rights appeared strengthened. Japanese diplomacy received support from other powers which, although envious of Japanese power in Manchuria, had their own rights to defend elsewhere in China and thus tended to back the principle of imperialist right.[44]

These successes, though, proved short-lived as particularistic concessions and the practice of railway imperialism itself fell out of favor in great power diplomacy in the decade after the Russo-Japanese War. Expectations that had risen high during the "scramble for concessions" between 1895 and 1905 suffered disappointment in the years that followed. Official and popular Chinese resistance made the exploitation of extracted rights difficult. Foreign powers with economic aspirations in China saw a return to the Open Door as more conducive to their interests than partition. Mounting tensions in Europe also drew the Europeans' attention away from competition in the East. Japanese diplomacy found itself increasingly isolated not only in its insistence on traditional imperialist rights, but in its success in the practice of railway imperialism as well.

The Knox scheme of 1910 represented a shot across the bow. Little more than a decade later, the era of concession-hunting and exclusive railway rights appeared to come to a definitive end with successful American-led initiatives leading to the Washington treaties in which all powers, including Japan, renounced claims to spheres of influence in China. Japan managed to preserve a core of its claims in Manchuria, including its exclusive ownership of the SMR, but at the cost of significant curbs on further expansion and reduced protection against competition. With a substantial weakening of the political and legal framework of railway imperialism, those in Japan with a persistent commitment to expansion in Manchuria began looking for supplemental and even alternative strategies.[45]

Growing disappointment in some of the promised results of railway imperialism further fueled the search for other strategies. The slow progress of immigration, often blamed on SMR policies, but due more broadly to a paucity of attractive opportunity, drew persistent criticism. The acquisition of land rights in Manchuria, a key feature of the Twenty-One Demands of 1915, some argued, would resolve this problem, But, in fact, a declining proportion of Japanese relative to Chinese residents of the Railway Zone, where Japanese property rights were not in question, pointed to deeper difficulties.[46] The question of who benefited from Japanese railway investment, noted earlier, also contributed to skepticism and highlighted yet again the problem of immigration. The only way that Japanese would gain directly from the SMR's development work would entail settling in large numbers in southern Manchuria.

Thus, the project of imperial integration, of binding Manchuria more closely to Japan through the development of railway connections through Korea, made little substantive progress, despite the completion of the network itself. Even after the SMR took over the management of the Korean railway system on a contractual basis, the economic amalgamation of Korea and Manchuria failed to advance.[47]

Manchuria's soybean economy, although certainly engaging Japan, remained more broadly linked to international markets, including high demand for margarine in Europe and soy-cake fertilizer in China south of the Great Wall.[48] Wary of high expectations and of becoming the brunt of criticism in failing to realize them, the SMR launched a public relations campaign in the 1920s to redress exaggerated claims and tone down unrealistic hopes in a series of pamphlets entitled, *What Should We Expect from Manchuria?*[49]

Among possible alternative and supplemental strategies in Manchuria during the 1920s, the army came to favor the development of a client relationship with Zhang

Zuolin, one of so-called warlords contending for power in the fragmented Chinese republic, whose primary base lay in Northeast China. The strategy of cultivating Zhang as a client suffered from ambiguities, however, from the start. Did the primary purpose of linking up with Zhang lie in using his authority to shore up the weakened framework of railway imperialism so that the SMR could continue to thrive? Or was a compliant, pro-Japanese client in Manchuria a more straightforward substitute for railway power that no longer offered much promise? Such ambiguities contributed to tensions between Zhang and his handlers in the Japanese army, as well as among the handlers themselves. These problems culminated in the assassination of Zhang by a disgruntled Japanese officer in 1928. Zhang's son and successor, motivated by nationalist sympathies as well as a desire to shore up his regional power and revenue base, launched an aggressive effort to build a new railway system that would end the monopoly of the SMR.

The end result of Zhang's assassination was a simultaneous collapse of both railway imperialism and client management as strategies for controlling Manchuria.[50] Japanese hardliners saw both the opportunity and need for direct action. It is in this context that the Kwantung Army launched a military initiative in the Manchurian Incident of 1931.

The South Manchuria Railway in Manchukuo

The armed occupation of Manchuria and the subsequent creation of the puppet state of Manchukuo marked a great divide in the history of Japanese expansion in the region.[51] Formal control through partition and state building displaced informal control of the territory through railway power. To be sure, the SMR continued to stand close to the center of the Japanese project during the 1930s. The strategic importance of the railway, in fact, increased, given a Soviet military buildup in the Far East in response to the developments of 1931 and tenuous Japanese control of a vast Manchurian countryside. The economic aims of the new state continued to rely on the SMR's role as an engine of development in agriculture, commerce, and natural resource extraction. The company's branch and subsidiary operations in manufacturing and refining formed the core of modern industry in the territory, and the army regarded the SMR's heavy industrial plant as vital to schemes for a self-sufficient empire.

Given its past performance, the company also served as the most reliable conduit for private investment into the region. The SMR provided much of the material foundations for economic planning in Manchukuo as well as experience and know-how. Early planning bodies organized by the army on behalf of the fledgling state leaned heavily on the company's economic research and technical staff.[52] In many respects, territorial economic management under the SMR segued almost seamlessly into state planning in Manchukuo.

The transition between an era when the SMR stood on the foundations of railway power as a near-sovereign entity and one in which the company formed a vital yet subordinate component of a colonial state apparatus, however, proved less than entirely smooth. Conflict between the SMR and the Japanese army, Manchukuo's puppet masters, indeed, became a serious political issue in the early 1930s. Insofar as this conflict offers a particularly revealing, albeit ironic, look at the dynamics of railway power, it warrants a brief examination.

For most intents and purposes, the nominally independent Manchurian state was an entity controlled by the Japanese army, which, moreover, shielded the army from direct accountability to civilian authorities in Tokyo. Yet, as much as its sovereignty might be a fiction, the legal framework of relations between Japan and Manchukuo sought, insofar as possible, to follow the norms of relations between sovereign states, governed by formal, international treaties. These treaty agreements, interestingly, preserved most of the old rights that the SMR, as a Japanese-owned entity, enjoyed before 1931, including extraterritoriality and its control of the Railway Zone. These circumstances provided the SMR immunity from the Manchurian state and, accordingly, army control in the same way that imperialist rights had protected it earlier from Chinese authority. The preservation of the company's special, extraterritorial status represented more than an unforeseen glitch in the new institutional arrangements, because that status provided a vehicle for civilian officials in Tokyo with jurisdiction over the SMR to check an otherwise unbridled army in Manchuria. Given the magnitude and far-reaching ramifications of railway power, civilian control of the SMR from Tokyo represented a significant encroachment on the "sovereignty" of army-controlled Manchukuo.[53]

Tensions came to head in 1933, when the army launched an initiative to "reorganize" the SMR in a manner that would, in effect, dismantle the company into separate operational units managing railways, coal mining, steel production, machine building, chemical refining, and other industrial enterprises. Army planners sought to nationalize some of these units under the Manchurian state while placing others under control cartels that would facilitate direct army supervision and, not incidentally, give military authorities greater leverage over economic planning in the home islands. The initiative of 1933, which roiled public opinion to the embarrassment of the army, proved premature. But over the next few years, taking advantage of increasing political influence at home, the army gradually managed to bring the SMR under its control.

This confrontation between the army and the SMR formed part of a larger story of civil-military conflict in the Japanese empire during 1930s, but it also revealed a peculiar pattern of Japanese on Japanese imperialism or, alternatively, of two rival imperialisms in Manchuria, one centered on railway power and the other, on managing a puppet state. At the same time, viewed from a broader perspective, the dynamics of this conflict resonated with the politics of railway regulation elsewhere and highlights railway power as a challenge to sovereignty that transcended traditional contexts of imperialism.[54]

Conclusions

The SMR provided the "bones and sinews" of Manchukuo, as well as the material and technological resources that made Japan's experiment in "imperial socialism" on the continent possible. It also made important contributions to the culture of Manchukuo. The ethos of the "brave new empire," as Louise Young describes it, had its proximal sources in the intellectual ferment of the 1920s and in the radicalism shaped by the crisis environment of the early 1930s.[55]

Its distal origins, however, arguably lie in what might be described as "railway culture." One aspect of that culture exhibited inherently imperial qualities in the monumental architecture of railway stations, in ostentatious displays of engineering feats, and in the hubris of conquering nature reflected in the construction of luxury hotels in the wilderness, like the Canadian Pacific Railroad's Hotel Lake Louise.[56]

Another aspect, and perhaps the source of the first, however, lay in an abiding faith in technology and the limitless wonders it could work. The age of the railway brought forth an engineer's vision of the world to come, well captured, as Raymond Betts has noted, in the writings of Jules Verne. In this respect, railways of the early twentieth century enjoyed a substantial leavening of the "brave" and the "new" from the start.[57] That ethos and the vision of great transformation seem to have permeated the SMR's promotional literature from early on, which reveled in such contrasts as the smokestacks of Anshan towering against a blank Manchurian horizon. A sleek Asia Express racing across the prairie became an important icon of the new Manchukuo. Yet in one form or another, that image had symbolized Japan in Manchuria since 1905.[58]

Notes

1. I first encountered the term, a variant of which is attributed to Sergei Witte, in Huenemann, *The Dragon and the Iron Horse,* 57.
2. The basic description of the SMR's organization is draw from official company history, Minami Manshū tetsudō kabushikigaisha, *Minami Manshū tetsudō kabushikigaisha 10 nen shi* (Dairen: Manshū nichinichi shinbunsha, 1919, abbreviated hereafter as SMR I). For an overview of the SMR in English, see Herbert P. Bix, "Japanese Imperialism and Manchuria, 1890–1931" (Ph.D.

dissertation, Harvard University, 1972); Ramon H. Myers, "Japanese Imperialism in Manchuria: The South Manchuria Railway Company," in *The Japanese Informal Empire in China*, ed. Peter Duus et al. (Princeton: Princeton University Press, 1989), 101–32; Y. Tak Matsusaka, *The Making of Japanese Manchuria* (Cambridge, MA: Harvard Asia Center, 2001). For a sampling of work in Japanese, see *Mantetsu: Nihon teikokushugi to Chūgoku*, ed. Andō Hikotarō (Waseda study group, Tokyo: Ochanomizu shobō, 1965); Harada Katsumasa, *Mantetsu* (Tokyo: Iwanami shoten, 1981); Kaneko Fumio, "Sōgyōki no Minami Manshū tetsudō, 1906–1916," *Shakai kagaku kenkyū*, Vol. 31, No. 4 (January 1980): 171–201; *Kindai Nihon to Mantetsu*, ed. Kobayashi Hideo (Tokyo: Yoshikawa kōbunkan, 2000).

3. For general background on the Chinese Eastern Railway, see Chinese Eastern Railway Printing Office, *North Manchuria and the Chinese Eastern Railway* (Reprint of an original volume published in English in Harbin, 1924. New York: Garland Publishing, 1982). For an early assessment of the relative strengths of the two branches of the CER, see Kantō totokufu minseibu, *Manshū sangyō chōsa shiryō*, 8 unnumbered volumes, volume on commerce and manufacturing (Tokyo: Kokkōsha, 1906), 101–2. On the problematic connections at Changchun, see Kaneko, "Sōgyōki no Minami Manshū tetsudō," 193–94.

4. Kitaoka Shin'ichi, *Nihon rikugun to tairiku seisaku* (Tokyo: Tokyō daigaku shuppankai, 1978), 103–9; Kaneko, "Sōgyōki no Minami Manshū tetsudō," 195–97.

5. On these two categories of railway concessions, see Huenemann, *Dragon and the Iron Horse*, 58–59.

6. On railway diplomacy immediately following the Russo-Japanese War, see Baba Akira, "Nichi-Ro sengo ni okeru dai 1 ji Saionji naikaku no tai-Man seisaku to Shinkoku," in *Tai-Manmō seisaku shi no ichimen*, ed. Kurihara Ken (Tokyo: Hara shobō, 1967), 67–73; Inoue Yūichi, *Higashi Ajia tetsudō kokusai kankei shi* (Tokyo: Keiō tsūshin, 1991), 155–79; for examples of later negotiations of loan concessions, see Matsusaka, *Making of Japanese Manchuria*, 163–71.

7. *Manshū sangyō chōsa shiryō*, volume on mining, 143–44. SMR I, 603–26.

8. SMR I, 629–43.

9. SMR I, 369–70, 375–86. Hoshino Tokuji, *Economic History of Manchuria* (Seoul: Bank of Chōsen, 1920), 123.

10. Nagura Bunji, *Nihon tekkōgyō shi no kenkyū* (Tokyo: Kondō shuppansha, 1984), 271–77; Seiichirō Yonekura, *The Japanese Iron and Steel Industry* (New York: St. Martin's Press, 1994), 117–32.

11. Chinese Eastern Railway, *North Manchuria and the Chinese Eastern Railway*, 42.

12. SMR I, 691–897. Tetsudōin kantokukyoku, *Mantetsu shisatsu hōkokusho* (1913, No publication data, University of Tokyo Social Science Institute Library), 70–72.

13. The construction contract and statutes governing the CER are reproduced in MacMurray, Vol. 1, 74–77, 84–91.

14. Kurihara Ken, "Kantō totokufu mondai teiyō," in *Tai-Man seisaku shi no ichimen,* 57–59, (shiryō 1) 275–84; Suzuki Takashi, *Nihon teikokushugi to Manshū, I* (2 vols., Tokyo: Hanawa shobō, 1992), 334–40.

15. See for example, Hoshino Tokuji, *Economic History of Manchuria*; C. Walter Young, *Japanese Jurisdiction in the South Manchuria Railway Areas* (Baltimore: Johns Hopkins, 1931).

16. Sanbō honbu, *Meiji 40 nendo Nihon teikoku rikugun sakusen keikaku* (March, 1907 [Japan] National Defense Research Institute Library). 1907 is the earliest year for which complete operations plans in Manchuria have survived. On specifications, Sanbō honbu, *Man-Kan kōtsū kikan jūbi kansei no kyūmu* (Miyazaki Collection, item 23, [Japan] National Defense Research Institute Library). Also see Kobayashi Michihiko, "'Teikoku kokubō hōshin' saikō: Nichi-Ro sengo ni okeru riku-kai gun no kyōchō," *Shigaku zasshi*, Vol. 98, No. 4 (April 1989): 36–71; Matsusaka, *Making of Japanese Manchuria*, 104–14.

17. Sanbō honbu, *Futatabi waga kuni rikugun sentō nōryoku o zōka sezarubekarazaru yuen o ronji, awasete Chōsen, Manshū ni okeru yusō kikan seibi no hitsuyō ni oyobu* (5/1911, Miyazaki Collection, item 48, [Japan] National Defense Research Institute Library).

18. On army plans, Rikugunshō gunmukyoku gunjika, "Tōnan tetsudō ni kansuru ken," (1/1914), *Mitsu dai nikki* 1914, Vol. 4, unyu-tsūshin 3; Army Chief of Staff Hasegawa Yoshimichi to Army Vice Minister Kusunose Sachihiko, "Shina ni oite gunjijō waga kibō suru tetsudō mō," (3/16/1914), *Mitsu dai nikki,* 1914 Vol.4, unyu tsūshin 4 ([Japan] National Defense Research Institute Library); Director Matsuoka Yōsuke to Prime Minister Katō (12/11/25) in Matsuoka Yōsuke denki kankō kai, *Matsuoka Yōsuke–sono hito to shōgai* (Tokyo: Kōzasha, 1974), 171.

19. During the 1920s, for example, the Kwantung Army designated Shanhaiguan as the point at which it would forcefully disarm any Chinese troops attempting to cross into Manchuria without Japanese permission. Shimada Toshihiko, *Kantōgun* (Tokyo: Chūōkōronsha, 1965), 56–72.

20. Gavan McCormack, *Chang Tso-lin in Northeast China: China, Japan and the Manchurian Idea* (Stanford: Stanford University Press, 1977), 146–87. Suzuki, *Nihon teikokushugi to Manshū I,* 421–32. Bannō Junji, *Kindai Nihon no gaikō to seiji* (Tokyo: Kenbun shuppan, 1985), 137–41.

21. Rather precise boundaries for Russian and Japanese spheres based on railway operations in Manchuria were defined in a succession of agreements. Cabinet resolution, "Nichi-Ro dai 1 kai kyōyaku," (7/30/07), 280–82; Cabinet Resolution, "Dai 2 kai Nichi-Ro kyōyaku ni kansuru ken," (3/1910), 332–36; both in Gaimushō, *Nihon gaikō nenpyō narabini shuyō bunsho, I* (2 vols., Tokyo: Hara shobō, 1965–66). For a discussion of the distinction between "spheres of influence" and "spheres of interest," see W.W. Willoughby, *Foreign Rights and Interests in China* (Baltimore: Johns Hopkins Press, 1920), 270–73.

22. Kaneko, "Sōgyōki no Minami Manshū tetsudō," 193–94.

23. Kaneko Fumio, *Kindai Nihon ni okeru tai-Man tōshi no kenkyū* (Tokyo: Kondō shuppansha, 1991; hereafter, *Tai-Man tōshi*), 132–137, 235–46; Kitaoka, *Nihon rikugun to tairiku seisaku,* 235–46.

24. Understanding that the business success of the railway depended, at least initially, on diverting existing movements of goods, SMR and other Japanese researchers studied traditional trade routes extensively. They paid special attention to the Liao River route. For example, Minami Manshū tetsudō kabushikigaisha chōsaka (Ueda Kenzo), *Ryōga no sui'un* (Dairen: SMR, 1911). Drawing all export traffic to Dairen was a central element in the SMR's business strategy. Kaneko, *Tai-Man tōshi no kenkyū*, 111–14.

25. On the SMR and the development of Manchuria's "soybean economy," see Kaneko, *Tai-Man tōshi no kenkyū*, 45–49; idem, "Sōgyōki no Minami Manshū tetsudō," 80–90; Su Chungmin, *Mantie shi* (Beijing: Zhonghua shuqu, 1990), 90–184.

26. SMR I, 878–93.

27. A detailed listing of travel itineraries and stations embargoed for certain categories of Chinese and Korean travelers as part of the plague control effort (based on unapologetic ethnic and class "profiling" with regard to propensities for carrying disease) may be found in Minami Manshū tetsudō kabushikigaisha, *Dai 8 kai eigyō hōkokusho* (annual stockholder report for 1910, reprints, Tokyo: Ryūkei shoseki, 1977), 18–19.

28. Matsusaka, *The Making of Japanese Manchuria*, 140. Chinese railway competition, discussed below, was partly driven by this rivalry.

29. On "plan rationality," see Chalmers Johnson, *MITI and the Japanese Miracle* (Stanford: Stanford University Press, 1981), 19–23.

30. Kaneko Fumio, "1920 nendai ni okeru Nihon teikokushugi to 'Manshū' (1)," *Shakai kagaku kenkyū*, Vol. 32, No. 4 (February 1981): 149–219, 151. The visionary first governor of the SMR, Gotō Shinpei, received a rude awakening and a lesson in the primacy of this mandate when the finance ministry rejected his initial budget proposal, which included operating deficits for the first five years. Tsurumi Yūsuke, *Gotō Shinpei, II* (4 vols., original, 1942, Tokyo: Keisō shobō, 1965), 772–73, 1023–24.

31. See note 6.

32. Matsusaka, *Making of Japanese Manchuria*, 229–35, 281–304, 316–26.

33. Matsusaka, *Making of Japanese Manchuria*, 141–45, 162–64; Kitaoka, *Nihon rikugun to tairiku seisaku*, 103–09; Kaneko Fumio, "Sogyōki no Minami Manshū tetsudō," 195–97.

34. On complaints about competition in coal, see Tetsdōin, Kantokukyoku, *Mantetsu shisatsu hōkokusho*, 61–63; on iron, see SMR, *Honpō seitekkō saku jūritsu to Minami Manshū* (Dairen: SMR, 1924).

35. SMR I, 135–38; *Mantetsu: Nihon teikokushugi to Chūgoku*, 112–13. Preference for low-wage Chinese labor extended to other Japanese businesses as well. Nishimura Shigeo, *Chūgoku kindai tōhoku chiiki shi kenkyū* (Tokyo: Hōritsu bunkasha, 1984), 175. Minami Manshū tetsudō kabushikigaisha, *Dai 8 kai eigyō hōkokusho* (1910) 18.

36. For example, see "Akiyama Saneyuki danwa, Minami Manshū keiei hōshin; fu, dō danwa Ōshima Ken'ichi iyaku," ca. early 1913, in *Terauchi Masatake kankei monjo*, ed. Yamamoto Jirō (Kyoto: Kyoto joshi daigaku, 1984), 713–15.

56   Y. TAK MATSUSAKA

37. SMR director Matsuoka Yōsuke rationalized this orientation by arguing that what was good economically for Manchuria was good, in the long run, for Japan, even if it required some sacrifice in the short run. Matsuoka Yōsuke, *Ugoku Manmō* (Tokyo: Senshinsha, 1931), 24–29.

38. See, for example, Austin Kerr, *Railroad Politics, 1914–1920: Rates, Wages and Efficiency* (Pittsburgh: University of Pittburgh Press, 1968); on motivations for local Chinese investment in competing railways, see Hirano Kenichirō, "1923 nen no Manshū," in *Kindai Nihon to Ajia–bunka no kōryū to masatsu* (Tokyo: Tokyo daigaku shuppankai, 1984), 250–52; Su, *Man-tie shi*, 401–08; McCormack, *Chang Tso-lin in Northeast China*, 87–100, 190–91.

39. For example, petition from the Federation of Residents' Committees of the SMR Zone (4/10/29), transmitted by Mukden Consul General Hayashi Kyūjirō to Foreign/Prime Minister Tanaka (5/28/29), Gaimushō microfilm, S61921, ff. 3991–93.

40. On policy conflicts in Manchuria, see Tsunoda Jun, *Manshū mondai to kokubō hōshin*, (Tokyo: Hara shobō, 1967), and the collection *Tai-Man-Mō seisaku no ichimen*.

41. This is a central theme in Matsusaka, *The Making of Japanese Manchuria*; see esp. 103–148.

42. Matsusaka, *The Making of Japanese Manchuria*, 77–102.

43. On schemes for autarky, see Michael A. Barnhart, *Japan Prepares for Total War* (Ithaca: Cornell University Press, 1987). Examples of SMR-inspired projects may be found in Sanbō honbu (Koiso Kuniaki), *Teikoku kokubō shigen* (1917, [Japan] National Defense Research Institute Library).

44. On the rise of Chinese "railway nationalism," see Lee En-han, *China's Quest for Railway Autonomy, 1904–1911* (Singapore: Singapore University Press, 1977). On railway diplomacy in this era, see E-tu Zen Sun, *Chinese Railways and British Interests, 1898–1911* (New York: King's Crown Press, 1954), 148–64; Michael Hunt, *Frontier Defense and the Open Door* (New Haven, CT: Yale University Press, 1973), 188–229; Tsunoda, *Manshū mondai to kokubō hōshin*, 480–83; Inoue, *Higashi Ajia tetsudō kokusai kankei shi*, 265–74.

45. These developments are traced in Matsusaka, *Making of Japanese Manchuria*, 205–250.

46. Minami Manshū tetsudō kabushikigaisha chōsaka (Kudō Takeo), *Waga kuni jinkō mondai to Manmō* (Dairen: SMR, 1928), a detailed study of Japanese migration and settlement conducted by the SMR. Also see Matsusaka, *Making of Japanese Manchuria*, 174–85, 189–92, 305–11.

47. Hashitani, "Chōsen tetsudō no Mantetsu e no itaku keiei o megutte–dai 1 ji taisen zengo no Nittei shokuminchi seisaku no 1 danmen," *Chōsenshi kenkyūkai ronbunshū*, no. 19 (March 1982): 159–78; Kaneko, *Tai-Man tōshi no kenkyū*, 235–42.

48. In 1909, for example, 18 percent of Manchurian soybean exports went to Japan, 25 percent to China, and more than 34 percent to Europe and the United States. Kaneko, *Tai-Man tōshi no kenkyū*, 41. Matsumoto Toshirō points out that Japanese economic activity in Kwantung and the Railway Zone constituted more an element of the regional Chinese economy than an imperial extension of Japan's.

Matsumoto Toshirō, *Shinryaku to kaihatsu: Nihon shihonshugi to Chūgoku shokuminchika* (Tokyo: Ochanomizu shobō, 1988), 36–37.

49. Minami Manshū tetsudō kabushikigaisha chōsaka (Nonaka Tokio), *Manmō yori nani o kitai subeki ka* (Dairen: SMR, 1924, 1929, 1930).

50. On Zhang and his troubled relations with the Japanese, see McCormack, *Chang Tso-lin in Northeast China*; on Zhang Xueliang in this period, see Nishimura Shigeo, *Chō Gakurō* (Tokyo: Iwanami Shoten, 1996), 51–77; on railway competition, Ogata Yōichi, "Tōhoku kōtsū iinkai to iwayuru 'Mantetsu hōi tetsudō mō keikaku'," *Shigaku zasshi*, dai 86 kan, dai 8 gō (August 1977): 39–72. Also see Matsusaka, 312–48, 363–77.

51. There is a large volume of work dealing with the founding of Manchukuo which include among earlier works, Sadako Ogata, *Defiance in Manchuria: The Making of Japanese Foreign Policy, 1931–1932* (Berkeley: University of California Press, 1964); Mark R. Peattie, *Ishiwara Kanji and Japan's Confrontation with the West* (Princeton: Princeton University Press, 1975); and more recently, Louise Young, *Japan's Total Empire: Manchuria and the Culture of Wartime Imperialism* (Berkeley: University of California Press, 1997).

52. A plan in which the SMR would serve as the principal economic planning and development agency in Manchukuo was drafted in early 1932. Hōjō Shūichi, "Manshū keizai tōsei an (kōhen, seisaku hen)" (6/1932), in Minami Manshū tetsudō kabushikigaisha-keizai chōsakai, *Manshū keizai tōsei hōsaku* (Dairen: SMR, 1935). The army, at minimum, sought to use the SMR to underwrite both military and development costs. Katakura Diary (12/6/1931), *Gendai shi shiryō 7: Manshū jihen*, ed. Kobayashi Tatsuo and Shimada Toshihiko (Tokyo: Misuzu shobō, 1964), 287–90.

53. Y. Tak Matsusaka, "Managing Occupied Manchuria, 1931–1934." In *The Japanese Wartime Empire, 1931–1945*, eds. Peter Duus, Ramon H. Myers and Mark R. Peattie (Princeton: Princeton University Press, 1996), 97–135.

54. See Makita Kensuke, "1930 nen dai ni okeru Mantetsu kaiso mondai," *Rekishi hyōron*, No. 289 (May 1974): 36–50; Hara Akira, "'Manshū' ni okeru keizai tōsei seisaku no tenkai—Mantetsu kaiso to Mangyō setsuritsu o megutte," in *Nihon keizai seisaku shiron, II*, ed. Andō Yoshio (Tokyo: Tokyo daigaku shuppankai, 1976), 211–28; and Takahashi Yasutaka, "Minami Manshū tetsudō kabushiki kaisha no kaiso keikaku ni tsuite," *Shakai kagaku tōkyū* Vol. 27, No. 2 (April 1982): 53–112. In English, Joshua Fogel (trans.) *Life Along the South Manchurian Railway: The Memoirs of Itō Takeo* (Armonk: M.E. Sharpe, 1988), 124–32; Matsusaka, "Managing Occupied Manchuria," 120–27. A forthcoming work by Emer O'Dwyer examines this development.

55. Young, *Total Empire*, chapter 6.

56. The novelist Natsume Sōseki observes some of these qualities in the SMR's facilities during his 1909 tour of the company's facilities at the invitation of his friend, Vice Governor Nakamura Zekō. Natsume Sōseki, *Man-Kan tokorodokoro* (orig. 1910), in *Meiji hoppō chōsa tanken ki shūsei 10* (Tokyo: Yumani shobō, 1989), 209–10, 215, 218–19.

57. Raymond Betts, *Uncertain Dimensions: Western Overseas Empires in the Twentieth Century* (Minneapolis: University of Minnesota Press, 1985), 80–81.

58. Matsusaka, *Making of Japanese Manchuria*, 394–95.

3

Sino-Soviet Tensions and Soviet Administrative Control over the Chinese Eastern Railway, 1917–25

Bruce A. Elleman

Following the October Revolution in 1917, the Soviet Union regained majority control over the strategically-located Chinese Eastern Railway (CER), which ran through northern Manchuria, by signing two secret agreements: the first with the Beijing government on 31 May 1924, and the second with Zhang Zuolin's government in Manchuria on 20 September 1924.[1] To consolidate Soviet power over this railway, the USSR then signed a 20 January 1925 convention with Japan that recognized Japan's authority over the South Manchuria Railway in return for Japan's acquiescence to full Soviet authority over the Chinese Eastern Railway. The final step in the Soviet Union's rejection of its earlier promises of equality with China was reached on 26 February 1925, when the Soviet government's ambassador to China, Lev Karakhan, recognized the validity of Japan's Twenty-one Demands, considered by many Chinese to be the most humiliating example of China's mistreatment by the capitalist countries.

The Geostrategic Importance of the Chinese Eastern Railway

The nineteenth century struggle to partition Manchuria ended in war between Russia and Japan. After Russia's defeat in 1905, Washington offered its services to negotiate a peace treaty. Taking advantage of its role as broker, the United States convinced Russia and Japan to declare that "they have not in Manchuria any territorial advantages or preferential or exclusive concessions in impairment of Chinese sovereignty or inconsistent with the principle of equal opportunity."[2] But the Portsmouth Treaty publicly stated that Russia retained the Chinese Eastern Railway, while Japan acquired the South Manchuria Railway. In practical terms, therefore, Manchuria was divided into Russian and Japanese spheres of influence.

Ignoring all attempts by the United States to enforce the treaty, Russia and Japan continued to carve up China, even signing several secret agreements—in 1907, 1910, 1912, and 1916—which delimited their respective spheres of influence. When the 1911 Chinese revolution divided and weakened China, Russia used this opportunity to negotiate an advantageous treaty with Outer Mongolia in 1912 and then pressured China to sign an agreement in 1913 that limited her rights in Outer Mongolia. Russia then convinced China to sign a tripartite treaty with Russia and Outer Mongolia in 1915, by which Outer Mongolia recognized the *suzerainty* of China in exchange for China recognizing the *autonomy* of Outer Mongolia.[3] The immediate effect of the tripartite treaties was that Outer Mongolia, which formerly had been internationally recognized as part of China, fell under the sway of the stronger Russian government.[4]

With the European nations already embroiled in World War I, and with the United States' attention also directed mainly across the Atlantic, Japan carried out similarly expansionist policies in southern Manchuria, Shandong, and Inner Mongolia. In January 1915, Japan presented China with "Twenty-one Demands," that pressured Beijing to cede a long list of territorial and economic rights, including the transfer of Germany's former rights in Shandong province to Japan. The United States condemned the Twenty-one Demands as a violation of the political and territorial integrity of the Republic of China. But Yuan Shikai accepted Japan's demands to prop up his own authority as President. Several of the resulting Sino-Japanese agreements were outlined in secret treaties signed by the president of the Republic of China, Yuan Shikai.[5]

In an attempt to capitalize on the 1919 May Fourth Movement, which opposed the Paris Peace Conference's decision that Germany should cede Japan the Shandong concession before Japan returned it to China, Lev Karakhan, the Soviet government's assistant commissar of foreign affairs, issued a manifesto to China on 25 July 1919. The Karakhan Manifesto offered to fulfill all of the requests that China had just had rejected by the Paris Peace Conference, including the abolition of all of Russia's extraterritorial rights in China, the return of territorial concessions, abolition of all unequal treaties, and cancellation of the Boxer indemnity. Karakhan's most important promise was to return the Chinese Eastern Railway to China free of charge:

> The Soviet government restores to the Chinese people without exacting any kind of compensation, the Chinese Eastern Railway, as well as all concessions of minerals, forests, gold, and others which were seized from them by the government of Tsars, the

government of Kerensky, and the brigands Horvath, Semenov, Kolchak, the former generals, merchants, and capitalists of Russia.[6]

The Karakhan Manifesto was an attempt to obtain the Chinese people's sympathy for the diplomatically-isolated new Soviet state, as well as the first step in opening diplomatic negotiations with the Beijing government. Later controversy between the Soviet Union and China over the Karakhan Manifesto revolved around the fact that when this 25 July 1919 document was published in the Soviet press under the title "Obrashchenie Sovetskoi Rossii k Kitaiu" (Appeal from Soviet Russia to China), the 26 August 1919 *Izvestiia* edition did not contain the crucial sentence about returning the CER without compensation; Soviet diplomats later used this second version initially to demand payment for the CER, and then to refuse to return the railway to China altogether.

In addition to the original Soviet telegram, however, a 1919 pamphlet published by Vladimir Vilenskii, a Soviet Foreign Ministry official, confirmed that the original version of the Karakhan Manifesto promised to return the CER free of charge.[7] A third published document from the 24 April 1921 *Bulletin of the Far Eastern Secretariat of the Comintern* also conforms to these other two sources.[8] These three sources—the original telegram, the Vilenskii pamphlet, and the version published in the Communist International's own Siberian journal in 1921—prove that the Soviet Union did initially offer to return the CER to China without compensation.

The two versions of the Karakhan Manifesto allowed the Soviet government to present the more liberal manifesto to the Chinese government and populace between 1919 and 1921, and then the less generous manifesto after 1921. The Soviet government made two versions of the Karakhan Manifesto on purpose—one to satisfy its propaganda requirements and the other to satisfy its diplomatic requirements—and then proceeded to pick and choose the manifesto that suited its purposes. Ignatii Iurin was the first Soviet representative to travel to Beijing to attempt to open diplomatic relations between China and the Soviet Union.[9] Simultaneously, the Soviet Union helped Chinese intellectuals organize a Chinese Communist Party during July 1921.[10] Both of these events were used to open Sino-Soviet diplomatic negotiations over the status of the Chinese Eastern Railway.

Opening Sino-Soviet Diplomatic Negotiations

The Bolsheviks' first problem during 1920 and early 1921 was to renew diplomatic relations with the internationally-recognized Chinese government in Beijing. The Beijing government was especially interested in Karakhan's promise to return the

CER to China. It responded positively to Karakhan's first manifesto during September 1920 by breaking relations with officials of Kerensky's Provisional Russian government in preparation for receiving the first of many Soviet representatives to China.

China's preeminent railway expert, Wang Jinzhun, wrote a letter to Foreign Minister W. W. Yan not long afterwards, in which he advocated that China take advantage of the current situation to solve the sticky ownership disputes that revolved around the CER: "Today presents the only and most unexpected opportunity for some solution of the problem, for it is the first time for many years that Russia and Japan are really at logger heads, while other Powers are in no position to interfere as they used to do." In addition, Wang warned that further conflict over the Chinese Eastern Railway might arise: "Manchuria has twice been the battle field in recent years, and will be the bone of contention for more international conflicts, unless the statesmen of today can arrange matters in such a way as will ameliorate the situation. The Chinese Eastern [Railway] plays a most important part and constitutes a most important factor in the Manchuria question."[11]

On 2 October 1920, Karakhan met with a Chinese military mission in Moscow, and presented it with an entirely new program under which the Soviet government would be willing to open relations with China (often referred to as the second Karakhan Manifesto, or the 1920 Karakhan Manifesto). Besides repeating that all former Sino-Russian treaties were now abolished, this manifesto once again renounced the Boxer indemnity, returned to China without compensation all Russian concession areas, and revoked extraterritoriality for Russians living in China. But, the promise to return the CER was not repeated. Instead Karakhan stated that the Soviet Union wanted to maintain some control over the railway by signing a "special treaty on the way of working the Chinese Eastern Railway with regard to the needs of the Russian Socialist Federative Soviet Republic."[12]

While Karakhan's new offer still looked generous to China, it negatively affected the White Russians who were living in China. Moscow's frequent declarations that it was abolishing Russia's special privileges and concessions in China actually meant little, since abolishing the Boxer indemnity would have cut some $3,000,000 a year in Chinese funds supporting the continued activities of the defunct Russian Provisional government's consulates in China, the remaining consulates in Japan, and was even suspected of also being a source of income for the Provisional government's embassy in Washington.[13] Furthermore, by 1920, much of the territory in the Russian concessions in China was owned by non-Russians, as confirmed in a letter dated 5 October 1920, from American Minister Charles Crane to Foreign Minister Yan, informing him that in the Tianjin concession "the bulk of the property in the Russian Concession is owned not by Russians but by Americans and subjects of other nations."[14]

The Soviet government also publicly renounced special privileges that it was later able to retain secretly under new names: for example, with the nationalization of all the USSR's foreign trade in 1923, all Soviet businessmen in China immediately became government officials and claimed diplomatic immunity in place of the former extraterritoriality rights.[15] Karakhan's previous assurances that the USSR would return the CER to China, therefore, was the only promise that actually gave China something that it did not have already.

Although Karakhan's new proposal concerning the CER was not nearly as advantageous to China as the offer made in his original manifesto, it was vaguely enough worded that it did not seem to contradict the intent of his former promise. Only after the Soviet government's first official diplomat, Aleksandr Paikes, arrived in Beijing in December 1921, did the Soviet government's true intentions start to become clear. During April 1922, Paikes told a Chinese official: "My government formerly announced that all of the tsarist treaties were abolished, it did not say that the basis for these treaties was abolished, because these matters have to be studied. But your government mistakenly thought that the 1919 manifesto unconditionally canceled the 1915 treaty; at the same time it never said that Outer Mongolia's autonomy was abolished and that the Chinese Eastern Railway was already returned to China's control. On these matters your government is mistaken."[16]

According to Paikes's interpretation, the Soviet government's former declaration that it would annul all of the tsarist unequal treaties clearly had no meaning so long as China could be convinced to agree to the old terms. In addition, Paikes had given the first hint that not only was Moscow no longer willing to return the railway to China, but that all previous indications to the contrary would be blamed on China's "misunderstanding" of the Karakhan Manifesto. Considering that Vladimir Vilenskii, the author of the pamphlet that had first printed the promise to return the CER to China without compensation, had also been sent to Beijing as Paikes's counselor, it cannot be doubted that Paikes knew of the contents of the original Karakhan Manifesto.[17]

When Adolf Joffe replaced Paikes later in 1922 as the Soviet Union's official envoy, he tried unsuccessfully to convince the Beijing government to agree to the joint management of the CER. Joffe now swore that the Soviet government had never promised to return the CER to China, denying that this promise was "contained either in the authentic text of the Declaration of 25th July, 1919, which the Plenipotentiary Mission has in its possession, or in the text of the same published at the time in the official collection of the People's Commissariat of Nationalities."[18]

The Soviet Union's use of generous promises to return the Chinese Eastern Railway convinced the Beijing government to open negotiations. However, Joffe's denial that the USSR had ever made this promise was the final step in the long process of using Karakhan's promise to start Sino-Soviet negotiations and then gradually disclaiming the original 25 July 1919 Karakhan Manifesto and putting the published 26 August 1919, version, which did not include the promise to return the CER, in its place.

Origins of the First United Front

Karakhan's original manifesto served another purpose, by helping the Soviet-supported Communist International sponsor the creation of a communist party in China during 1921, and then promoting its rapid growth in the following years. The Soviet Union's generous promises to China was a mainstay of the Comintern's propaganda. For example, during August 1922, Vilenskii published an article in *Izvestiia* stating that the CER was being returned "to China without redemption."[19] Meanwhile, in China, Cai Hesen, a member of the Chinese Communist Party, wrote in the party's journal, *Guide Weekly*, during the fall of 1922, that the Soviets had offered to return to China all of the tsarist holdings in Manchuria, including, "land, mines, and the Chinese Eastern Railway."[20]

The impact that Karakhan's promise had on the formation of a pro-Soviet communist movement in China was very important. But of even greater impact was that these beneficent offers paved the way for an alliance between the Soviet Union and Sun Yat-sen, the leader of the Guomindang (GMD), and at that time the head of the opposition Canton government. When Adolf Joffe could not get the Beijing government to agree to joint Sino-Soviet management of the CER, he turned to Sun Yat-sen for help.

Sun's open support proved to be a great advantage to the Soviet diplomats carrying out negotiations in Beijing. Moscow's hope of playing the two governments off each other are referred to in letters from the Soviet consul, Adolf Joffe, to the Comintern representative in China, Henk Sneevliet, better known as Maring (*Malin* in Chinese). During the fall of 1922, for example, Joffe discussed at length the need for Sun Yat-sen to change "his passive policy to an active one," so as to intervene "in affairs of the central government."[21] The importance of gaining Sun's assistance in reneging on earlier promises to give up Soviet control over Outer Mongolia and the Chinese Eastern Railway was mentioned in a second letter, when Joffe said: "Moreover, I ask you to inform Sun that I rely strongly on his support at the negotiations (especially on the Mongolian and East-China railways questions)."[22]

Sun Yat-sen's decision to back the Soviet diplomats was crucial to the USSR's success in regaining majority control over this railway. On 26 January 1923, Sun and Joffe signed a four-point public declaration in which Sun backed the Soviet position by agreeing that the railway should be managed jointly by Russia and China. Sun Yat-sen's decision implied that each country would have five seats on the board of directors, since all decisions were to be made on the basis of "true rights and special interests."[23]

Sun Yat-sen's agreement caused no little embarrassment to the Nationalist party after it became anti-communist. To try to soften the Sun's responsibility in this matter, the version of this four point agreement published in volume nine of *Geming Wenxuan* translates this point by saying that decisions on the railway would be made "temporarily;" meanwhile, an original Chinese-language copy of these four points uses the word "definitely."[24] By agreeing to this declaration, Sun tacitly acknowledged that even though Moscow had formerly promised to return the railway to China "without compensation," it could now be managed jointly. Considering that this railway was valued at between 500 and 700 million gold rubles, it is impossible to deny that Sun Yat-sen's support for the Soviet position conflicted with China's national interests.

Even though the Sun-Joffe declaration implied that the railway would be managed equally by the two countries, Moscow actually wanted to obtain Sun Yat-sen's support in regaining majority control over the Chinese Eastern Railway. Secret communications between the Comintern representatives in China even referred to a plan to invade Manchuria during the fall of 1922, in order to take control of the Chinese Eastern Railway by force. In a letter from Joffe to Maring dated 7 November 1922, Joffe stated quite clearly: "I have reported to Moscow . . . that as long as Dr. Sun is not an official figure of the Central Chinese state, we cannot, even by appealing to him, attempt an occupation in China." This reference to an "occupation" was then clarified in a report written by Maring of his conversation with P.A. Kobozev, former Chairman of the Far Eastern Republic Council of Ministers, in Chita during February 1923: "Three months ago it would have been possible to occupy the railway but now the good opportunity has already been lost."[25]

Although no military occupation of the Chinese Eastern Railway took place, it is important to clarify that a Soviet military campaign into Manchuria was seriously considered during the fall of 1922. Its very proposal belied the USSR's constant protestations that it did not intend to infringe on China's sovereignty. In fact, Moscow hoped to use its new alliance with Sun Yat-sen to retake majority control of this railway. Soon after Sun Yat-sen agreed to the USSR's terms, Maring visited Zhang Zuolin, the main warlord in Manchuria, in order to discuss the railway's return to Soviet control. On 15 February 1923, Maring reported his progress in a telegram addressed to the Politburo in Moscow. Arriving in Mukden, Manchuria, with a letter of introduction from Sun Yat-sen, Maring described how this was sufficient "to open doors quickly for me." After an hour-long meeting with Zhang Zuolin, Maring determined that Sun appeared to have a great deal of influence over Zhang. Maring therefore recommended: "I gained the strong impression that a lot can be achieved with Zhang through Sun Yat-sen. This situation should be made use of."[26]

Acting on Maring's recommendation, the Soviet government authorized him to negotiate with Sun Yat-sen, who desperately needed Moscow's help to prop up his newly-formed government in Canton. On 1 May 1923, Joffe sent a telegram telling Maring to offer Sun "ideological and political" help, a loan of up to two million gold rubles, and then "assistance in organizing an outstanding military unit," which would be trained in Northwest China and provided with "eight thousand Japanese rifles, fifteen machine-guns, four 'Oriska' guns, and two armored cars." Since Joffe clearly realized that public knowledge of these terms would have tarnished Sun's political credibility, he cautioned Maring to make sure that news of this aid would "remain strictly secret."[27]

In what appears to have been a simple exchange of Soviet military and financial aid in return for Sun Yat-sen's help in regaining the Chinese Eastern Railway, Maring succeeded in convincing Sun to approach Zhang Zuolin. On 31 May 1923, Maring wrote a report addressed not only to Joffe but also to Gregory Zinoviev, the head of the Comintern in Moscow, explaining the outcome of these negotiations. In this report, Maring explained that Sun had sent two important Guomindang officials, Wang Jingwei and Chang Chih, to talk to Zhang Zuolin about the Soviet Union's intentions, and he could now report: "On the question of the Chinese Eastern Railway, I have received news today that Wang Jingwei and Chang Chih have returned from Mukden without getting the 7-3 demand adopted. Zhang Zuolin has declared that first Russia wanted 5-5 and he thinks that [the Chinese warlord] Wu Peifu could very easily agitate against him if he adopts 7-3."[28]

Maring's report confirms that Sun Yat-sen actively helped the Soviet Union try to regain seven of the ten seats on the CER's managing board of directors. The Soviet attempt to regain majority control is further proof that its initial promise to return the railway to China without compensation was mere a ploy to open diplomatic relations. When Beijing proved unwilling to negotiate, the Soviet government turned to Sun Yat-sen, who publicly signed away China's rights to all of the CER—which represented over 40 percent of all of the foreign-managed railways in China—in exchange for promises of Soviet military and financial support. This exchange is especially noteworthy since the Soviet-supported Guomindang soon afterwards began to criticize the other great powers for retaining their territorial and railway concessions in China; in point of fact, the 1,073 mile-long CER and its 250,000 acres of associated property made it one of the largest foreign concessions in all of China.

Karakhan Takes Charge of the Sino-Soviet Negotiations

Since Adolf Joffe had failed to convince the Beijing government to manage the CER jointly, the Soviet government decided to appoint Lev Karakhan as the Soviet Union's plenipotentiary to China, charged with strengthening the "friendly bonds" between the two countries.[29] After arriving in Beijing, Karakhan gave a speech in which he repeated that the Soviet government hoped to maintain relations with China on the basis of "complete and absolute equality," and he was greeted with a round of applause when he reiterated that his two manifestoes of 1919 and 1920 were still in force and were "the basis for his future work in China."[30] During December 1923, Karakhan sent the Beijing government an English-language copy of his 1919 manifesto. It turned out that this copy was based on the text published in *Izvestiia* on 26 August 1919, which did not include the promise to return the CER to China without compensation. It was marked "True to the original," however, was then stamped with the official Soviet seal, and signed by the first secretary of the mission.[31]

In a note to Karakhan dated 9 January 1924, the Chinese negotiator, Wang Zhengting (better known as C.T. Wang), pointed out the discrepancy between the copy that the Soviet mission had given to him and the original telegram the Beijing government had received on 26 March 1920, which was also "signed certifying that there were no mistakes in the copy." Since Wang now had two different copies of the 1919 Karakhan Manifesto, both of which claimed to be true to the original, he suggested that Karakhan might want to clear this problem up before the Chinese people began to doubt the "sincerity" of the Soviet offers.[32] In reply, on 17 January 1924, Karakhan expressed his "deep amazement" that Wang would want to discuss the 1919 declaration since he had just "handed over authentic texts of the 1919 and 1920 declarations." Karakhan then called the original telegram that Beijing had received a "false version of the 1919 declaration," and stated that it did not "give any kind of rights to China."[33]

In an attempt to break this stalemate, Li Jiaao, the newly-appointed Chinese consul to Moscow, informed Foreign Minister Gu Weijun (better known as Wellington Koo) on 18 January 1924, of an off-the-record talk with Karakhan, where Karakhan listed four reasons why the Soviet Union did not want to return the CER to China: 1) the Russian people would lose their capital investment in the CER; 2) the continued existence of the Guomindang government in Canton showed that China was not yet united and so could not manage the railway herself; 3) the CER was still in the hands of White Russian factions that opposed the Soviet government; and 4) after the CER was returned to China it might fall prey to Japan's attempts to gain control over it.[34]

In reality, the first reason was complicated by the fact that French investors owned 60 percent of the shares of the Russo-Asiatic Bank, which had actually built the railway, while the tsarist government had invested money to guard the railway line.[35] Even though the Soviet government had earlier renounced all tsarist debts, it now apparently wanted to take credit for these tsarist expenditures. As for the second point, the Moscow-controlled Communist International was actively supporting and funding the Nationalists in Canton, and so using the existence of the Canton government as an excuse for why the CER should stay under Soviet control was hardly convincing. Third, although the White Russians did have some influence over the CER, Karakhan greatly exaggerated their military power and knew that they were no match for the Red Army. Finally, Karakhan's fear that the Japanese would take over the CER actually worked better in reverse, since if the Soviet Union regained full control over the CER, Japan's economic interests in South Manchuria would be directly threatened and Japan might feel compelled to respond.

Although these four reasons do not stand up under close scrutiny, the Beijing government had no way—short of war—of forcing Karakhan to live up to his earlier promise to return the CER to China without compensation. Then, on 27 February 1924, Karakhan appeared to indicate a sudden willingness to exchange mutual recognition simultaneously with a general agreement resolving Sino-Soviet problems. Retreating from his former proposal that China and the USSR jointly manage the CER, Karakhan now agreed that China would have full authority over the CER as well as over the territory along the railway line. He also stated that China could buy back the railway from the Soviet government in exchange for continued Soviet use of the CER to transport goods from Manzhouli to Vladivostok. Until the terms of its return were decided, however, Karakhan suggested temporary joint management of the railway with China, with a managing board composed of five Russians and five Chinese members. Karakhan further proposed that the price and the terms of the sale and return of the CER to China should be decided at a Sino-Soviet conference which would follow one month after official relations were opened.[36]

Li Jiaao once again supported Karakhan in a long letter from Moscow: "If China tried to pay for the complete return of the Railway then it would create a whole range of difficult problems which would not exist if China and the Soviet Union jointly managed the Railway." Li also praised Karakhan's plan as "comparatively secure," "very fair," and "comparatively easy."[37] Since the Soviet government had already convinced Sun Yat-sen and the Guomindang to support joint Sino-Soviet management of the CER, Koo was left with few viable alternatives and so accepted Karakhan's proposal.

China's decision to agree to joint management over the CER seemed to promise the railway's eventual return to China, but in fact merely proved the efficacy of using two versions of the 1919 Karakhan Manifesto, since the Soviet government had pulled off a propaganda coup by promising to return the same railway that it was now being allowed to manage jointly. Once the Beijing government agreed to this solution, Karakhan and Wang quickly hammered out a draft agreement by 1 March 1924. Koo telegraphed an order to Li Jiaao in Moscow on 7 March, telling him to talk to Foreign Minister Gregorii Chicherin about several outstanding problems, including China's desire to fix the price and immediately determine new management regulations for the CER.[38] As ordered, Li Jiaao met with Chicherin for a three-hour discussion on 9 March 1924. He requested that Chicherin encourage Karakhan to be more "amiable" and willing to make concessions, so that "the future of our two countries' friendship will really be close."[39] But Chicherin also wanted to decide these important problems only at the Sino-Soviet conference following the opening of official relations.

The Beijing government's cabinet met on 13 March, and agreed with the basic points of this 1 March draft, although it suggested that all Sino-Russian treaties be abolished immediately and that the status of the White Russians in China be defined more clearly as jointly under Sino-Soviet responsibility. Meanwhile, the Chinese Ministry of Foreign Affairs had circulated "top secret" copies of the 1 March draft Sino-Soviet agreement to the different ministries in the Beijing government. Responses were returned from several ministries that cautioned Wang that he should eliminate an oft-repeated clause stating that all new Sino-Soviet treaties should "be decided at the conference," since by simply delaying the upcoming Sino-Soviet conference, Moscow could avoid abolishing all of the old unequal treaties. The Ministry of Education and the Ministry of Finance then both warned that all former treaties should be abolished immediately, and the Ministry of Education further recommended that an additional clause be added: "Prior to the convening of the conference, all treaties, agreements, protocols, contracts, will no longer be in effect."[40]

The problem with these new suggestions was that the draft treaty stated that annulling the old treaties and replacing them with new treaties should happen simultaneously, ensuring that treaty relations would continue unbroken. The Chinese officials were worried, however, that if it was not made clear that the old treaties had been abolished prior to recognition, then the Soviet Union might try to retain the former treaties at the upcoming conference. Thus, the Ministry of Education's suggestion to agree that all of the old treaties were no longer in effect from the signing of the Sino-Soviet agreement to the convening of the conference actually left a one month gap during which time China and the Soviet Union would have no operative treaties. But, this undoubtedly appeared to be a minor problem at the time and following what seemed to be almost total support within the Beijing government, Karakhan and Wang met again on 14 March 1924, to finalize the draft treaty.

Signing the Secret Protocol and the CER

When Karakhan and Wang met on 14 March, it is unknown whether Wang tried to take out the phrase "to be decided at the conference," but, in any case, it remained unchanged in the later versions of the treaty. Although Wang was unsuccessful in making this change, he did convince Karakhan to agree to add a new clause stating that all former agreements would not be enforced. It was decided not to make this change in the text, but to sign a separate protocol instead.

This protocol was very simple, but was destined to have far-reaching consequences for China, since it stated that all former conventions, treaties, agreements, protocols, contracts, etc, would be annulled at the upcoming Sino-Soviet Conference, at which time new treaties would also be adopted, but then added: "It is agreed that pending the conclusion of such new Treaties, Agreements, etcetera, all the old Conventions, Treaties, Agreements, Protocols, Contracts, etcetera, will not be enforced." This protocol was then signed by Karakhan and Wang, but it was not dated, and did not have a seal, which meant that this protocol would only take effect if ratified by the Beijing government.[41]

This secret protocol was never previously published with the treaty, but the original signed copy is included with the other treaty provisions.[42] Although there is no way to know for sure, it might have been decided to make this protocol secret so that outsiders could not take advantage of the one month period during which none of the Sino-Russian treaties would be valid; apparently Wang never seriously considered that the Soviet government might try to take advantage of this suspension.

By including only one of the Ministry of Education's two suggested amendments, however, Wang altered the whole intent of these suggestions. Now, the draft agreement clearly stated that all former Sino-Russian agreements would not be enforced until after the official Sino-Soviet conference convened and concluded new treaties, thus making the revision of China's and the Soviet Union's commercial, consular, and border relations all dependent on the convening of the conference. The wording of this secret protocol was all-important, since the previous agreements were not eliminated, they were simply not enforced. This proved to be an important distinction, since the Beijing government had now recognized the legitimacy of these earlier agreements, even though both sides agreed that they were suspended. If the Soviet Union violated the old agreements, as later happened, the Beijing government could not publicly protest, because a public announcement would immediately expose Beijing's complicity in signing a secret protocol that had actually reaffirmed the validity of these former Sino-Russian agreements.

While the Beijing government literally made dozens of protests to the Soviet government during the following years about treaty infractions, therefore, these protests were all confidential. Numerous copies of China's private remonstrances against Soviet mistreatment are located in the Foreign Ministry Archives in Taiwan. The most important include the 14 October 1924 protest against Moscow's signing of the 20 September 1924 supplemental agreement concerning the CER with Zhang Zuolin,[43] as well as verbal protests against the Soviet Union's 20 January 1925 Convention with Japan, dated 21 February 1925.[44] The Soviet Union could and did ignore China's objections with impunity, however, since it could not very well break a treaty that both sides had agreed not to enforce.

By signing this secret protocol, while failing to eliminate the clause specifying that all new agreements could only be made at the upcoming Sino-Soviet conference, Wang unintentionally placed enormous power in the Soviet government's hands. Since China was too weak to oppose the Soviet Union on its own, it could not back up its protests with actions; if China had later turned to other countries for help, such as Great Britain, the United States, or Japan, it would have had to confess that it had signed a secret agreement with the Soviet Union. But, admitting the existence of a secret protocol with Moscow would have called the legitimacy of the Beijing government into question, and would have undermined the very support that Beijing hoped to gain from these other countries.

Karakhan understood quite well the power that this secret protocol gave him and was willing to take many risks to make sure that the draft treaty was ratified without changes. When it looked as if the Beijing government might not accept this draft agreement, Karakhan sent an ultimatum to Foreign Minister Koo on 16 March, insisting that the Beijing government recognize the draft treaty unchanged within three days or else all further negotiations would end.[45] Karakhan also published the contents of the 14 March draft treaty in the local Chinese press—minus the crucial secret protocol, of course. The Chinese Communist Party and the Guomindang led the way in condemning the Beijing government for caving into foreign pressure not to ratify the draft Sino-Soviet treaty. As a result, the Beijing government was subjected to enormous public pressure to sign the treaty.

Karakhan's three-day ultimatum harkened back to similar ultimatums forced upon China by Imperial Russian diplomats, as well as to the pressure tactics that Japan had used to coerce China into accepting the Twenty-one Demands. But, the Soviet government added a new twist by marshalling Chinese public opinion against the

Beijing government. Since the secret protocol was never published along with the other parts of the draft Sino-Soviet treaty, it is ironic that Chinese public support for the Soviet government's position proved to be so important in securing the Beijing government's ratification of the secret protocol.

After almost two months of delay, the official version of the Sino-Soviet treaty was signed on 31 May 1924, by Lev Karakhan, ambassador extraordinary of the USSR, and Dr. Wellington Koo, the minister of foreign affairs, Republic of China. The final treaty included all of the 14 March 1924 draft treaty verbatim as well as "one Protocol, seven Declarations, and one exchange of Notes."[46] The inclusion of the "one Protocol," agreeing not to enforce all of the "old Conventions, Treaties, Agreements, Protocols, Contracts, etcetera," meant that the Soviet government did not have to do anything to continue enjoying its special rights and privileges in China. All it had to do was delay the convening of the official Sino-Soviet conference, which it did for fourteen months after the official treaty was signed on 31 May 1924. During this period, the Soviet government managed to retake majority control over the CER.

The USSR's Retakes Control of the CER

With the complete suspension of all prior Sino-Russian agreements on 31 May 1924, the Soviet government was in a strong position to force China to put the CER under joint control. To put pressure on Beijing, the Soviet Union signed a supplemental agreement with the Manchurian "Autonomous Three Eastern Provinces" on 20 September 1924. This new treaty in fact transferred full control of the Chinese share of the CER to Zhang Zuolin. Because the supplemental agreement's secret protocol was not previously published, scholars have falsely concluded that this supplemental agreement did not depart "in principle from the terms of the earlier Beijing agreement."[47]

This subterfuge was accomplished by way of a secret protocol that clarified that where the term "China" appeared in clauses six and seven of the first section of the agreement, its actual meaning was the "Government of the Autonomous Three Eastern Provinces of the Republic of China," the official name of Zhang Zuolin's government.[48] This new agreement was written to sound as if it were an addition to the former 31 May 1924 agreement with Beijing. But, the inclusion of a secret protocol actually meant that the Soviet Union's agreement with Zhang Zuolin superseded its agreement with Beijing and so gave Zhang Zuolin the power to choose which Chinese officials would represent China in the joint commission that ran the railway, thus giving him absolute control over the Chinese half of the CER.

In addition, while the original agreement signed by Karakhan and Koo stated that the joint management of the railway would continue only until the Sino-Soviet conference met, at which time terms for purchasing the railway from the Soviet Union would be determined, the supplemental agreement only admitted that China had the "right" to buy back the railway. This statement was much weaker than the former clause stating it would be sold back, effectively negating Karakhan's numerous promises that the Soviet government would give or sell the railway back to China. Even when the Sino-Soviet conference was finally convened, therefore, the Soviet Union no longer felt obliged to discuss terms for selling the CER to China.

In exchange for helping the Soviet Union retain control over the railway, the Soviet government rewarded Zhang Zuolin by changing the terms of the 1896 railway contract to reduce the original eighty-year lease to sixty years. At the end of sixty years the Autonomous Three Eastern Provinces of the Republic of China would receive back the railway and the surrounding railway property free of charge. Other changes included the provision that all profits from the management of the CER would be divided equally between the Soviet Union and the Mukden government, or really Zhang Zuolin.

The joint management of the railway was patterned on the May agreement with Beijing: a committee composed of five Russians and five Chinese, with the executive manager being selected by the Chinese and the assistant manager selected by the Soviets, would run the railway. All details pertaining to the management of the railway were to be decided by special commissions that were to meet within a month after the agreement was signed, and would finish their work within six months.[49]

The similarity in these terms with the May agreement with Beijing meant that delays in the convening of these special commissions would have given the Soviet government leverage over Zhang Zuolin, in the same way that it had established diplomatic leverage over Beijing.

On 18 October 1924, Foreign Minister Chicherin gave a speech in Moscow in which he praised the Soviet government for its enormous diplomatic victory in regaining partial control over a railway line which was valued in excess of half a billion gold rubles. He portrayed this success as "one of the most remarkable instances of return of Soviet property that was seized by its enemies who hoped to use it against the workers and peasants of the USSR." Turning a blind eye to the Soviet government's secret diplomacy in China, Chicherin then predicted that "the aggressive policy of imperialism towards Eastern peoples and its attacks on them strengthen their friendly links with us." This was especially true in China, and Chicherin optimistically stated that the "Soviet-Chinese friendship has already become a weighty factor in international politics."[50]

The vast chasm between Chicherin's public statements and his private actions was merely emphasized by the fact that Li Jiaao had already presented an official, although secret, protest from the Beijing government to the Soviet government only four days before, condemning Moscow's decision to sign the supplemental agreement with Zhang Zuolin. In particular, Li denounced a statement made by Chicherin on 27 September 1924 that the supplemental agreement had been negotiated with the "previous approval of the Minister of Foreign Affairs Mr. Koo."[51] To date, no evidence that Koo agreed to the supplemental agreement in advance has appeared, while there is much evidence that he opposed it from June all the way through September 1924 and beyond.

The USSR's Secret Diplomacy and the 1925 Convention with Japan

The second secret agreement might have made it appear that Zhang Zuolin would retain half control over the management of the CER, but the Soviet government used two techniques to take majority control away from Zhang. In the 31 May 1924 CER agreement with Beijing, Article V stated that: "The employment of persons in the various departments of the railway shall be in accordance with the principle of equal representation between the nationals of the Union of Soviet Socialist Republics and those of the Republic of China." In order to circumvent this provision, in the separate agreement with Zhang the following note was added: "In carrying out the principle of equal representation the normal course of life and activities of the Railway shall in no case be interrupted or injured, that is to say the employment of the people of both nationalities shall be based in accordance with experience, personal qualifications and fitness of the applicants."[52]

Since Russians had traditionally run the railway, it was a foregone conclusion that they would take the majority of the positions on the railway, claiming that any other solution would interrupt or injure the railway. In the months following the signing of this supplemental agreement, therefore, the Soviet government rapidly reorganized the administration of the railway so as to increase the number of Russian employees of the CER from 10,833 to 11,251, while the number of Chinese employees fell from 5,912 to 5,556.[53]

A second method of taking full control of the CER was simply to make use of the 31 May 1924 secret protocol with the Beijing government, which specified that all former contracts between China and Russia would not be enforced. Zhang Zuolin clearly did not know about this secret protocol, because the 20 September 1924 supplemental agreement specified that the 1896 CER contract would continue to be valid during the first four months of operation. Since only the Soviet diplomats knew that the secret protocol had suspended this 1896 contract, Soviet officials immediately began to fill the majority of the administrative posts on the CER.

Although the president of the railway was Chinese, this official was evidently little better than a figurehead and it was reported that he never even went to the railway headquarters in Harbin. The real control of the Chinese Eastern Railway resided in its eight main committees and eighteen subcommittees. Soviet officials eventually took charge of twenty-four of these twenty-six committees and they also greatly outnumbered their Chinese counterparts; there were a total of 120 Soviet officials to 80 Chinese officials in the railway administration.[54]

By making use of these two techniques—the agreement not to fire skilled workers and the secret protocol—the Soviet government soon not only controlled the most important positions within the railway management, but its officials outnumbered the Chinese officials by a ratio of three to two. This was hardly the equal joint management that had been promised in the 31 May 1924 Treaty, since the Soviet government now controlled approximately 67 percent of all of the positions on the railway, which almost exactly fulfilled its 1923 goal of gaining seven of the ten seats on the CER's board of directors. Thus, by playing the two secret protocols off of each other, the Soviet Union was able to regain majority control of the CER.

To add insult to injury, the Soviet government used its renewed influence in Manchuria to negotiate a new treaty with Japan on 20 January 1925, which, by recognizing the validity of the 1905 Portsmouth Peace Convention, actually reaffirmed the former Russian and Japanese spheres of influence in Manchuria. When China protested, Karakhan's reply, dated 26 February 1925, confirmed that the USSR now also recognized the validity of Japan's Twenty-one Demands, considered by many Chinese to be the most humiliating example of China's mistreatment by the capitalist countries. By 1925, therefore, the Soviet Union and Japan had renewed almost exactly the same state of affairs that had existed prior to World War I.

All of these events flew in the face of the Soviet Union's public propaganda in China proclaiming Sino-Soviet equality. When the USSR succeeded in winning back control of the Chinese Eastern Railway in 1924 it still represented 14 percent of all of China's railway mileage, or about a sixth of the total. From the time that the Soviet government first promised to return the railway in July 1919, to the signing of its agreement with Japan in January 1925, less than six years passed. During this time the Soviet government gradually reneged on its former promises to treat China equally. All of these actions were kept secret from the Chinese public, however, and in the mass anti-imperialist movements in China during 1925, the focus of the Chinese people's anger was directed largely at Great Britain, Japan, and the United States, not at the Soviet Union.

Conclusions

On 25 July 1919, Karakhan had opened his first manifesto to China by annulling all of the tsarist government's former treaties with Japan, China, and the other great powers, treaties through which the Imperial Russian government had "enslaved" the people of China. Karakhan warned China that the Versailles powers were working "to transform it into a second Korea or a second India," a fate that could only be avoided by joining with the Soviet Union. Karakhan ended his manifesto by telling China that its only "allies and brothers" in the struggle for liberty from imperialism are the "Russian worker and peasant and the Red Army of Russia."[55]

By February 1925, however, Karakhan had not only helped to negotiate two secret agreements to retake control over the CER, he had secretly defended the legitimacy of his agreement with Japan by upholding the infamous Twenty-one Demands, demands that the United States government, for example, had quickly condemned as a violation of the political and territorial integrity of the Republic of China, and had afterwards consistently pressed Japan to revoke. Furthermore, the Chinese Communist Party was founded in 1921 based, in part at least, on the Chinese rejection of Japan's demands.

As a result of Karkahan's secret diplomacy, friction between the two countries increased. During January 1926, Zhang Zuolin threatened to take control of the CER by force, making it appear that war could erupt at any time between China and the Soviet Union. In Moscow, Leon Trotsky proposed the return of the railway to China, but Joseph Stalin denounced Trotsky and eventually used differences over the China policy to oust him from the Bolshevik Party.[56] Meanwhile, increased Sino-Soviet tensions over the CER helped prompt Jiang Jieshi (Chiang Kai-shek) to conduct the March 1926 "political" purge of the Chinese Communists, followed a year later by the April 1927 "physical" purge, which ended the United Front policy. Throughout the rest of the 1920s, China tried in vain to pressure the USSR to return the CER, as it had promised to do in the Sino-Soviet Treaty signed on 31 May 1924. As the next chapter will discuss, these tensions over the CER eventually resulted in Sino-Soviet conflict during 1929.

Notes

1. This chapter expands on research first presented in Bruce A. Elleman, "The Soviet Union's Secret Diplomacy Concerning the Chinese Eastern Railway,1924–1925," *The Journal of Asian Studies,* Volume 53, No. 2 (May 1994), 459–86.

2. 5 September 1905, "Treaty of Peace–Russia and Japan," commonly called the Portsmouth Peace Treaty. MacMurray, Vol. 1, 522–25.

3. 5 November 1913, "Declaration, and accompanying Exchange of Notes, in regard to Outer Mongolia–Russia and China," 7 June 1915, "Tripartite agreement in regard to Outer Mongolia–Russia, Mongolia, and China." Ibid., 1066–67, 1240–45.

4. See Bruce A. Elleman, "The Final Consolidation of the USSR's Sphere of Interest in Outer Mongolia," in Stephen Kotkin and Bruce A. Elleman (eds.), *Mongolia in the Twentieth Century: Landlocked Cosmopolitan* (Armonk, NY: M.E. Sharpe, 1999), 124.

5. See Bruce A. Elleman, *Wilson and China: A Revised History of the 1919 Shandong Question* (Armonk, NY: M.E. Sharpe, 2002).

6. The Soviet government's original French-language telegram of the Karakhan Manifesto to the Beijing government, dated 26 March 1920, is located in the Foreign Ministry Archives at the Institute for Modern History, Academia Sinica, Nankang, Taiwan (Waijiao dang'an, or WJDA below), collection 03–32, volume 463(1).

7. Vladimir Vilenskii, *Kitaia I Sovietskaia Rossia* (China and Soviet Russia) (Moscow: Gos. Izd-vo. 1919), 15.

8. *Biulleteni Dal'ne-Vostochnogo Sekretariata Kominterna* (Bulletin of the Far Eastern Secretariat of the Comintern) Irkutsk, 24 April 1921, # 5, 3; This journal was restricted in the Soviet Union, because the republication in 1921 of the Soviet government's 1919 promise to return the Chinese Eastern Railway to China without compensation confirmed that the Soviet Union did initially make this promise to China.

9. Ignatii Iurin, the diplomatic representative from the Soviet-sponsored buffer state, the Far Eastern Republic, played an important role in this process, as outlined in Bruce Elleman, "The Iurin Mission to China: The Prelude to Sino-Soviet Diplomatic Relations." *The Soviet and Post-Soviet Review*, Volume 19, Nos. 1–3 (1992).

10. See Bruce A. Elleman, "Soviet Diplomacy and the First United Front in China," *Modern China*, Volume 21, No. 4 (October 1995).

11. Commonly called C.C. Wang, he had received his education through the doctorate level at Peking University, Yale University, and the University of Illinois, and in January, 1920, had been appointed Director-General of the Chinese Eastern Railway. 3 May 1921, English-language letter from C.C. Wang to W.W. Yan, WJDA, 03–32, 242(2).

12. 2 October 1920, Chinese-language copy of Karakhan's second manifesto, dated 27 September 1920, WJDA, 03–32, 479(1); These proposals were officially dated 27 September 1920, but seem to have been publicly announced in Moscow on 27 October 1920, which caused a certain amount of confusion about the dating of this second Karakhan Manifesto, not dissimilar to the dating problems of the first Karakhan Manifesto, but for entirely different reasons; it is even possible that this second dating problem was intended to help cover up the intentional use of two versions of the first Karakhan Manifesto the year earlier.

13. George Alexander Lensen, ed., *Revelations of a Russian Diplomat: The Memoirs of Dmitri I. Abrikossov* (Seattle, WA: University of Washington Press, 1965), 258.

14. 5 October 1920, American embassy memo #62 and #63, signed by the American ambassador to China, Charles R. Crane. WJDA, 03–32, 438(1).

15. The Beijing government protested this practice during January 1926: "The Chinese Delegation is astonished to learn that the Soviet Delegation is seeking to invest the so-called Russian Trade Mission in China with a diplomatic character." 10 January 1926, Confidential Beijing government response to Soviet proposal, entitled: "General Observation on the Preliminary Soviet Draft on Trade and Navigation," WJDA, 03–32, 536(4).

16. 26 April 1922, Chinese-language minutes of Paikes's meeting with Chinese officials, WJDA, 03–32, 200(3).

17. 27 March 1922, English-language memorandum No. 311, signed by Paikes, listed Vladimir D. Vilenskii as the "counselor" of the Soviet mission in Beijing, WJDA, 03–32, 470(2).

18. *New Russia*, Volume 1, #10, 6 January 1923, 305.

19. Allen Whiting, *Soviet Policies in China, 1917–1924* (New York: Columbia University Press, 1954), 210.

20. *Xiangdao Zhoubao*, #3, 27 September 1922.

21. Letter from Joffe to Maring, dated 7 November 1922, Tony Saich, *The Origins of the First United Front in China The Role of Sneevliet (Alias Maring)*, (Leiden: E.J. Brill, 1991), Vol. 1, 352–53.

22. Letter from Joffe to Maring, dated 17 November 1922, Saich, Vol. 1, 356–59.

23. Jane Degras, *Soviet Documents on Foreign Policy* (New York: Oxford University Press, 1952), Vol. 1, 370–71.

24. Archives of the Historical Commission of the Central Committee of the Guomindang Party, Taipei, Taiwan, #047/2.

25. Saich, Vol. 1, 351–53; 400–1.

26. Secret Report from Maring to "Comrades Karakhan and Joffe, Copy for Members of the Politburo," entitled "Report Concerning My Trip to Mukden and My Discussions with Marshall Chang Tso-lin," 15 February 1923, Saich, Vol. 1, 407–8.

27. Telegram from Joffe to Maring, 1 May 1923, Ibid., Vol. 2, 527.

28. Letter from Maring to "Comrades Joffe, Davtian, and Zinoviev," 31 May 1923, Ibid., Vol. 2, 545; also see telegram from Maring to Joffe, 30 April 1923, Ibid., Vol. 1, 414.

29. 1 August 1923, French-language copy of Karakhan's credentials, signed by the head of the Central Executive Committee, N. Narimanov, and the Foreign Minister, G. Chicherin, WJDA, 03–32, 470 (3).

30. 4 September 1923, Russian-language text of Karakhan's speech at the luncheon given by C.T. Wang, WJDA, 03–32, 467 (1).

31. 2 December 1923, English-language copies of the 1919 and 1920 Karakhan manifestoes, provided by the Soviet Mission in Beijing and marked "True to the original," WJDA, 03–32, 481 (3).

32. 9 January 1924, Chinese-language letter from Wang to Karakhan, WJDA, 03–32, 477(1).

33. 17 January 1924, Russian-language signed letter from Karakhan to Wang, WJDA, 03–32, 483(2).

34. 18 January 1924, Chinese-language report written by Li Jiaao, the Chinese Consul in Moscow, to Foreign Minister Wellington Koo, WJDA, 03–32, 461(3).

35. *The China Yearbook*, 1923, 613.

36. 27 February 1924, Chinese-language minutes of a meeting with Karakhan, WJDA, 03–32, 487(1).

37. 24 February 1924, Chinese-language letter from Li Jiaao to Foreign Minister Koo, WJDA, 03–32, 461(3).

38. 7 March 1924, Chinese-language telegram signed by Wellington Koo to Li Jiaao, WJDA, 03–32, 487(1).

39. 9 March 1924, Chinese-language copy of minutes of meeting between Li Jiaao and Foreign Minister Chicherin, WJDA, 03–32, 483(1).

40. 1 March 1924, Numerous departments in the Beijing government responded to 1 March 1924 draft treaty, WJDA, 03–32, 488(1).

41. 14 March 1924, Draft Treaty—Secret Protocol, WJDA, 03–32, 506(5).

42. Sow-theng Leong, *Sino-Soviet Diplomatic Relation, 1917–1926* (Canberra: Australian National University Press, 1976), 264–65.

43. 14 October 1924, Russian-language letter No. 575 to Foreign Minister Chicherin from Li Jiaao, WJDA, 03–32, 494(3).

44. 21 February 1925, Chinese-language minutes of a meeting between Li Jiaao and Chicherin, WJDA, 03–32, 498(1).

45. 16 March 1924, Russian-language original of Karakhan's signed three day ultimatum, letter No. 1011, WJDA, 03–32 483(2).

46. 30 May 1924, English-language copy of the "Certificate of Full Power Given to VI Kyuin Wellington Koo Plenipotentiary," signed by President Cao Kun and countersigned by Wellington Koo, as Minister for Foreign Affairs. This certificate stated that Koo was authorized to sign with Karakhan an "Agreement on General Questions . . . (15 Articles)," an "Agreement for the Provisional Management of the Chinese Eastern Railway (11 Articles)," "one Protocol," and then "seven Declarations, and one exchange of Notes," WJDA, 03–32, 495(2).

47. McCormack, *Chang Tso-lin*, 114–15.

48. Leong, 274–75; Two signed copies of this secret protocol are now available to scholars, one copy in the PRC and the other in Taiwan. Nanking, File 1039, #99; WJDA 03–32, 491(2).

49. Nanjing, File 1039, #99.

50. Degras, Vol. 1, 459–69.

51. 14 October 1924, Russian-language letter No. 575 to Foreign Minister Chicherin from Li Jiaao, WJDA, 03–32, 494(3).

52. Nanjing, File 1039, #99.

53. McCormack, *Chang Tso-lin*, 115.

54. The administrative breakdown of the Chinese Eastern Railway was explained by a volume entitled *Zhong-e Guanyu Zhongdonglu zhi Jiaoshe Shilüe* (A History of Sino-Russian Negotiations on the Chinese Eastern Railway), published by the *Zhongguo Guomindang Zhongyang Zhixing Weiyuanhui Xuanzhuan Buyin* 1929.11, 20–21; A copy of this rare volume is located in the Guomindang archives in Taipei, Taiwan.

55. 26 March 1920, Original French-language telegram to the Beijing government, WJDA, 03–32, 463(1).

56. Bruce A. Elleman, *Moscow and the Emergence of Communist Power in China, 1925–30: The Nanchang Uprising and the Birth of the Red Army* (London: Routledge Press, 2009), 20.

4

Railway as Political Catalyst: The Chinese Eastern Railway and the 1929 Sino-Soviet Conflict

Felix Patrikeeff

China's modern history has been defined by railway-building and for good reason: "As with Russia, railway lines in China . . . [opened] up a Pandora's box that few other instruments of modernization could."[1] Building the Trans-Siberian and Chinese Eastern Railways (CER) constituted the height of planning, execution, and technology.[2] The CER, in particular, in the years through 1914 had absorbed an estimated 182 million gold rubles in subsidies from St. Petersburg.[3] But the project was plagued by strategic concerns from very early on,[4] and after 1905 Russia and Japan used their competing railways to increase their respective spheres of interest.[5] Following the signing of the 1924 Sino-Soviet treaty, the central Chinese authorities exerted pressure on Moscow to hand over the CER to China. Meanwhile, the Manchurian warlord Zhang Zuolin worked to build up his own position in Manchuria, a legacy his son, Zhang Xueliang, tried to continue.[6] However, within a year of his coming to power, Zhang Xueliang was locked in a military struggle with the USSR over control of the CER. In part, this was the result of his own indelicate manner and inept methods, but it also was a sign of China's desire to erode the visibly swelling Soviet economic and political influence in the region.[7]

The Origins of the Sino-Soviet Railway War

Despite the diplomatic agreements it has signed with the USSR, the Chinese government continued to demand that the CER be return to China. This situation came to a head in mid-1929. The result was a near-classical example of Clausewitzian "continuation of politics by other means."

Early post-revolutionary years of jostling for *de facto* Chinese influence over the railway line had led to uncomfortable agreements, and then to five further years of difficult, often ill-tempered, political co-habitation, and, finally, resulted in Chinese authorities taking a radical path to oust the Soviet presence in the management of the line. Confronting what the Soviet Union interpreted as a political-organizational coup, it first resisted and then opted to launch a dramatic, sweeping military strike into northern Manchuria to correct the situation. In this regard, it was no different, at least on the surface, to a number of incidents in modern neo-colonial Chinese history, in which Western powers for a time endured incursions into their perceived political power, and then responded with the blunt language of military force.

But the crisis and conflict of 1929 was different to the normal pattern, as is evidenced by its not being comfortably shaped by any traditional interpretative mould.[8] Such approaches have failed to recognize the complex political, economic, and social mix of the situation. The essays in this book have taken a more nuanced approach to the railway conflict, elevating the conflict from epiphenomenon to a watershed event in modern Chinese history.

Ostensibly, the crisis sprang, as earlier suggested, from the Chinese authorities' response to the Soviet Union's efforts to reassert control over the CER. The other cause, and one that the Soviet Union gave as a reason for its concern—and ultimately military intervention—was the inability of the Chinese authorities to prevent Russian white-guard and warlord military intrusions into Soviet territory.[9] In fact, the crisis may be seen as the military response to a long history of Chinese attempts to displace Russian, and later Soviet, predominance in Manchurian.[10]

The diplomatic prelude to military conflict was a complicated one, but may be summed up in a chronological sketch. In May 1929, there was a raid by the Manchurian authorities on the Soviet Consulate at Harbin, much like that on its embassy at Beijing two years earlier. As a result of the Harbin raid, some Soviet citizens, including the General Manager of the CER, Emshanov, and his assistant Eismont, were removed from their posts and, in some cases, arrested. Soviet retaliation took the form of the arrest of a number of Chinese citizens, including businessmen, living in the USSR. However, Moscow's formal response came only on 13 July, in the form of a three-point ultimatum: 1) A conference was to be convened for the settlement of all questions concerning the CER; 2) Chinese authorities were to cease at once all unilateral acts committed in respect of the CER; 3) All arrested Soviet citizens were to be freed immediately, and the rights of the Soviet citizens and institutions alike to be restored.

Simultaneously, a note was issued by Karakhan, who was by then the Acting Commissar for Foreign Affairs in Moscow, personally warning the Chinese authorities of the consequences of their having frequently reneged on treaties he himself had helped to engineer. On 19 July, the Soviet government severed diplomatic relations with China, suspending railway communication and "inviting" Chinese diplomatic and consular representatives to leave Soviet territory.

By 20 July, all White Russians employed by the Chinese Maritime Customs left Suifenhe—over which Soviet military planes made frequent flights to demoralize the populace—and Lahasusu—where Soviet warships had their guns trained on the

Customs House and the vicinity.[11] *Dal'bank*, the USSR's financial instrument in the region, began to transfer funds to New York. The offices of Soviet companies in Harbin, the capital of Northern Manchuria, began to close and the German Consul-General was requested to take charge of local Soviet interests.[12]

Between late July and the first week of August, there were negotiations between the two sides, with communications to Karakhan being sent by C.T. Wang, China's Minister of Foreign Affairs, as well as Zhang Xueliang, calling for the initiation of talks. Despite the prolongation of discussions between the two sides, Karakhan intervened with a note to the Mukden authorities, accusing the Chinese of "bad faith." Instead of *status quo ante,* China had proposed legislation based on the prevailing, and what the Soviet government considered changing, conditions. Karakhan concluded his communication on an ominous note: "A situation is developing that is pregnant with weighty consequences, the entire responsibility for which rests fully with the Mukden and Nanjing governments."[13]

On 8 August, American consular reports indicated that General Boldyrev had been appointed Commander of the Soviet Army of occupation and Beikker, a former director of the railway, was to serve as Chief of Staff.[14] Two days earlier, the Soviet military commander Bliukher—a former adviser to the Nationalists—and N.E. Donenko—a member of the Revolutionary Military Council—were charged with the formation of the Special Far Eastern Army (*Osobaia Dal'nevostochnaia armiia* or ODVA) by the Revolutionary Military Council (RMC). Bliukher was to be its Commander-in-Chief.[15] This order showed that the USSR was willing to resort to military force to retain its control over the CER.

The 1929 Sino-Soviet War

Aside from isolated skirmishes in July, military action proper began on 17 August, with an "official notification" reaching the Manchurian government of 10,000 troops and 30 guns attacking between Manzhouli and Chalainor, with 50 Chinese soldiers killed in a separate incident at Manzhouli itself on the same day. The attack on Chalainor is interesting in that "either by design or fluke" Chinese troops retreated some 400 yards to an entrenchment, which was well supported by machine gun emplacements, and as a consequence inflicted heavy losses on the Russian forces.[16] This was the first and last occasion on which Soviet forces suffered significant casualties in the Manchurian conflict.

In mid-October, Soviet naval vessels forced their way up to the confluence of the Amur and Sungari (Songhua Jiang) Rivers in the Northeast, and captured Lahasusu, shattering Chinese ranks and forcing their opponents to Fujin, where the Chinese soldiers killed inhabitants who crossed their path and plundered all stores in the area.[17] The Red Army, on the other hand, took only military supplies and stores, but did not touch the civilian population or property.[18] On 16 October a public meeting was held in which the Chinese were invited to enlist in the Red Army and move with it to Khabarovsk.[19]

A tense, but relatively stable, period ensued until 17 November, when the main thrust into Manchuria began, involving the Transbaikal Group of the ODVA, which comprised ten divisions.[20] The stratagem was to divide the action into two stages, with a maximum emphasis on surprise, as it was to be again in 1945, but on that occasion against the Japanese. There was to be no smoking by Soviet troops, no use of bullets, only bayonets, and wheels on their vehicles were muffled.[21] The tactics were, in the first stage, to sweep past Manzhouli and to strike at the fortified region of Chalainor. Having captured the latter, the forces were then to wheel around and take the westward-facing fortifications at Manzhouli by an assault from the East.[22]

With the exception of heavy resistance near Hailar, the plan was carried out quickly. By the morning of 20 November, troops had surrounded the township of Manchuria Station and the local *Tupan* was given an ultimatum, with two hours to decide on his response. However, without waiting for a peace envoy, or the two hours to elapse, Stepan S. Vostretsov, the head of the Transbaikal Group, entered the city with several commanders and two vehicles. They arrived to find that the remaining Chinese troops defending the settlement were too busy looting to interfere. The city itself had already been totally destroyed: not one window was intact and the streets were littered with abandoned weapons and equipment. The Chinese troops had begun their panic-stricken looting with the impact of the first bombs. Many soldiers had stolen civilian dress, including women's clothing and foreign dresses and bonnets, presumably to disguise themselves while escaping.[23]

The Russian forces gave chase to the routed Chinese army in an easterly direction to Bukhedu. In complete disarray, the Chinese soldiers moved towards Tsitsihar (Qiqihar)—even further East—plundering as they went.[24] Only 10 miles away from Tsitsihar, General Wan Fulin, who was charged with holding the bridge over the Nonni River (Nen Jiang), was able to stop them, shooting down hundreds of his own army, thereby preventing their entry into Harbin.[25]

The Soviet military campaign was a complete success: within 48 hours of the invasion, Zhang Xueliang was ready to sue for peace on Soviet terms, and on 26 November had already acknowledged the Soviet demand that the three-point ultimatum of July be the basis for negotiation. On 30 November, Tsai Yun-sheng left Harbin for Nikol'sk-Ussuriisk and there concluded a provisional agreement with Simanovskii (the representative of the Soviet Foreign Commissariat), and this was signed by the two men on 3 December. Two days later, once Tsai had returned to Mukden, Marshal Zhang telegraphed his acceptance with the exception of a return of Emshanov and Eismont to senior positions in the CER. After a Soviet threat of a resumption of hostilities, including the bombing of Tsitsihar, Zhang finally agreed to return of the two men; upon having won this point, Narkomindel (the Soviet Commissariat of Foreign Affairs) soon replaced them.[26]

On 13 December, Tsai arrived in Khabarovsk with plenipotentiary powers from both Mukden and Nanjing governments and, finally, on 22 December affixed his signature to the Khabarovsk Protocol. In effect, the protocol restored peace along the border and *status quo ante* (embodied in the 1924 position) to the situation in Northern Manchuria as a whole. All orders and instructions issued after 10 July 1929 were, thereby, declared null and void "unless properly confirmed by the lawful board and administration of the railway."[27] The Khabarovsk Protocol, unlike the initial agreement arrived at Nikol'sk-Ussuriisk, was not accepted by the Chinese authorities; a cause for further disturbance in the North Manchurian situation.

The Red Army's performance was impressive. Russian forces were under strict instructions to inflict minimal damage to the non-military sector. Their primary objectives were: 1) the destruction of opposing armies; 2) smashing of military fortifications and installations; and 3) destruction of prisons and the release of inmates. Special emphasis was placed on the requirement that there should be no damage done to hospitals, schools, cultural institutions, and national shrines. Slogans employed in pursuing this line included: "The Red Army—the friend of the workers of China."[28] The army was instructed, moreover, ". . . to ensure the highest degree of self-control with respect to all strata of the population, and especially the workers."[29] Another aim of the command was to ". . . forbid categorically the appropriation by military personnel of even the smallest things, as well as any purchases on enemy territory."[30] During the campaign itself, there were meetings of political agitators with Komsomol members, and even "socialist competition" between companies.[31]

During the month of occupation, Russian sappers demolished Chinese military installations and emplacements. Communist Party workers put up posters blaming the "White Chinese Generals" of trying to trample on Soviet territory. Propaganda, apart from posters, took the form of the Red Army trying "to win friends" by its conduct. There were well-organized campaigns conducted by Communist Party agitators, as "Political life boiled over in the Chinese towns temporarily occupied by the Red Army."[32] Efforts were also made to influence prisoners held in Chita, including the creation of a wall newspaper, *Krasnyi kitaiskii soldat* (Red Chinese Soldier). The efforts soon paid dividends: within two days, 47 prisoners had filed membership applications for the Komsomol (the Soviet youth organization), and 1,240 lodged applications to remain in the USSR.[33]

The Soviet military action itself had been a striking example of *voennoe iskusstvo* (military art), a major element of military science concerned with "the theory and practice of preparing for and conducting military operations on land, at sea, and in the air."[34] Indeed, one could go even farther by interpreting the action as a major stage in the development of the USSR's Operational Art, which had been in gestation since 1927. Its military forces combined carefully measured use of depth and variety, coordinated in the fashion of a swift action designed to achieve the precise goal of "[a]n annihilating offensive under complex conditions" against enemy forces.[35]

The Manchurian operation was also important in that in its style, and in its disciplined achievement of seemingly very clear objectives, it had for the first time since the military humiliation of 1904 restored Russian military prestige outside its own territorial limits in the Asian region. This, together with the extensive use of demoralizing and confusing propaganda both through radio broadcasts and spread of printed literature, gave the Red Army the image of being an advanced form of war-machine.[36]

The Soviet campaign in Northern Manchuria convinced some Western observers of the USSR's ability to coordinate military and diplomatic technique. One influential observer, the British Envoy Sir Miles W. Lampson, summed up the Soviet tactical achievement in the following analysis:[37]

> . . . it is impossible not to pay a tribute to the extraordinary skill with which Russia handled the dispute. The restraint, the knowledge of psychology, Chinese and foreign, shown by the Soviet Government, and the manner in which their measures were adopted to the end in view and the means at their disposal were surprising. The situation with which they were faced in July, 1929, was one of which other Powers have had all too common experience—a forcible attack upon rights secured by treaty but which were represented as an infringement of China's sovereignty. An immediate invasion of Manchuria would not only have mobilised the whole opinion of the world against her and possibly provoked the armed intervention of Japan, but as a piece of "imperialist" aggression it would have aroused the violent opposition of Chinese nationalism . . .

The diplomatic crisis in itself had strengthened the foreigners' position in China, by demonstrating that Manchuria—and by extension China itself—clearly remained vulnerable to Western action, and perhaps even more so than in the past.

More importantly, while the diplomatic crisis had shown that the notion of a unified Chinese negotiating position was non-existent, the ensuing military conflict also showed quite clearly the weakness of the Chinese armed forces and their inability to resist modern military *matériel* and tactics. China had been shown to be a "paper tiger." Japan, in particular, took note how easily Soviet troops had defeated their Chinese opponents.

The Political Impact of the War

The 1929 Sino-Soviet conflict had an enormous political impact in both countries. Moscow, the clear victor, was quick to point out that war had not been declared and that the Kellogg Pact outlawing war was not violated.[38] By contrast, the Chinese foreign and domestic policies were in disarray. In particular, the differences between the central Chinese government in Nanjing and Zhang Xueliang's government in Mukden were highlighted, and it became clear that various Chinese officials had been working at cross-purposes during the conflict. For example, Sun Fo, Sun Yat-sen's son and the Nationalist Minister of Railways, had published an article in the *North China Standard*, rallying the people, when, at the same time, Chinese ministers in Washington and Berlin were requesting foreign intervention.[39] C.T. Wang, the Chinese Foreign Minister, also issued conflicting statements at the time.[40] Among other things, he appealed to Japan to intervene against the USSR's "armed invasion" of Manchuria.[41] Concurrently, Zhang Xueliang began to make independent proposals to the Soviet Union. By 14 November, when Wang sued for peace via consular links to Moscow, Commissar Litvinov replied that Nanjing's proposals were pointless as Zhang Xueliang had already accepted preliminary conditions for a peace.

Although successful on the battlefield, the Soviet Union was to incur severe short- and long-term losses as a result of its intervention. The military victory was undoubtedly a success, establishing the Red Army as a force to be reckoned with in the broader Northeast Asian region. However, it was on the ideological side that the intervention was ultimately found to be profoundly wanting. The Soviet action was accompanied by a very full, and single-minded, propaganda campaign. The underpinnings of this propaganda were less clear-cut in the Soviet Union itself. Judging by the positions taken within the Soviet Communist Party's Central Committee concerning the methods to be employed in dealing with the crisis, the Soviet leadership appears to have been divided.

The policies emanating from Moscow were not quite as sure-footed as its actions in late 1929 suggested. On 25 July 1929, Coleman, the American representative in Latvia, reported that at its most recent meeting of the Soviet Central Committee there had been a most pronounced division in its ranks. One member, Ia. E. Rudzutak, argued that China, with the aid of England and Japan, was preparing to go to war. At this point, K.I. Voroshilov, the Soviet Commissar of War, considered that the peasants would rise up against the Chinese government, since Russian tactics were defensive, and therefore recommended military action. Kalinin, on the other hand, recommended a peaceful solution through the application of external pressure on China. A.P. Smirnov, P.G. Smidovich, and N.P. Briukhanov, too, all spoke in favor of a peaceful resolution of the crisis. War would, they argued, upset the grain-stocking campaign and the internal situation in Russia itself.

On the other side of the debate, Mikoyan countered by saying that the government could, despite the waging of war, arrange grain supplies for the Army and industrial centers. Piatnitskii argued that there was a chance they could instigate a revolutionary uprising that might overthrow the Nationalist Government in China. He went on to reason that such an uprising was already being prepared in South China and that war in the Far East was an excellent opportunity for the sparking of revolution in China, and especially so if the Soviet Union were not an aggressor.

Following this debate, Stalin was reportedly "extremely annoyed" by the speeches of Smirnov, Smidovich, and Briukhanov, with the latter on the verge of being dismissed. In the end, resolutions were passed recommending "needful measures to combat Chinese rapacity," *or* the organization of protest demonstrations and the mobilization of all organs in Siberia.[42]

The tension in the Soviet leadership over the direction that their policies should take was subsequently revealed in the tone adopted in publications by Soviet "house" journals in articles stressing the need for stability: "If the CER is allowed, peacefully, to fulfill its role and spread its already very considerable economic influence deeper into N. Manchuria, the faster will be the development of the region, the faster its colonization and, as a consequence, the more rapid its growth as an import center."[43] In spirit this view was entirely right, but whether the Soviet leadership understood the possible repercussions that its action might have on the Soviet Union's long-term economic interests in the region is not clear, although the possible damage to the CER may have been considered.

The irony is that, along with the plea for level-headedness in the Soviet Union's public utterances, this is a precise echo of the line that the tsarist Minister of Finance S.I. Witte had taken at the time the Trans-Siberian and its Manchurian extension were first begun: that such an extension of the railway had to be based on principles of peaceful, economically cooperative coexistence. It was a line that had also been pressed very strongly—and entirely appropriately, as it came to pass—by Russian settlers in the region since the late nineteenth century, and more often than not against the thinking of the incumbent Russian government. At the core of this proposition was the idea that all of the interested powers should focus on the most important element in the complex Manchurian question, its economy.[44]

As it happened, both positions in the internal debate within the Central Committee were evident in the political dimension of the conflict. There was a strong element of *realpolitik* present, but also a "revolutionary half-life" to the intervention. Neither, however, was present in strong enough proportions in Manchuria itself. The revolutionary aspect of the conflict drew a fair amount of enthusiasm from the Chinese population of Northern Manchuria, as is evidenced by the soldiers crossing over to the Soviet side. However, the numbers influenced by the Soviet propaganda decrying the warlord rule in Northern Manchuria, and by the military operation itself, were insufficient to precipitate the revolutionary overturn that some members of the Soviet leadership desired and, indeed, thought likely. The broader result in Northern Manchuria was therefore inconclusive.

At the same time, the dominant aspect of *realpolitik*—the one to which much of the foreign praise was addressed—was also flawed. In his musings on the evolution of operational art, Isserson noted of the German penetration of March 1918 that:[45]

> [T]here was no one among the attackers to prolong the attack through the formed breach into the depth, so that the tactical breakthrough of the front could turn into an operational penetration and rout. All grandiose efforts of tactical organization of the penetration, all technical progress in arms, all the enormous concentration of forces and means of suppression—all these turned out to be, essentially, in vain, if tactical success was powerless to develop into operational achievement. *It is senseless to break down the door if there is no one to go through it.* But this is just what happened with the 1918 penetrations. The imperialist war did not resolve the problem of penetration: it ended without having demonstrated the ability to implement this on an operational scale.

Painted on the larger canvas, the image that Isserson presents of the German failure is one that applies also to the Soviet action in Manchuria. The new rules of engagement had been adhered to by the Soviet forces, and the door had been broken down, but nobody went in the door.

However, Northern Manchurian action displayed one further facet of modern warfare: breaking into the enemy's territory "through the door" had to be done for an achievable purpose. In this case, the successful military lunge had resulted in nothing more than further diplomacy and debilitating uncertainty. The limited gains from the victory could not be adequately secured, nor the situation on the ground in Northern Manchuria dramatically transformed. One further quote from Isserson is instructive in this respect: "The German front," he writes, "collapsed in 1918 not so much from without, but from within, under the influence of general economic desolation and the powerful process of the revolution of the masses, which led not only to the downfall of the front, but also to the overthrow of the monarchy."[46] With one adjustment—the revolution of the masses that, finally, did not come to pass in Manchuria—the analysis could as easily be a mirror image for Northern Manchurian situation, and the Soviet Union's part in it.

In sum, the Soviet campaign showed itself to be neither an outright imperialist venture, which, in the case of the Great Powers in China, was usually launched in order to stabilize a given situation, nor was it the actions of a revolutionary vanguard. In the case of the latter, the care that Soviet forces had taken not to disturb the Chinese population had probably helped to create the image that their war was indeed against the "White Chinese Generals," and not against the Chinese peasant or worker. However, while this ensured that there was no lasting sense of resentment in the Manchurian populace towards what might otherwise have been seen as a belligerent act, there was no evidence at all of Manchuria's or China's masses using this opportunity to rise against their own Chinese political masters.[47]

The Economic Impact of the War

One of the most important results of the war were the conflict's effects on the Soviet Union itself, and this takes us to the second, economic plane of the discussion. The USSR had until 1929 been building up its trading position in Manchuria steadily, and remarkably successfully, especially considering the shaky foundations left by the tsarist government, and the chaos of the Russian revolutions and civil war. By the late 1920s the Soviet Union had reversed these negative effects, and strikingly so.

The Soviet government, in particular, had shown a very strong inclination to claim a share in Manchurian growth, this being most clearly evident in the lively activities of *Dal'bank*, which showed a pronounced keenness in its activities on the local market. By employing distinctly Chinese methods of banking—allowing loans on the basis of personal references from well-known members of the business community rather than collateral—*Dal'bank* secured an active financial role in over half of Harbin's bean-oil refineries and bean mills by the end of 1926. Furthermore, by 1929 all the refineries and mills processing beans in the entire region had at some stage received its credit.[48]

Between 1927 and 1928 *Dal'bank* eased its credit requirements by not tying loans to overall plans of operations. As a result of such policies, *Dal'bank* came to finance virtually all large European firms involved in the bean trade, and this was done, moreover, on a regular basis.[49] As a consequence, the bank's turnover in 1927 and 1928 was ¥2.5 million as opposed to ¥1.9 million in the previous financial year. Its active current accounts rose by a similar margin in that year.[50]

In hindsight, the Soviet Union could not have chosen a *less* opportune moment to invade Manchuria. For a start, the Sino-Soviet conflict overlapped with the start of the international economic crisis beginning with the Wall Street Crash in late October 1929. As a result, the economic effects of the crisis were severely compounded. The importance of this point can be seen in increased hardship experienced by northern Manchuria's highly specialized economy as a fully dependent, near monoculture economy. While the market for soybeans, its staple export, remained steady, the region's position was one of prodigious success and dizzying potential. Manchuria had, in fact, not even begun to explore the various other paths of development open to it.

By the time the initial shock-waves from the markets in Germany and England reached Harbin, however, the Sino-Soviet conflict was instrumental in creating the conditions for the region's almost complete economic collapse. The disruption of trade caused by the conflict had reminded the major banks of the dangers inherent in maintaining too casual a credit policy, and they acted to correct it. This correction, as so often happens in such circumstances, quickly became an over-correction and merely exacerbated an already dire economic situation.[51]

The conflict also broke the delicate trade link—maintained through the years of prosperity—between center and periphery. Provincial buyers, for example, did not reappear after the cessation of hostilities between China and the Soviet Union, while the periphery was by then already overstocked with produce, but with little likelihood of a sufficient volume of sales to meet maturing bills.[52] Provincial cities such as Hailar were still suffering from the recession instigated by the conflict when the major international financial tremors shook the region.[53] Even one of the most important engines of economic growth, the movement of labor into northern Manchuria, dried up at source: resettlement in the region fell by almost half in 1929 and its decline accelerated in 1930.[54]

The final collapse of the Manchurian economy, after the growth and interweaving of the underlying weaknesses, came in a crowded, intense sequence. Following the months of retardation resulting from the Sino-Soviet conflict, the economy in northern Manchuria for a time appeared to be returning to its previous footing: banks resumed normal operation in February 1930;[55] grain prices began to creep up; the impact of the bankruptcies reported in months of crisis were softened by reports of potential renewed investment in the region.[56] As late as May 1930, and despite a prolonged slackness in the Harbin market, business circles remained quite optimistic in their view that the depressed condition of the local economy would last just a few weeks, or a few months at the most.[57]

For a time such optimistic predictions seemed justified, when, a few weeks later, London prices for soybeans began to edge up. The improvement, however, was fleeting: on 16 June 1930 London prices fell to levels unheard of in the post-1910 period. With them, the Manchurian grain market collapsed, closely followed by the local import/export trade.[58] The decline continued virtually unabated in the remaining months of 1930, and by early 1931 bean prices were down by 135 percent from those of September 1929.[59]

Conditions in the countryside were by then in a state of deep crisis. Wealthier farmers had begun to use up their capital stock, while for the poorer sectors calamity had already been spelt by plummeting earnings.[60] Compounding the effect of the decrease in prices and export trade was the collapse of silver: its fall by 60 percent brought with it an equivalent reduction in local capital, savings and the value of sales of goods made to foreigners before the collapse.[61] In other Manchurian centers the impact of the trade crisis verged on the spectacular, with the population of Manchuria Station, for instance, being halved as a result.[62] By August 1931, the price quoted in London for Manchurian beans was 20 percent lower than that of 1908 through 1909.[63]

The market slump and crash, introducing the initial phase of economic reversal to the region, rapidly revealed a gaping chasm. With the onset of the financial crisis in China proper, commercial and banking organizations there had formulated projects to counter its effects.[64] However, no such measures were conceivable in northern Manchuria, as the credit and currency systems were too disparate to allow any immediate, formal unified action. Joint action by the banks, insofar as this existed in Russian-dominated northern Manchuria, at least, came in the form of their response to the Sino-Soviet Conflict. When the crisis matured into open conflict, and *Dal'bank* ceased its operations altogether, the remaining banks adopted the informal policy of restricting or withdrawing credit, with the result that bank credit disappeared completely, thereby leaving the business community at the mercy of moneylenders and usurers. With the worsening of the financial situation at the very start of 1930, foreign banks realized that the Manchurian bean exporter was in dire straits and so intervened "collectively" in the hope that trade might be resuscitated in the process.[65]

Many local Russian companies began to dip into their capital—and more often than not their reserves too—to weather the economic hardships. Because of the prolonged nature of the political crisis, a proportion of them were soon on the brink of bankruptcy.[66] For some of the businesses, the alternative to bankruptcy was to reduce the number of employees; a situation that led to a dramatic increase in unemployment figures for Russians in particular, as they were the key nationality involved in the trade of the region.[67] Wages too tumbled, partly due to the crisis itself, and partly through the Soviet ascendancy.[68]

Foreign companies, many of which were affected by the economic crisis, notably American firms, began to regard the political instability as an added liability and, therefore, were encouraged to transfer operations, leaving much of their predominantly Russian staff behind. Some major Russian capitalists joined their number, and in a few cases withdrew from trade altogether, transferring capital in the process. In the case of the latter, an interview with a Russian accountant based in Harbin at the time showed that the company he worked for just "packed up and left" in the course of the 1929 crisis, leaving him to keep the operation going "in some measure." The company did not return to Harbin.[69] Many of these commercial operations had already been thinking about moving in the past, so the crisis simply confirmed their earlier fears and hurried them on in the process of relocation.

Manchuria finally emerged on the path towards unification and stabilization, but under Japanese tutelage following the success of the September 1931 Manchurian Incident. By the mid-1930s the local market was at last showing signs of revival. By then, however, the region had transformed from an essentially export-orientated zone to one with an excess of imports. In the process, banks had suffered great losses, although those that had invested heavily in the local export industry, amongst their number *Dal'bank*, bore losses "several times larger" than those of the more cautious institutions, which helps to explain its withdrawal from Manchuria.

The Economic Plight of the Chinese Eastern Railway

Because of the political crisis in 1929, and notably its protracted character, the import and export figures of the region temporarily collapsed. As a result, the Soviet Union's economic position in Manchuria was on the verge of suffering irreversible damage. Of great importance in this respect was the fact that the resolution of the crisis, while it may have appeared to be a Soviet military and diplomatic coup, created unbearable pressures on the CER itself. These did not find outlet until, finally, the railway came under Japanese control in 1935.

With the agricultural base growing from strength to strength in the 1920s, outstanding soybean harvests behind it, and export figures soaring, even the inherently conservative giant, the CER, had cause for some optimism, and, perhaps more significantly, reason to take risks with its own future well-being. At the height of the economic boom in Manchuria the CER appeared to conclude that there would be an extension of this success through to the end of the decade and well into the next, thereby inspiring it to invest massively in reconstruction, new construction, and rolling stock purchases.

However, not everyone shared this unbridled enthusiasm. Some two years before the dramatic reversal in Manchuria's fortunes, Professor G.K. Gins, a distinguished Russian economist working in Harbin, had warned the CER against capital investment of this magnitude. Voicing his misgivings in *Vestnik Man'chzhurii* (*The*

Manchurian Messenger), he issued an oblique criticism of the railway for having invested away its liquid assets without having created a sinking fund. Almost prophetically, he pointed out the danger in the railway's not having kept a separate repository for the workers' pension fund.[70]

The dangers of the former were fairly obvious, while the latter became painfully clear for the CER in the wake of the combined political and economic crises. Without liquid assets, the company would leave itself exposed in the event of a severe economic crisis; so much so that in such a case it could conceivably have been able to cover only its own operating needs, but certainly not a sudden run on the pension fund. The catastrophe that followed, and not long after Gins's warning was published, was greater than even this astute commentator might have imagined.

The global economic depression, triggered by the Wall Street Crash, was subtle, and insidiously so, in the way that it first touched the Manchurian economy:[71]

> On the surface nothing appeared to have changed in the commercial life. The Chinese ER still remained under the joint management of Soviet and Chinese Administration, its thousands of Russian and Chinese employees appeared to have the same purchasing capacity, import and export was at its height and yet the crisis was coming imperceptibly.

The economic disturbances in America and Europe had initially passed virtually unnoticed in Manchuria, the events obscured by the Sino-Soviet dispute, which, as shown above, at first smoldered for months, before erupting into open conflict.

The biggest economic losses were those associated with the CER, which, being at the core of economic activity and development in the region, suffered greatly, and doubly so. First of all, there had been the loss in carriage. Second, activities of the railway's commercial agencies and auxiliary enterprises, the latter stunted even before the crisis gripped the region, came to a complete standstill.[72]

Having found itself in such a poor financial position, the CER's economic woes soon came to be translated into the further dimension of political friction. A major area for the interplay between the economic and the political was that of the staff dismissals that took place in the wake of the crisis, which occurred in tandem with the return of Soviet officials to the CER's administration. The warnings issued by Professor Gins in 1927 returned to haunt the company later. With the company's financial situation already under strain, staff dismissals became a logical step to take, but this was fraught with political complications as many of those targeted were Russian émigrés, and the latter suspected that they were the focus of political repression. A similar problem arose over refusals to repay outstanding CER debts to

Russian creditors, the majority of whom were émigrés too. In combination, these elements made up a strong and persistent political undercurrent.

When the League of Nations-sponsored Lytton Commission came to Harbin in 1932 to examine the situation after Japan's precipitous assumption of control of Manchuria as a whole in 1931 to 1932, it received a letter from CER employees dismissed after the 1929 conflict. Highlighted in the petition were the return of the Soviet "vanquishers" to the CER administration, and the "illegal" sackings of Russian employees. "[T]housands of . . . poor people," the letter suggested plaintively and with simmering anger, "do not stretch out their hands to beg."[73]

Whether this was true or not, the *belief* that the Russian émigré railwaymen were being starved and humiliated by Soviet efforts was sufficient to generate a great deal of resentment and hostility; much of it, it must be said, in a fog of confusion— no mention had been made in the petition itself, or in any popular medium, of the suspect financial methods employed by the CER, as highlighted by Gins.

Therefore, by intervening militarily, the Soviet Union heightened internal tensions not only between Russians and Chinese, but also between "White" Russian and Soviet citizens. The latter point is most important, as the non-Soviet Russians constituted 50 percent of the total Russian population and held important positions in municipal councils. A combination of these factors, and notably the last, led to a marked deterioration in the political mood throughout northern Manchuria.[74] This, in turn, led to enormous social changes in rural areas throughout Manchuria dominated by Russian immigrants.

The Social Impact of the War

The dislocation and turmoil in Harbin caused by the Sino-Soviet conflict was minimal by comparison with its effect on Russian émigrés in the Manchurian countryside and northern provincial centers. There, the Soviet military effort was under no orders to exercise restraint, as it had been with Chinese settlements, or in Harbin. Indeed, a key goal of the 1929 incursion was to allow Soviet forces to deal systematically with pockets of actual, and perceived, "White" activity in the border areas roughly delimited by Manzhouli, Chalainor, Hailar, Bukhedu, and *Trekhrech'e.*[75]

Such was the efficiency of the Soviet efforts to locate suspected enemies that many small Russian settlements, which otherwise might have escaped the full brunt of the economic depression by reverting to basic agricultural production essential to supporting themselves, were sucked into the political and economic maelstrom instead. Most of these villages and towns were populated by peasants, many of whom were *Starovery* (Old Believers). The Soviet action targeted such villages with a ferocity that caused them to splinter, forcing nearly 10,000 Russians ". . . to abandon their hard-earned belongings . . . and save their lives afresh."[76]

Their departure was much like it had been for the many thousands who had crossed the Sino-Soviet border into China ten years earlier: rough-built carts filled with a few personal belongings, drawn by a horse, and accompanied by whatever livestock that could negotiate the difficult trek. Their departure on this occasion was clouded not only by the specter of the Bolsheviks, but also of roaming bands of Chinese deserters and avaricious local officials who preyed on the helpless convoys as they passed through their bailiwick. "Never," a report on the 1929 conflict concluded, "has the absence of rights and the helplessness of Russian émigrés been as clearly seen as in these days." The report further suggests that it was difficult to estimate under whose abuse the refugees suffered more: "the tyranny and violence of the Bolsheviks, or that of the Chinese authorities and soldiers."[77]

The damage to the provincial sector of Russian life in Northern Manchuria was such that an aid agency estimated total Russian losses to be over 200 killed, many hundreds injured, over 800 forcibly "repatriated" for trial and punishment in the Soviet Union, and the seizure of over three million silver dollars in lost possessions.[78] Hundreds of families, the agency observed, were still not in a position to recover and depended entirely on whatever aid could be provided by its very limited resources.[79]

Cases of cruelty and atrocities at the hands of Soviet forces, notably in the *Trekhrech'e* area, remained unaddressed.[80] Much of the infrastructure vital to the conduct of Russian economic and administrative activity in the periphery had been seized by the Chinese authorities themselves.[81] Items seized by the local authorities included boats and steamers belonging to private individuals and the CER, a local telephone company, premises of the Museum of OIMK (*Organizatsiia izuchennie Manchzhurskago kraia* [Organization for the Study of the Manchurian Region]), a Russian think-tank engaged in social, economic, and historical research, and even the Russian Red Cross. "All had been arbitrarily seized by former representatives of local authorities," a report stated, with there being little chance of their return, despite strenuous protests and repeated requests.[82]

Conclusions

In the wake of the Sino-Soviet conflict over the CER, the USSR's actual control over northern Manchuria decreased rather than increased. The Russian refugee organizations' various petitions, while pointing their fingers at Soviet "pressure" as the root underlying cause, accused local Chinese authorities in the border areas of taking all forms of control into their own hands.[83] A Russian refugee publication concluded: "Deprived of the links with the railway and its aid, suffering from the destruction of enterprise, the absence of basic rights and the onset of anarchy, [the Russian Emigration] exhausted all hope of existence, irrespective of its loyalty to authority, love of peace and its work skills."[84]

After the 1929 crisis, it was stability that figured as the major focus of attention in the region. And, arguably, it was because of the desire for, and the pursuit of, stability rather than simply clear hegemonic or annexationist motives alone that Japan intruded into Northern Manchuria after the 1931 crisis. Nor was it simply a Japanese pretext that lay behind the move. By 1931 there were many sectors of northern Manchurian society that came to yearn for, and sought, political and economic stability. The indigenous Russians were amongst them and when Japanese forces reached the streets of Harbin in 1932, they were greeted with rousing *Banzais* from Russian onlookers crowding the pavements.[85]

Despite the consummate Soviet military performance in northern Manchuria during the 1929 conflict, it was the Japanese who were able to take *de facto* control of Manchuria within two years of the conflict. Soon afterwards, Japan initiated talks with the USSR leading to the 1935 sale of the CER to Japan's South Manchuria Railway. Not only did this help consolidate Japan's control over all of Manchuria, but as the following chapters will show, this success had a profound effect on China's own internal railway development in Central China and in Manchuria, not to mention adjoining railway systems like those located on the Shandong peninsula directly to the South.

Notes

1. Felix Patrikeeff and Harold Shukman, *Railways and the Russo-Japanese War: Transporting War* (London: Routledge, 2007), 30.

2. S. Avenarius, "80 let KVzhd (1898–1978): Istoricheskii ocherk," *Politekhnik* (Sydney, 1979), No.10, 58–64.

3. *The China Weekly Review* (formerly *Millard's Review*), Shanghai, 23 October 1920.

4. Felix Patrikeeff, *Russian Politics in Exile: The Northeast Asian Balance of Power, 1924–1931* (Houndmills: Palgrave Macmillan, 2002), Chapter 1.

5. *Ekonomicheskii Biuliten'* 1928, No. 20, 14; Felix Patrikeeff, "Prosperity and Collapse: Banking And the Manchurian Economy in the 1920s and 1930s," F.H.H. King (ed.) *Eastern Banking: Essays in the History of the Hongkong and Shanghai Banking Corporation* (London: The Athlone Press, 1983), 265–78.

6. For a comparison of the two, see H.W. Kinney, *Confidential Report*, Mukden, 25 September 1931, Hoover Institution Archives [HIA], Pastuhov Collection, Box 21, 6.

7. B.G. Tours, the British Consul General at Mukden, reported that as early as August 1929, Zhang Xueliang had begun to "lose interest" in the crisis over the

railway, preferring ". . . to devote all his attention to 'movie-tone' pictures, which are being demonstrated to him by special agents of the American Fox Company." Tours to Lampson, No. 50, Mukden, 2 August, 1929, FO 371/13954–632.

8. See, for example, the work on the 1929 Conflict by E.H. Carr, *The Russian Revolution from Lenin to Stalin, 1917–1929* (London: Macmillan, 1979); James W. Christopher, *Conflict in the Far East: American Diplomacy in China from 1928–1933* (New York: Ayer, 1970); Lensen, *The Damned Inheritance*; and Tang, *Russian and Soviet Policy in Manchuria and Outer Mongolia.*

9. *Sovetsko-Kitaiskii konflikt 1929 g.: Sbornik dokumentov* (Moscow: 1930), 3–4.

10. H.L. Kingman, *Effects of Chinese Nationalism upon Manchurian Railway Developments, 1925–1931* (Berkeley: University of California Press, 1932), especially 61–70.

11. Over a year after the conflict had run its course, "White" Russian captains of steamers on the river system would hand over the ships to their Chinese seconds after they had cleared the Lahasusu Customs point and the vessels were ready to continue on the Amur portion of their trip, the captains "themselves remaining on the Sungari, the commercially navigable river running through Harbin, ready to take over their ships on their return." Gibbes, *Memorandum on Trade*, Lahasusu, September Qr., 1930, 3.

12. Hongkong and Shanghai Banking Corporation (hereafter HSBC), Archives, Vol. 91, Wood to de Courcy, Harbin, 11/12.7.29; Tsao Lien-en, *The CER: An Analytical Study* (Shanghai, 1930), 121; Lensen, *The Damned Inheritance*, 54.

13. "*Oblastnik*" *Statia KVzhd (O Kitaiskoi Vostochnoi zheleznoi doroge)*, n.p. (Harbin?), n.d. (1929?), 12; GARF, 5869, No.1, Khr. No. 9.

14. Department of State, *Papers Relating to the Foreign Relations of the United States*, 1929, Vol. II, Washington: 1943 [FRUS], 274.

15. V. Dushen'kin, *ot soldata do marshala* (Moscow: 1964), 178; The text of the order for the formation of the force can be found in *Sovetsko-Kitaiskii konflikt 1929 g.*, op. cit., 37–38.

16. Badham-Thornhill to Lampson, Peking, 24 September 1929, "Secret," FO 376/13955.

17. FRUS, op. cit., 337–38. Similar reports exist for other northwestern areas: at Bukhedu Station, between Tsitsihar (Qiqihar) and Hailar, Soviet planes bombed Chinese encampments on 28–29 November, causing an immediate rash of looting and violence as the troops made their chaotic retreat. ("Delegates of the European population of the District of Station Boohedoo C.E.Rly." to the Lytton Commission of Enquiry, 11 May 1932, HIA, Pastuhov Collection, Box 52, 1.)

18. Dushen'kin, op. cit., 182, 194–95.

19. FRUS, op. cit., 338.

20. Since the units were not on a war footing, the numbers were not more than 6,033 infantry and 1,599 cavalry.

21. George Alexander Lensen, *The Strange Neutrality: Soviet-Japanese Relations during the Second World War, 1941–1945* (Tallahassee, FL: The Diplomatic Press, 1972), 156–73.

22. Lensen, *The Damned Inheritance*, 62–65.

23. Russian troops filmed this bizarre spectacle, showing it to the population of Manzhouli and, some time later, in Moscow; Kinney to Pratt, 3 February 1930, FO 371/14700.

24. "Delegates of the European Population. . .," op. cit., 1.

25. Badham-Thornhill to Lampson, Peking, 13 January 1930, 'Secret,' FO 371/14700.

26. FRUS, 1929, II, 392–93, 397; *Sovetsko-Kitaiskii konflikt*, 86–7.

27. *Izvestiia*, 23 December 1929; Also, all employees who had been dismissed were to be reinstated, or pensioned off if they were unwilling to resume their work; all former Russian subjects—not citizens of the USSR—hired by the CER during the conflict were to be dismissed; White Guard detachments were to be disarmed by the Chinese and their organizers and leaders deported from the Three Northeastern Provinces; diplomatic links were left to the Moscow Conference to consider, however Soviet consulates in the provinces and Chinese consulates in the Russian Far East were opened immediately.

28. V.M. Kulagin and N.N. Iakovlev, *Podvig Osoboi Dal'nevostochnoi* (Moscow: 1970), 124; This slogan was, by all accounts, adhered to, with gratitude being expressed by Chinese civilians for the treatment they received from the soldiers of the Red Army. See, for example, the vote of thanks from the Chinese Municipal Council of Hailar, Dushen'kin, 194–95; Similar treatment, according to one account, was accorded to captured Chinese soldiers, with whom Red Army personnel shared bread, tobacco, and sugar. Ibid., 194.

29. Kulagin and Iakovlev, 124. The directives appear to have been obeyed: "We received not so much as one complaint about the conduct of our soldiers with the civilian population," reported Bliukher upon completion of the military action. Dushen'kin, 194.

30. Ibid. It is interesting to observe that the policies of non-interference and non-exploitation employed by the Red Army in Northern Manchuria in 1929 anticipated by a number of years the very successful political methods (subsumed under the body of theory known as the "Yenan Way") introduced by Mao Zedong to the People's Liberation Army after the Yenan period.

31. Lensen, *The Damned Inheritance*, 64.

32. Kulagin and Iakovlev, 166.

33. Ibid., 158–66.

34. S.P. Ivanov and A.I. Evseev, "Voennoe iskusstvo," *Sovetskaia voennaia entsiklopediia*, 1976, Vol. 2, 211.

35. A.A. Svechin, "Strategy and Operational Art," 2nd edition of *Strategiia* (Moscow: 1927), in H.S. Orenstein (tr.) and D.M. Glantz (foreword and introductions), *The Evolution of Soviet Operational Art, 1927–1991: The Documentary Basis* (London: Frank Cass, 1995), Vol. 1, 10.

36. *China Weekly Review*, Shanghai, 11 January 1930, No. 6.

37. Lampson to Henderson, No. 930, 2 July 1930, FO 371/14699.

38. While the Chinese government frequently invoked the pact, signed just a year earlier (27 August 1928), in the course of the crisis, the Soviet Union was able to negate the thrust of these complaints by referring to the Chinese incursions onto its

own territory; raids which were much-publicized by Soviet media. Thus, Moscow argued that the Soviet Union was not engaging in war-like action, but rather adopting measures essential to repel an aggressor; *China Weekly Review*, 11 January 1930.

39. FRUS, 263; For a further description of the ragged Chinese diplomatic effort, see "Kto otvetstvenen za razryv?" (Translated from *Weekly Review*, 25 January 1930) GARF, Fond 5878, no.1, Khr. no.173.

40. Christopher, *Conflict in the Far East,* 110–11.

41. Bruce Elleman, *Modern Chinese Warfare, 1795–1989* (London: Routledge Press, 2001), 187.

42. Christopher, op. cit., 99–100.

43. V.F. Shchepin, "Severnaia Man'chzhuriia kak importnyi tsentr," *Vestnik Man'chzhurii* [hereafter *VM*], No.1, 1930, 68.

44. Felix Patrikeeff, "Russian and Soviet Economic Penetration of Northern China, 1895–1933," in John W. Strong (ed.) *Essays on Revolutionary Culture and Stalinism* (Columbus, OH: Slavica Publishers, 1990).

45. G. Isserson, "Evoliutsiia operativnogo iskusstva," *Voina i revoliutsiia*, 5–6, 1932, 25–52, in Orenstein and Glantz, 76.

46. Ibid.

47. If anything, the competing forms of Soviet and Chinese propaganda must have been the cause of considerable confusion for the civilian population watching the conflict from the sidelines. One Russian, who was an engineering student at *KhPI* (the Harbin Polytechnical Institute) at the time, remembered a particularly confusing example of the Chinese propaganda. The Chinese authorities had, he said, sent up an aeroplane with the large markings *Pekin-Moskva* on it, with the intention of using it as the "vanguard for Chinese forces in their thrust towards Moscow." The plane managed to get as far as the border, where Soviet aircraft forced it to land; B. Koreneff, Interview, Sydney, 13 March 1981.

48. *Ekonomicheskii Biuliten'* [hereafter *EB*], 1929, Nos 15–16, 1–4; Information comes from Mr Ishiga, the Assistant Director of the Bank of Chosen.

49. A.V.M., "Eksport Man'chzhurskikh bobov i ego finansirovanie," *VM*, 1928, No. 3, 10.

50. K.P. Kursel', "Dal'bank v 1927 g.," *VM*, 1928, No. 4, 20.

51. Harbin market reports for the first half of 1930 show a very sharp decline across the board, but notably in soybean trade. *EB* for 1 June 1930 showed that crop prospects for the first half of the year were very good, but that the European market had "almost altogether" stopped purchasing Manchurian beans; No.10, 11–14. Later in the same month, an All-Manchurian Conference of Chinese Commercial Associations began to hold emergency sessions in Mukden in order to find ways in which to protect Manchurian trade and industry; Ibid., 8 August 1930, No.14, 1–3.

52. *EB*, 1931, No. 2, 1–5.

53. Hailar, an agricultural centre, in 1930 shipped only 68 percent of wool supply (compared with the previous year's figures) and experienced a 50 percent fall in the price of hay. *EB*, 1930, No. 5, 19–20.

54. Figures for those dispatched from Dairen, for example: 1928 –73,983; 1929–48,724; 1930 (first five months) –9,717. *EB*, 1930, No. 7, 7.

55. *EB*, 1930, No. 3, 27.

56. *EB*, 1929, Nos 15–16, 20.

57. "Harbin Market Review," *EB*, 1930, No. 7, 14–18.

58. N.M. Dobrokhotov, "Ekonomicheskiie zatrudneniia v Kharbine," *VM*, 1930, No. 6, 12.

59. L.I. Liubimov, "Krizis sbyta bobov i poteri Man'chzhurskogo krest'ianina," *VM*, 1930, No. 6, 6.

60. Between 30 September 1929 and May 1931 prices in Harbin fell from 104 to 82 *Sen* per pood. Cited in Ibid., 7.

61. Dobrokhotov, 13.

62. *EB*, 1931, No. 5, 14; On 1929 figures (1924 population = 92,000).

63. *EB*, 1931, No. 16, 10–12. In late November–December, London prices were not quoted at all. (See *EB*, No. 22, 7–9).

64. The meeting was held in mid-January 1930. Present were: representatives of the Bank of China, the Chinese Chamber of Commerce, the Federation of Banks and the Chinese Stock Exchange. At this meeting, a directive was issued abolishing the *Tael* as from 1 July 1930, the Chinese Dollar thereby becoming the sole currency. In A.I. Pogrebetskii, "Na puti k zolotomu standartu," *VM*, 1930, No. 2, 8.

65. *VM*, 1930, No. 2, 83. The banks taking part in this action were: Chosen, Yokohama Specie, HSBC, *Dal'bank* (Harbin Office), National City, and, later, the Standard Chartered (but on a small scale).

66. One Russian businessman was working for a fur company in Mongolia in 1929. The owner of the company had, in his words, transformed ". . . from a millionaire to a pauper, but a pauper with accumulated debts." The businessman himself found out about the collapse when he attempted to buy some goods on credit, but discovered that his company had not paid its existing debts. Finally, after queries from his Chinese customers, he travelled to Kalgan (where the head office was based) only to find an empty office, with a cold stove. There was insufficient money left even to heat the office. His stock of furs had for some time been sold off to local Chinese buyers, who sewed hats from the most exotic of furs, replacing the cheap fabric caps worn in the area; A.P. Zanozin, Interview, 5 March 1981.

67. Numerous retail businesses in Harbin were forced to run their operations on skeleton staff of 1–2 employees, shedding the remainder in the course of 1929–1930; See "Harbin Market Reports," *EB*, 1930, No. 9–1931, No. 1.; A.M. Pagudin, Interview, San Francisco, 7 July 1979.

68. Pagudin, Interview, July 1979.

69. Pagudin, Interview, July 1979. The sharp slump in trading figures would have encouraged companies to transfer their operations. One report (for early 1930) observes that the activities of trading companies in the region had fallen to 40 percent of those recorded for the same period in 1929; N.M. Dobrokhotov, "Depressiia na Man'chzhurskom rynke," *VM*, 1930, No. 3, 13.

70. G.K. Gins, "Osnovnye cherty khoziaistva KVzhd'," *VM*, 1927, No. 2, 21; Gins, a professor of economics in Harbin, was especially critical of the CER's

refusal to run a sinking fund when, at the same time, it had gone into debt to its own employees' Savings Fund.

71. HSBC, Letter/report from Ostrenko to J.R. Jones, 12 March 1955.

72. Tsao notes that "[a]side from seizure and damage to its rolling stock, the Railway also suffers the loss of huge revenue, which, according to the yearly rate of increase, should have surpassed that of preceding years during corresponding periods to a very great extent." Tsao, 78.

73. S.A. Poperek, "To the Inquiry Committee of the League of Nations from the Delegation of discharged employees of the CER," 9 May 1932, HIA, Pastuhov Collection, Box 3.

74. V.G. Savchik, Interview, 14 February 1981.

75. *Kharbinskii komitet pomoshchi Russkim bezhentsam* [Harbin Committee for Aid to Russian Refugees], Survey, HIA, Pastuhov Collection, Box 3, 6.

76. Ibid., 7

77. Ibid.; Reports on specific incidents involving the seizure of refugees' property by Chinese soldiers is to be found in *On the Condition of Russian Emigrants in Northern Manchuria,* Submission to the Lytton Commission, 6 May 1932, No. 1850, HIA Pastuhov Collection, Box 3.

78. *Kharbinskii komitet pomoshchi*, 8; Regarding the forced repatriation of Russians, one case, that of General K.M. Aslamov, especially stands out: the man in question was returned to the Soviet Union on the pretext of bearing an expired passport; *On the Condition of Russian Emigrants in Northern Manchuria,* Submission to the Lytton Commission, 6 May 1932, No. 1850, HIA, Pastuhov Collection, Box 3.

79. *Kharbinskii komitet pomoshchi*, 8.

80. Atrocities are focused upon by Tang, 226–27; V.I. Ivachev, the head of the Russian emigrants' group at *Trekhrech'e*, reported on the excesses and explicit cruelty of both Soviet and Chinese forces; *On the Condition of Russian Emigrants.*

81. The evolution of full control, which this in effect appeared to be, took various forms. The *KhkpRb* recommended to Chinese authorities as early as December 1929 that suitable plots of land be transferred to displaced refugees in order that the latter might be able to "freely engage" in hunting, forestry, fishing, mining etc. Its efforts, however, were fruitless; Survey of the activities of the *Kharbinskii komitet pomoshchi Russkim bezhentsam,* n.d. [1931?], HIA, Pastuhov Collection, Box 3.

82. *On the Condition of Russian Emigrants.*

83. The *KhkpRb* listed a large number of steps that Chinese authorities had taken in order to inhibit Russian economic activity in the region. These ranged from restrictions on freedom of movement, to the prohibition of new enterprises in the provinces; Survey of the activities of the *Kharbinskii komitet pomoshchi Russkim bezhentsam,* n.d. [1931?], HIA, Pastuhov Collection, Box 3, Appendix 1.

84. Survey of the activities of the *Kharbinskii komitet pomoshchi Russkim bezhentsam,* op. cit.

85. Amleto Vespa, *Secret Agent for Japan: A Handbook to Japanese Imperialism* (London: V. Gollancz Ltd., 1938), 25.

PART II

Competing Railway Nationalisms

Rival railway imperialisms created enormous challenges for both the people of Manchuria and for the Chinese government's persistent claims of national sovereignty over this entire region. But during these years China was not standing still. As Chang Jui-te shows, railway construction continued apace, and by 1933 there were more than 6,000 miles (10,000 kilometers) of railway lines covering China's nineteen provinces. These railways represented the largest enterprise in modern China, employing 120,000 people, and transporting 45 million passengers and 27 kilotons of cargo annually. In many ways, it was the construction of railways that brought modern science and technology to China, and thus helped to create what observers took to calling "modern" China. In other words, strategic rivalry and bloodshed were not the only consequences of Manchurian railway building.

Chang examines China's railway modernization and technical development, showing the important effects of railways on Chinese society, and especially on its educational system. Transportation universities, backed by on-the-job training, created a substantial group of technical and managerial personnel in China's government and in its rapidly modernizing private sector. As a result, railways helped promote the development of a new class of Western-trained professionals, a trend that was new in Chinese history. From the end of the Qing dynasty in 1911 through the creation of the People's Republic in 1949, this shift in Chinese society's evaluation of professionals was destined to play an enormously important role.

Elisabeth Köll shows the important impact of this societal shift by focusing on the construction of the Tianjin-Pukou railroad, in the northern province of Shandong province. The Tianjin-Pukou as well as the Qingdao-Jinan railway lines helped to connect North and South China. According to Köll, the Shandong railways also maintained maritime lines of communication with Manchuria, thereby linking the commercial and political centers of Republican China with the Northeast. Beyond helping create the underlying infrastructure necessary for economic growth, commercial agriculture, and economic integration with neighboring provinces, including Manchuria, the Shandong province rail lines became an essential part of the Nationalist government's attempts to centralize its administration and integration into a nation-wide railway network. After 1937, the Japanese military used the Shandong railways to invade North China. This was a strategy that the Chinese Communists would follow with equal success during the late 1940s, when they used the combined Manchuria-Shandong lines to seize power.

Rather than view railway lines as targets to attack, the Communist military leadership valued them for their logistical benefits and strategic leverage. As Harold M. Tanner shows, beginning in mid-August 1945, the Chinese Communist Party (CCP) transferred units of its Eighth Route and New Fourth Armies from the backward rural areas of northern China to Manchuria. After relocating to Manchuria, Communist forces quickly occupied the main railway lines, and via a policy of using some lines and cutting others, isolated and eventually destroyed the Nationalist forces. The Communist Ministry of Railways was so important that it was subordinated directly to the Central Military Affairs Commission and proved crucial to the delivery of supplies and war materiel to the Communist armies south of the Great Wall. By mid-November 1948 the Communist forces had defeated the Nationalist troops and taken control of all of Manchuria. From beginning to end, the civil war in Manchuria revolved around the railway lines, and following their victory in the Northeast the Chinese Communists could use its control over the railway links with North and Central China to dominate all of mainland China and create the People's Republic of China (PRC). After 1949 railroad companies were quickly turned into socialist work units (*danwei*) and the railways' well-known administrative efficiency and discipline were praised as socialist virtues.

In 1952, more than fifty-five years after the original Sino-Russian agreement to allow construction of the Chinese Eastern Railway (CER), the Soviet government finally agreed to return the unified Manchurian railway lines, now called the Chinese Changchun Railway, to the PRC. Zhang Shengfa examines the tense Sino-Soviet negotiations leading up to the final handover of this railway and the subsequent fate of the port cities of Lüshun (formerly Port Arthur) and Dalian (formerly Dairen). Despite a delay of some thirty years in the promised return of the Manchurian railways, as recorded in the 1924 treaty, the act helped reduce friction between the two countries. The return also graphically highlighted the end of "Red Imperialism" in Manchuria, perhaps best shown by the rapid decline in the Russian/Soviet émigré community in Northeastern China, historically centered in Harbin. During the 1950s, tens of thousands of Soviets either repatriated to the USSR or emigrated to Western countries. This precipitous decline of the émigré community revealed that, after sixty years of foreign domination, including nearly constant political and military turmoil, Manchuria was becoming an integral part of China. The trajectory from railway imperialism to national consolidation appeared complete.

5

Technology Transfer in Modern China: The Case of Railway Enterprises in Central China and Manchuria

Chang Jui-te

After more than half a century of development beginning at the end of the nineteenth century, railway construction made considerable progress in China. According to statistics, in 1933 a total mileage of more than 10,000 kilometers covering 19 provinces had been completed. Total railway assets reached 860 million yuan and liabilities were more than 1.2 billion. Although still a very minor operation compared to other industrialized countries, this was the largest enterprise in modern China, employing 120,000 people and transporting 45 million passengers and 27 kilotons of cargo annually. Railway operating incomes had reached 148 million yuan, and the output was 160 million yuan. Railways, being a product of modern science and technology, differed from other institutions in their organization, and therefore required a highly integrated and differentiated administration.[1] With regards to personnel, qualified technology specialists and administrators were required to carry out construction and operation of the railway. In China, the railway was a new enterprise, and research on the technology transfer of this enterprise helps to understand the nature of Sino-foreign economic relations in modern China.

Railway Building in China

Most contemporary scholars involved in economic development research think that the government should play an important role in the technology transfer being carried out in developing countries. However, during the end of the Qing Dynasty no plan for large-scale technology transfer was adopted, owing to financial difficulties, and railways were the only enterprise that proceeded at a constant rate. By the end of the Qing Dynasty, it was railways—in the eyes of most government officials and the gentry—that would lead the way in promoting the development of various industrial sectors, as well as benefit the national defense, to help reach their objective of making China strong and wealthy.

In the West, railway building was the product of years of constant research and development. In China, however, the most advanced railway technology could be adopted immediately without spending equal amounts of energy and money. Reformer Ma Jianzhong (1844–1900) understood this and in 1879 wrote in his "On Railways": "The train, in its early creation, was fraught with many short-comings and was improved to the perfection of today by repeated correction. We are lucky enough to take advantage of the availability at this time."[2] Clearly Ma had fully acknowledged the "advantages of backwardness," as pointed out by the economic historian Alexander Gershenkron, as exhibited by nineteenth century China.[3]

In modern China, railway technology transfer included both "hardware" technology in engineering and "software" technology in management. As a result of China's initial lack of knowledge of railway accounting and the expenditure of foreign loans, China's railway finance in the early years of its establishment was controlled by foreign capitalists. Whenever a railway was constructed, various systems of accounting and book keeping much more rigid than those traditionally practiced by the Chinese government were set up by the foreign accounting general of the country from which the loan came.[4]

After the Republic was founded in 1912, the Ministry of Communications, under the assistance of U.S. Advisor Henry C. Adams (1851–1921), completed the unification of the railways' different accounting systems. Adams was a founder and early president of the American Economic Association and president of the American Statistical Association. From 1887 to 1911, he was associated with the Interstate Commerce Commission, developing the system of accounts and statistics that provided the factual basis for railroad regulation. From 1913 he performed a similar service for the Chinese government. Adams had spent more than ten years in charge of unifying accounting systems in the United States, but owing to his experience finished the same job in China in less than two years. Ever since then, perfect annual railway accounts were available—these were precise to a degree not only second to none in China, but regarded as excellent worldwide.[5]

Although modern China's employment of Western railway technology saved a great deal of time and expenditure, a tremendous cost was paid as well. As regards the introduction of the technology itself, the greatest shortcoming was the lack of standardization. When the railway was invented, each country, with its different industrial foundations and development, had a different standard that could not be uniformly recognized internationally. Most of the foundations for construction of China's railways in early times came from loans made by the United Kingdom, France, Belgium, Germany, and Japan. According to contract, engineers from the lending country were hired to supervise construction, while required materials were also purchased from the lending country; in other words, the equipment and construction standards would be the same as those of the lending country.

China had no choice but to accept the standards of the different countries as she did not have her own standard at the time. By doing so, differences in equipment installation existed between different railways. Even operational regulations, nomenclature, and telegram systems differed between English, French, Japanese, and Russian sections. This created great obstacles for the railway administrators, as well as their joint transportation with other railroads. These sorts of obstacles became increasingly serious with the gradual construction and opening of the railways.

In 1917, the Ministry of Communications set up the Committee of Railway Technology for which domestic and foreign railways specialists were hired to discuss the unification of operational procedures.[6] Although the Ministry of Communications in the early period of the Republic had already started to prepare for the standardization of railroads, the actual implementation of this plan was mainly the work of the Nationalist government. The construction of railroads henceforth was entirely in the hands of Chinese engineers, regardless of the source of funds and materials. This led to a gradual movement toward construction standardization.[7]

Construction of Modern Railways

The construction of the railways of modern China, with one or two exceptions, was funded by loans from foreign countries guaranteed by the railway's assets and operating income. According to statistics, up to the year 1936, the total of foreign loans was 1.4 billion yuan, most of which came from the United Kingdom and was followed by Belgium and Germany.[8]

In general commercial practice, loan conditions should be limited to interest, discounts, commissions, repayment time, and mortgage, but in China at that time foreign loan agreements were subject to many more special clauses than typical ones, and this resulted in the loss of many rights. After its establishment, the Nationalist government made a great attempt at promoting the reconstruction of the war-damaged railways, but it ran into too many difficulties, the most serious of which was the shortage of capital.

But in sharp contrast to the late nineteenth century, all initiatives for new foreign loans came from China itself. The Ministry of Railways was the prime mover in planning most of the lines, and the execution of this process was largely in the hands of the Ministry itself or of Chinese companies organized under its auspices. Foreign credits were sought by China to carry out her own designs rather than those pressed upon her to further the ambitions of other.[9]

The railway loans were made on a commercial rather than a political basis, so the right to determine the railroad routes was solely in Chinese hands. The Nationalist government could make plans for railroad construction according to its own needs and enforce them according to its own pre-determined sequence of priorities. Although the various countries had an historical interest in China, the concept of "spheres of influence" was no longer as important as it had been previously. For example, during the period of construction, foreign creditors only had the right to audit expenditures, while management and construction were completely under Chinese control.

More skilled Chinese construction personnel also began to appear after the Republic was set up, who were capable of handling all the difficult tasks involved. The choice of materials and the solving of technical questions were left to Chinese. For all of these reasons, this period of railway construction marked a new period of international cooperation in China.[10]

Chinese Railway Management

From the beginning, a system of single railway management was adopted by China; each line had its own managing administration regardless of its length or volume of cargo. This was because most railways were constructed with foreign loans, with privately collected funds, or were nationalized individually. However, each individual railway was directly under the supervision of the Ministry of Communications.

Before the War of Resistance Against Japan, the more than 7,000 kilometers of China's railways were run by 13 separate administrative offices. Two of those had lengths of only 143 and 166 kilometers, while the longest was 1,300 kilometers. Although one administration's line may have been short, its administration was the same as that of a large line, simply in miniature. Each line developed its own separate system, which led to increased administrative and other operational expenditures.

In addition to these increased expenditures, other shortcomings included the fact that operations, personnel, and facilities could not be fully utilized. In 1909, there were 40 categories of railway cars employed, whereas only 6 categories would have been sufficient had all railways been combined.[11] According to estimates, 60 percent of the cars could have done the same amount of work if properly organized, and "great expenditure could have been saved."[12]

The single railway management system was also inefficient in not maximizing the use of cars. This system did not adhere to the two principles governing the dispatching of cars. First, utilization of cars is to be maximized while empty car operation is to be avoided, and second, to optimize efficiency good use of the rules of supply and demand is desired.[13]

The railway facilities had to be improved. Owing to the large number of managing administrations, mechanical shops and supply depots were especially numerous. When there were too many mechanical shops their scale was unavoidably smaller and their usefulness thereby lessened. If there were too many supply depots, necessary stock on hand in each would be enormous.

In finance, prior to the Sino-Japanese War all railways were under the supervision of the Ministry of Railways, but all financial income and outflow were strictly divided under their auspices according to creditor's rights and loan histories. Although the Railway Ministry sometimes might subsidize some of the poorer lines, the Chinese railways, generally speaking, could not develop in a balanced fashion, for while some lines had good financial resources, others did not.[14] The lines on which business was heavy could not only afford to expand their facilities but also to improve the quality of their work and increase their workers' pay. On lines where business was light, debts could not even be met, to say nothing of the facilities' improvement.

Two types of railway organization were used worldwide: one a departmental system and the other a divisional system. In the former, administration was divided into the departments of traffic, mechanics, and construction. The railway was divided into sections run by one section chief from each department, under the supervision of their department chief. In the latter system, the section chief was responsible for all dispatching, mechanics, and construction in his section as well as all working operations.

The departmental system had the advantage of clear responsibility for each section chief, but there was a tendency for lack of cooperation between the different section chiefs. This system was commonly used for railways of shorter length and smaller cargo volume such as those of Europe and the United Kingdom.[15] Most railways in the United States used the divisional system, which was more centralized than the departmental system and so U.S. railway administrators enjoyed more complete authority.[16] China's early railway organization was influenced by the United Kingdom and France, and the departmental system was therefore adopted. This system resulted in a lack of centralized authority, and disputes often occurred.[17]

Railway Administration

The transportation enterprises of the Qing Dynasty were originally administered by laymen officials with the assistance of foreign engineering personnel, but there were few Chinese experts even in subordinate positions.[18] Returned students who had studied railways abroad were not only small in number, but were often not even able to use their specialized services.

One good example of this was Jeme T'ien-yow, who studied railway engineering and construction at Yale University, and in the 1880s' was assigned to Fuzhou Dockyard for training in navigation. After his graduation, he was assigned to battleship service, eventually becoming an instructor in the Guangdong Naval and Military Officer's Academy.[19] Moreover, in early times, the students, with their limited foreign study, could at most only be skilled artisans. A few of them eventually were able to rise above this status and become China's first railway engineers.[20]

According to an 1897 investigation of all students returning from railway engineering study abroad to be assigned to the Tianjin-Shanhaiguan Railway for experience, only Jeme T'ien-yow and Kuang Jingyang were qualified to be engineers.[21] Therefore, before Jeme T'ien-yow became famous for construction on the Beijing-Kalgan Railway there were no Chinese railway engineering specialists to speak of. Moreover, railway construction required additional foreign loans. Consequently the railroad's engineering, dispatching, mechanics, and even accounting were often in the hands of foreigners.[22]

By the time the Ministry of Posts and Communications was functioning, the sources of personnel may have been broader but were still insufficient. Those few returned students who offered their services to the railways were assigned to the translation and research sections in the Ministry.[23] Few of them, with rare exceptions like Jeme T'ien-yow, were qualified to serve in technical positions owing to their lack of experience, even if they had studied engineering. The Sichuan-Hankou Railway Company hired an engineer, Hu Dongchao, a Cantonese who had studied engineering in the United States, as its chief engineer. But he was charged with incompetence in designing and executing the various engineering tasks required in the construction of the railway.[24]

Owing to the shortage of engineering personnel, the few experts available often moved among the railways, and on-the-job training provided by the railways themselves became an important way of training personnel. For example, in 1905 the Beijing-Kalgan Railway was started. At that time neither Beiyang University, Nanyang University, nor Tangshan University had any graduate students in either civil engineering or railway studies.

Assistant Manager Jeme T'ien-yow's subordinates mostly came from the Imperial Railways of North China. Some of them had graduated from Shanhaiguan Railway School. Of the engineering assistants, many were later assigned to important engineering posts on other lines.[25] Nevertheless, technical personnel were insufficient for the need, both in numbers and ability. Thus before 1911, less than 10 percent of Chinese railways were built by Chinese.[26]

As time went by, the engineers in the early Republic were increasingly capable of independently dealing with their heavy responsibilities. Some of the older railways, being used as a place to train engineers, contributed a lot. For example, in the late Qing period some engineers involved with the Beijing-Mukden Railway became engineering managers on other railways after the Republic was founded.[27]

At this time, engineering students sent abroad to Europe, the United States, and Japan were returning in increasing numbers. Those engineers trained in China for the most part graduated from Shanghai Specialized Industry School (later changed to Transportation University, Shanghai Campus), Tangshan Specialized Industry School (later, the Transportation University, Tangshan Campus), Beijing University, Bei Yang University, Qingdao High-Rank Specialized School, Tung Ji Medical-Industrial Specialized School (later, Tung Ji University), Beijing Transportation Institute (later, Transportation University, Beijing Campus), or several others.[28]

During the time of the Ministry of Posts and Communications in the late Qing Dynasty, most railways drew on these schools to hire workers. After the establishment of the Republic, most employers also required experience. Each line's mechanical, engineering, management, accounting, and other department heads such as department chiefs, section chiefs, and mechanic shop managers were for the most part specialists.[29]

When the Beijing-Kalgan Railway was completed in 1909, the ability of the Chinese engineers was generally recognized. After this, all railways built with Chinese capital, such as the Yichang-Guizhoufu, Guangzhou-Shaoguan, Kalgan-Baotou, Zhuzhou-Pingxiang, Mukden-Hailong, Jilin-Hailong, Hulan-Hailong, and other lines were built entirely by Chinese engineers. At the same time, these Chinese engineers were also acquiring a more important place with those lines built with foreign loans. In 1929, the Longhai line was constructed to Lingbao. After this point all the railways, regardless of whether they were built with domestic or foreign loans, were constructed by Chinese engineers at every level.[30]

During the Nanjing decade, the numbers of domestically trained specialists and foreign-study returnees increased until they were sufficient to meet the demand. The most important contribution was made by the Transportation University of the Communications Ministry. According to estimates from 1928, more than 700 railway personnel had graduated from the school's three campuses. Although this only amounted to 3 or 4 percent of railway personnel,[31] most were in leading responsible positions. In these early times domestically trained engineers were also able to take charge of their departments. After the establishment of the Ministry of

Railroads they were anxious to build new routes and repair old ones. Most of those employed in construction, management, and other important positions were students who had graduated from Transportation University's T'angshan and Shanghai campuses.[32]

Students from other universities employed on the railroad were also increasing daily.[33] According to the scattered railway management information of the early 1930s, excepting most of the general affairs managers who as before came from a military or a non-railway background, almost all the other managers were graduated from related departments of universities or colleges. Some of them even studied abroad and were had acquired specialized training.[34]

Owing to the progress in quality and quantity of railway personnel, all railways connected with loans at this time (for example the Longhai railway extension line, the Zhuzhou-Shaoguan section of the Guangzhou-Hankou railway, and the Hangzhou-Caoer section of Shanghai-Hangzhou-Ningbo railway) were constructed under the complete responsibility of Chinese engineers. This was an outstanding achievement. It was not inferior to the work of foreign engineers, and in fact was done in an economical, efficient, and speedy fashion.[35] The entire lines' traffic management was also nearly completely under Chinese control.[36]

Comparatively speaking, foreigners employed by the national railways were gradually decreasing in number. According to statistics, in 1926 the national railway system employed 378 foreigners. By 1935, that number had decreased to 59, most of whom were employed in accordance with loan agreements.[37] This meant that the comparative responsibilities shouldered by Chinese engineers increased dramatically over time.

Manchurian Railway Construction

When it comes to China's modern railway development, no region is more remarkable than Manchuria. Manchuria's railway construction began in 1891, when Li Hongzhang created the Imperial Railways of North China. The principal railways in Manchuria were completed by the end of the nineteenth century, and in the early twentieth century it was divided into the Chinese Eastern Railway (CER) and the South Manchuria Railway (SMR).

From 1891 through 1911, construction of the Manchurian railways totaled 3,387.1 km, which represented approximately 37 percent if the entire country's railway network of 9,137.2 km.[38] But the Manchurian railway gauges were not unified, and ownership of the railways was divided into Chinese government, private, and foreign-operated railways. In addition to China, the most important of the foreign railways were those managed by Russia, Japan, and England, and included the CER, the SMR, and the Beijing-Mukden transportation systems.

From the formation of the Republic of China in 1912, until the 18 September 1931 Manchurian Incident, there were enormous changes in ownership from the end of the Qing Dynasty to the creation of Manchukuo. In particular, England's power gradually diminished, while the power of the Soviet government was replaced by Japan, as the power of the Chang-Bin (Changchun and Ha-er-bin) and CER lines gradually declined following the October 1917 Revolution. The Japanese government used the First World War, which distracted the European countries from the situation in China, to increase the scope of its power in Manchuria. Japan was able to encroach on China's sovereignty in Manchuria by providing loans to China to build railways, but demanding as a guarantee certain rights over the railways and the surrounding area; once China was unable to repay the railway loans on time, the Japanese used the terms of these treaties to demand joint control over railway operations. As time passed, the important Manchurian railways Ji-Chang (Jilin to Changchun), Ji-Dun (Jilin to Dunhua), Yao-Ang (Yaonan to Angangxi), X-Yao (Xiping to Yaonan), etc, all fell under Japanese control, and became little better than extender or "feeder" lines to the SMR.[39]

The Manchurian government, under pressure from both foreign and domestic parties, decided that they would construct railways on their own, in the process retaining the profits that had formerly gone to the CER and SMR. In May 1922, after the three northeast provinces had merged and declared independence from Beijing, using the Bei-Ning railway as the center from which to build the Three Provinces East-West Train Line. In May 1924, they formed the "Three Eastern Provinces Transportation Commission" (東三省交通委員會), which in 1929 was renamed the "Manchurian Transportation Commission" (東北交通委員會), to promote railway construction.

During the 1920s, the "Three Eastern Provinces Transportation Commission" built a number of railways, including the Shen-Hai (Shenyang to Hailong), the Ji-Hai (Jilin to Hailong), the Yao-Ang (Yaonan to Angangxi), the Chi-Ke (Chichihaer to Keshan), the Hu-Hai (Hulan to Hailun), and the Bei-Ning railway's branch line (Tahushan to Tungliao), etc. All together, this equaled 1,521.7 km of track, or 25 percent of all of Manchuria's railway business and over 10 percent of the entire country's railway network.[40]

These figures show the enormous success achieved in Chinese railway construction. Especially noteworthy is that in Manchuria all of the construction administrators, the route planners, the construction designers, etc, were all Chinese, which saved a tremendous amount of money. For example, the Shen-Hai railway saved over one-third of its construction costs by not hiring foreign engineers.[41]

When completed, this railway construction program created a transportation network that included:[42]

(1)   the "Dong-Da line" or "Eastern Main Line": Huludao-
        Fengtian-Hailong-Jilin-Hailin-Yilan-Tongjiang-Fuyuan

(2)   the "Xi-Da line" or "Western Main Line": Huludao-
        Dahushan-Tungliao-Yaonan-Chichihaer-Ningnian-
        Nenjiang

(3)   the "Nan-Da line" or "Southern Main Line": Jiaoyang-
        Chifeng-Duolun

All of these three lines terminated in the port of Huludao, which was ideal for the import/export trade, and so could compete successfully with the Japanese-controlled port of Dalian.

In 1929, the Manchurian Transportation Commission, using the Bei-Ning railway as the base, continued its construction program by building a number of new passenger and freight lines, including the "Xi-Ssu-Lu" (西四路) or "Four Western Lines." These were the Bei-Ning railway, the Xi-Yao railway, the Yao-Ang railway, and the Chi-Ke railway. It also began the "Dong-Ssu-Lu" (東四路) or "Four Eastern Lines." These included the Bei-Ning railway, the Shen-Hao railway, the Chi-Hai railway, and the Chi-Dun railway. Their goal was to surround the Japanese-run SMR, and in support of this effort the Manchurian government was assisted by the Chinese central government in Nanjing and by the Soviet-managed CER. Up until the September 1931 "Manchurian Incident," all of the Manchurian railways except the SMR and the An-Feng railways, were monitored, run, and managed directly by the Manchurian government.[43]

Through 1930, when they began to build the Hu-Lu railway line, the Manchurian Transportation Commission's plan of "surround the SMR, cut the CER" (包圍南滿、縱斷中東) was not yet complete. However, the policies of the Manchurian Transportation Commission to build the "Four Western Lines" and the "Four Eastern Lines" were already becoming an enormous threaten to the SMR and the CER. Several years later, a Japanese observer, reflecting on this situation, even observed:[44]

> Had all these schemes [supported by Zhang Xueliang] been
> successfully consummated, they would not only have destroyed
> the value of the S. M. R. and Dairen harbor but would have wiped
> out Japan's special interests in Manchuria from the very
> foundation . . . Japan was finally forced to the position where she

had to make the momentous decision either to stand by her rights
and remain in Manchuria or to renounce them and get out.

Under pressure to retain its railway franchise in Manchuria, Japan kept
demanding that China agree to negotiate a solution. The Russians also wanted to
protect their privileges along the CER, thus precipitating the "Chinese Eastern
Railway incident," mentioned in the previous chapters.[45] The failure of the Chinese-
Japanese and the Chinese-Russian railway negotiations in the end led to outbreak of
the 1931 "Manchurian incident."

Chinese Railway Pay Structure

Relative to the other administrative apparatuses, workers' pay on modern China's
railways was comparatively high. In 1906, after the completion of the Ministry of
Posts and Communications, the minister found enlisting the services of specialized
personnel difficult, so the better salary system of the Ministry of Foreign Affairs,
the Ministry of Agriculture, Industry and Commerce, and the Ministry of Finance
was adopted.[46] Under this salary system, a chief manager earned 12,000 taels
yearly,[47] higher than the income of a ministry president.[48] In classes of employees
under the level of chief manager, the salary was also good. Engineers, mechanics,
and similar technical personnel had higher salaries than regular staff members. After
1911, national railways lowered a bit in salary standards. However, workers' pay
before the Sino-Japanese War was said to have been high, owing to the stability of
business.[49]

Job security in modern China's railway enterprise could not be guaranteed by the
laws and regulations, and from the late Qing to the early 1930s cases of arbitrary
lay-offs existed constantly and were not uncommon. But the influence of this matter
on the professional employees was relatively small. The railway's emphasis on
technical skills and experience as well as the salary and benefits were looked upon
favorably. Therefore, the turnover rate was relatively low and many became lifetime
employees.[50]

The railroad enterprise, being highly technical, and general administration were
dissimilar. Therefore, regardless of the level of the post to which someone was
appointed, their knowledge and experience were first carefully evaluated. In judging
worth and capability solely on merits and qualifications, promotion could be granted
fairly. Railroad employee promotions may be divided into two categories:
leadership positions and general workers. The degree of autonomy in the leaders'
promotional system was, in fact, modest compared to those of the postal and
telegraph administrations. In the latter two the most important prerequisite was

qualifications. Postal workers first worked in mandatory subordinate positions before being promoted to postal chief positions. The telegraph administration had a similar system, so no matter what one's personal connections might be, these prerequisites could not be circumvented. However, regardless of one's individual service record any person could quickly become railway director or superintendent.[51]

Although the promotional system for personnel below office director was modest compared to the postal and electrical services, there was more soundness than in regular government organs, especially for those engineers and technicians. For example, in the late Qing when Jeme T'ien-yow was building the Beijing-Kalgan Railway, a technical training program (divided into six grades) was founded. Whenever untrained youth entered the railroad system they became intern students, receiving both work experience and basic engineering training.

Sixth level graduates were assigned associate or assistant engineer's jobs according to their behavior and record of service, and were given an excellent salary. Therefore when there were no engineering students graduating from domestic universities it was these students who built the railways.[52] This type of promotional system was quite popular among railways in the late Qing and in the early years of the Republic. From this time on, promotion standards were gradually raised owing to the increase of trained personnel.

For example, during the building of the Zhuzhou-Shaoguan section of the Guangzhou-Hankou Railway before the Sino-Japanese War, college graduates arriving on the railway were assigned first to be construction supervisors. After a year, high achievers were promoted to engineer's assistants. Students with foreign study or training experience also needed to begin as engineer's assistants, and after one year were given the opportunity to become assistant engineers.[53]

Chinese Railway Management

During the early part of the building of China's railways most engineering and management techniques came from other countries. This saved a great deal of time and expense for research and development, but a great price was also paid. Most of the money necessary for building the railways came from foreign loans. But the different forms of economic exploitation (like heavy interest payments, large discounts, penalties for early and late payback) were less harmful than was generally believed.[54]

The various types of loan limitations actually allowed China to reap benefits in the face of her unstable political condition. For example, outside inspection of the banks by the loaning countries made use of the money for unproductive business and internal warfare impossible. But on the other hand, the railroad's managerial rights (in administration, personnel, purchases, etc) were hurt by foreign intervention; economic interests (such as mining, forestry, agricultural reclamation, and postal and telegraph management) were also damaged. More importantly, China was thus unable to build its own railroad network according to its own development plan (regardless of its being right or wrong) specifically designed to meet its own needs.

The early construction of China's railways was begun for defense purposes. Afterwards, most of the railway construction was more haphazard. It was impossible to carry out overall planned construction. This led to uneven distribution as well as a lack of coordination in its railroad network. These characteristics of the location of modern China's railways were caused by the interplay of a number of factors; the most important being the scramble for concessions by the foreign powers at the end of the nineteenth century.

Regarding the railways' organizational structure, each railway's managerial mechanism had its own system. Each railway had a management office governing the railway itself. Although the ministry in charge of railway affairs had the right to examine their finances, eventually this lack of a centralized system of revenue and expenditure led to general deficiencies in the whole system's financial management. As there was no way to unify and control a system for transferring engines and cars, mechanic shops and supply depots could not be communally used, thereby creating a great deal of waste.

As mentioned above, one result of British and French influence was that each railway's office was organized on the departmental system. Its advantages lay in the clear distinction between the section chief's responsibilities for dispatch, construction, and mechanics. Its disadvantages lay in that each section did things its own way. This made cooperation difficult as one system was suitable only for those short lines with light traffic flow, and was not suitable to China's overall circumstances.

When the railway first began hiring workers it did not use examinations as did the Maritime Customs and postal services, and did not require certain education, as did the Telegraph Administration. Requirements for entrance were not rigorous. The salary of railway workers was similar to that of other departments' employees, such as postal, telegraph and customs workers. Together with sound channels for promotion, this salary system led to increased numbers of workers seeking jobs with the railway, many to become lifetime employees.

Conclusions

Looking back with a long-term historical perspective at the development of the railway enterprise in China's process of modernization and technical development, we can draw the following two conclusions. First, the railway enterprise built up a large quantity of industrial and commercial personnel for use in the future. When many of the developing countries began their modernization efforts, education could not be coordinated with demand, or there was a shortage of personnel, or study and usefulness on the job could not exist in concert. In China, the Transportation University's program, which was supported by their railway business, and the field training provided by the railways themselves, facilitated the production of a large group of technical and managerial personnel, and not only did this more than fill the ranks, it also cultivated a large number of talented personnel for the private sector.

Second, the railway enterprise promoted the development of professionalism. The railway enterprise in modern China was seriously handicapped by the unstable political environment. Railways were built according to military rather than commercial needs. Appointments to management positions were subject to considerations other than professional qualifications. The ministry in charge of railway affairs was heavily involved in warlord politics. However, from the macro-historical perspective, the railway enterprise did promote the development of professionalism. Traditional China's political institutions had elaborately specialized and differentiated sub-divisions, and were run by professional bureaucrats according to highly rational, fully documented regulations and precedents.[55] Although they had not even adopted a modern specialized post assignment, promotion, and training systems, they attached importance to length of service and specialized internship prior to appointment and some posts expected applicants with specialized experience. All these phenomena showed the traditional Chinese government's tendency towards specialization.[56]

Owing to the demands of rapidly changing circumstances, the late Qing government began to attach importance to specialized employees. The Ministries of Foreign Affairs, Posts and Communications, and Finance gave their administrators particularly high salaries. After the founding of the Republic the government established a special promotion and salary system for professional government employees. The systematic promotions of Western-trained professionals in a bureaucratic system was unprecedented in Chinese history. From the end of the Qing dynasty when Jeme T'ien-yow completed the Beijing-Kalgan Railway the position of the engineer in Chinese society immediately began to rise, and this shift in society's sense of the value of professionals has been of great influence. In particular, it shows that a strong tendency towards professionalization already existed among Chinese intellectuals in the late nineteenth and early twentieth centuries. Such tendencies were particularly notable on the Tianjin-Pukou line in Shandong province.

Notes

1. This chapter is an expanded and revised version of "Technology Transfer in Modern China: The Case of Railway Enterprise, 1876–1937," published in *Modern Asian Studies* 26 (May 1993), 281–96.

2. Ma Jianzhong, *Shike zhai jiyan jixing* (Ma Jianzhong's Essays), 1896, juan 1, 5b.

3. Alexander Gerschenkron, *Economic Backwardness in Historical Perspectives: A Book* of *Essays* (Cambridge, MA: Harvard University Press, 1962), 105.

4. On the system of bookkeeping and accounting traditionally used by the Chinese government, see Friedrich W.K. Otte, "The Evolution of Bookkeeping and Accounting in China," *Annalen der Betriebswirtschaft 2:*1 (1928), 160–80.

5. Yu Chengzhi (ed.), *Xiaan huigao* (Ye Gongchuo's Essays) (n.p., 1930), 277–8; Julean Arnold, *China: A Commercial and Industrial Handbook* (Washington, DC: Government Printing Office, 1926), 327.

6. Jiaotong tiedao bu, Jiaotong shi bianzhuan weiyuanhui (ed.), *Jiaotong shi luzheng bian* (A History of Communication, Road Administration) (Nanjing: n.p., 1935), ch. 1, 777–885.

7. H.H. Ling, "A Decade of Chinese Railroad Construction (1926–1936)," in Paul K.T. Shih (ed.), *The Strenuous Decade: China's Nation-Building Efforts, 1927–1937* (Jamaica, NY: St. John's University Press, 1970), 282.

8. Mi Rucheng, *Diguo zhuyi yu Zhongguo tielu (1847–1949)* (Imperialism and the Chinese Railroads) (Shanghai: Shanghai Renmin Chubanshe, 1980), 365.

9. Great Britain, Naval Intelligence Division, *China Proper,* Vol. III, *Economic Geography, Ports and Communications* (London, 1945), 465–6.

10. Ling, "A Decade of Chinese Railroad Construction," 283.

11. Arthur Rosenbaum, "Railway Enterprise and Economic Development: The Case of the Imperial Railways of North China, 1900–1911," *Modern China* 2:2 (April 1976), 242.

12. C.C. Wong, "Some Dangers of Railway Development in China and How to Prepare Against Them," in C.F. Remer (ed.), *Reading in Economics for China* (Shanghai: Commercial Press, Limited, 1922), 624.

13. For examples see Hong Ruitao, "Tie-dao zheng-li yu tie-dao tong-ji" (Railroad Reorganization and Railroad Control), *Jiao-tong za-zhi* 1:6 (April 1933), 51–2.

14. Jin Shixuan, *Tielu yunshu xue* (Railroad Transportation) (Chengdu, 1945), 407–8.

15. Ray Morris, *Railroad Administration* (London: D. Appleton and Company, 1930), ch. 6.

16. Alfred D. Chandler, Jr, "The United States: Seedbed of Managerial Capitalism," in Alfred D. Chandler, Jr. and Herman Daems (eds), *Managerial Hierarchies: Comparative Perspectives on the Rise of the Modern Industrial Enterprise* (Cambridge, MA: Harvard University Press, 1980), 16.

17. Some examples can be found in Hong, "Tiedao zhengli yu tiedao tongji," 51.

18. Yu (ed.), *Xiaan huigao,* 199.

19. H.H. Ling and Gao Zonglu (eds), *Zhan Tianyou yu zhongguo tielu* (Chan T'ien-yow and the Chinese Railroad) (Taibei: Zhongyang yanjiuyuan jindaishi yanjiusuo, 1977), 89–92, 259–60.

20. Thomas E. La Fargue, *China's First Hundred* (Pullman, WA: State College of Washington, 1942), 60.

21. Sheng Xuanhuai, *Sheng shangshu yuzhai conggao* (Collected Papers of Ministry President Sheng Xuanhuai), juan 2, 6–8.

22. H.H. Ling, *Zhongguo tielu zhi* (A History of Chinese Railroads) (Taibei, 1954), 137–8.

23. *Minli Bao* (The People's Automony) (Shanghai), 4 February 1911.

24. Lee En-han, *China's Quest for Railway Autonomy, 1904–1911* (Singapore: Singapore University Press, 1977), 135.

25. H.H. Ling (ed.), *Zhan Tianyou xiansheng nianpu* (A Chronological Biography of Chan T'ien-yow) (Taibei, 1961), 52.

26. Wang Shuhuai, "Qingmo tielu rencai wenti" (The supply of Railroad Talents in Late Qing China) in *Guoli taiwan shifan daxue lishi xuebao* (Bulletin of Historical Research), 9 (May 1981), 22.

27. *Jiaotong shi luzheng pian,* ch. 2, 177–8.

28. Sa Fujun, "Sanshi nian lai Zhongguo zhi tielu gongcheng" (Railroad Engineering in the Late Thirty Years) in Zhongguo gongcheng shi xuehui (ed.), *Sanshi nian lai zhi Zhongguo gongcheng* (Chinese Engineering in the Last Thirty Years) (Nanjing, 1946), 2.

29. Yu (ed.), *Xiaan huigao,* 200.

30. Sa, "San shi nian lai Zhongguo zhi tielu gongcheng," 1–2.

31. Tiedao bu, comp. *Tiedao nianjian* (The Railway Yearbook), juan I (Nanjing, 1934), 544–5.

32. H.H. Ling, "Tangxiao yu xin Zhongguo jianshe" (Tangshan School and New China's Construction) in *Guoli Jiaotong daxue bashi nian* (Eighty Years of Communication University) (Taibei, 1976), 111.

33. Sa, "San shi nian lai Zhongguo zhi tielu gongcheng," 2.

34. Chang Jui-te, *Zhongguo jindai tielu shiye guanli di yanjiu: zhengzhi cengmian di fenxi, 1876–1937* (Railroads in Modern China: Political Aspects of Railroad Administration, 1876–1937) (Taibei, 1991), Ch. V.

35. Sa, "Sanshi nian lai Zhongguo zhi tielu gongcheng," 2.

36. Ling, *Zhongguo tielu zhi,* 138.

37. Japan. Tedsudosho. Shanhai benjisho (ed.), *Tetsudobu seiritsugo no Shina tetsudo* (China's Railroads Following the Establishment of the Ministry of Railroads) (Shanghai, 1935), 9.

38. Li Shuyun, "Jiuyiba shibian qian di dongbei tielu jianshe" (Railroad Construction in Manchuria Before the Mukden Incident), *Liaoning daxue xuebao*, 3 (1999), 43.

39. Chen Hui, *Zhongguo tielu wenti* (China's Railroad Problems) (Shanghai, 1936), 279.

40. Li Shuyun, "Tielu jiaotong yu dongbei jinxiandai jingji fazhan" (Railroad Transportation and Economic Development in Modern Manchuria), *Liaoning shifan daxue xuebao*, 4 (1999), 85.

41. Wang Guizhong, *Zhang Xueliang yu dongbei tielu jianshe* (Zhang Xueliang and Railroad Construction in Manchuria) (Hong Kong, 1996), 93.

42. Zhang Zhenli, "Dongbei jiaotong weiyuanhui yu tielu jianshe (1924–1931)" (Manchurian Transportation Commission and Railroad Construction, 1924–1931), unpublished M.A. thesis, Graduate Institute of History, National Taiwan Normal University, 1986, 288.

43. Li Shuyun, "Tielu jiaotong yu dongbei jinxiandai jingji fazhan," 85.

44. Kadono Choryuro, *Development of Railways in Manchuria* (Tokyo: Japanese Council, Institute of Pacific Relations, 1936), 10.

45. Zhang Zhenli, "Dongbei jiaotong weiyuanhui yu tielu jianshe," 258–275; Yoshihisa Tak Matsusaka, *The Making of Japanese Manchuria, 1904–1932* (Cambridge, MA: Harvard University Press, 2001), 363–77.

46. Jiaotong tiedao bu jiaotong shi bianzhuan weiyuanhui (ed.), *Jiaotong shi zongwu pian* (A History of Communication, General Affairs Section) (Nanjing, 1935), ch. 1, 631–4.

47. *Zhengzhi guanbao* (Political Gazetteer), 458 (18 January 1908), 8.

48. Chung-li Chang, *The Income of the Chinese Gentry* (Seattle: University of Washington Press, 1962), 35, 41.

49. Ling, *Zhongguo tielu zhi,* 140; Stephen Lloyd Morgan, "Chinese Railway Lives, 1912–1937," unpublished Ph.D. dissertation, Australian National University, 1995, chapter V.

50. Yu (ed.), *Xiaan huigao,* 30.

51. Yuan Dexuan, "Jiaotong yao zheng gan ben jie jue chu yi" (A Draft Solution to the Problems of Communication Affairs), in *Jiaotong gong bao* (Communication Gazetteer), 925 (5 June 1925), Appendix, 16.

52. Ling, *Zhan Tianyou xiansheng nianpu,* 52.

53. H.H. Ling, *Longhai Yuehan Xianggui zhu lu huiyi* (Reminiscences on the Building of the Longhai, Yuehan and Xianggui Railroads) (Taibei, 1953), 27.

54. Huenemann, *The Dragon and the Iron Horse*, 119.

55. Gilbert Rozman (ed.), *The Modernization* of *China* (New York: Free Press, 1981), 205.

56. Thomas *A.* Metzger, *The Internal Organization of Ch'ing Bureaucracy: Legal, Normative, and Communication Aspects* (Cambridge, MA: Harvard University Press, 1973), 151–2; Benjamin Elman pointed out that strong tendencies towards professionalization among Chinese intellectuals existed already in the late

eighteenth and early nineteenth centuries. See Elman, *From Philosophy to Philology: Intellectual and Social Aspects of Change in Late Imperial China* (Cambridge, MA: Harvard University Press, 1984), 96–100.

6

Chinese Railroads, Local Society, and Foreign Presence: The Tianjin-Pukou Line in pre-1949, Shandong

Elisabeth Köll

The railroad system in Manchuria was not isolated, but interacted with other foreign-built railway systems in North China.[1] This chapter tries to address some of these issues by discussing the Tianjin-Pukou (hereafter JinPu) railroad in Shandong province from the early twentieth century to 1949. Initially financed and constructed by German and British colonial interests, the JinPu line became a Chinese national railway in the Republican period and a major factor of infrastructure and economic development in the province. The JinPu railroad provided the first trunk line in northern China that through railway connection with the Tianjin-Beijing and Nanjing-Shanghai lines and through maritime lines of communication with Manchuria, linked the commercial and political centers of Republican China. After 1937, Japan took control over the railways in Shandong and used them and the adjoining Manchurian railways to dominate North China, just as the Chinese Communists would subsequently do in their military campaigns in the late 1940s.

Historical Context: Railroad Development in Shandong

After the creation of a German sphere of interest in Shandong province in the late nineteenth century, with an administrative center in the Treaty Port of Qingdao, Germany and Great Britain obtained a joint concession in 1898 for constructing a railway line between the city of Tianjin and Pukou. The plan was to establish a transportation and communication artery linking the north of China from Tianjin, easily accessible from Beijing, to Nanjing in the south via Pukou, the crossover at the Yangzi river. The British would build and operate the southern part of the line within Jiangsu province, while the Germans were to be in charge of the northern part of the line within the borders of the Shandong and Zhili provinces. In 1899 the British-German syndicate entered an agreement with the Chinese government to build the railroad.[2]

However, it took several years to negotiate methods of financial control, construction, equipment selection, and operation of the line. In addition, construction was delayed by the events of the Boxer rebellion, which brought widespread turmoil and anxiety to northern Shandong and Zhili in 1900 and seriously challenged Chinese local government control over the area. After 1905, however, the construction of the line was carried out relatively swiftly, and both sections reached completion in 1912.[3] The financial terms for the JinPu railroad were finally worked out in 1908: the first loan arrangement of the so-called "Imperial Chinese Government 5 percent Tientsin-Pukow Railway Loan" consisted of a bond issue of £5 million on the London market, issued in two installments with 65 percent German capital and 35 percent British capital.[4] In 1910 a supplementary loan of £3 million at 5 percent interest was issued.[5]

In 1912, the JinPu line began full service and helped to transform Jinan, the provincial capital of Shandong province, into a commercial and industrial center; before 1904, when Jinan became a Treaty Port, the city had been mainly an administrative seat without significant commercial importance for eastern Shandong.[6] The German or northern section of the line was linked with the so-called southern, British section of the line using the same gauge. With its route parallel to the Grand Canal, the JinPu line soon became a serious competitor for goods transportation into Hebei, Shandong, and Anhui provinces and strengthened the commercial ties between Shanghai and eastern Shandong.

Linking Beijing, the political center, with Shanghai, the commercial center of Republican China, the JinPu line also attracted a major share of the passenger traffic headed for the lower Yangzi region, especially once Nanjing became the national capital following the success of the Nationalist "Northern Expedition" in 1927. The JinPu line together with the Beijing-Hankou railroad (completed in 1905) and later on the Guangzhou-Hankou railroad (completed in its entire length only in 1936) presented the backbone of China's strategic railroad development to expand commerce and industry, improve passenger transport, and strengthen the nation's communication networks in the early twentieth century.

With its location in Shandong, the JinPu line became exposed to changing political regimes in the province that affected its business operations and management, even if it did not involve an outright change in ownership. The Japanese were able to establish an imperialist presence in Shandong due to the events of World War I, replacing the previous German colonial power on the Shandong peninsula. In 1914, the Japanese took over the commercial hub and port of Qingdao, which was linked by ship to Port Arthur and Dairen to the north, and the railroad that connected the city to the provincial capital of Jinan. However, in sharp contrast to the South Manchurian Railway (SMR), the Qingdao-Jinan railroad was not invested with a similar level and scope of Japanese military and political power at this time and thus did not become the primary focus of Japanese civilian presence in Shandong. To use David Buck's phrase, the Japanese did not succeed in achieving "Manchurianization" of the Shandong area under their control.[7]

When the Japanese military authorities took control over the Qingdao-Jinan railroad, they set up garrisons close to major train stations, including a large garrison in Jinan city.[8] When combined with troops in Manchuria, the Japanese troops in Shandong could exert direct military pressure on Beijing from two directions. Accordingly, Shandong was used "to bring about Japanese domination of China."[9] To that effect, the Japanese government issued the infamous Twenty-One Demands in 1915 that, among other privileges, gave Japan the same special rights as Germany before 1914 and prevented the opening of new foreign leaseholds or land grants in Shandong.

During the months of intense Sino-Japanese negotiations, the Qingdao-Jinan railroad served as troop transporter for the Japanese military, which sent units to Jinan to prepare for a takeover should the Chinese refuse the Japanese position.[10] After the Chinese government signed the formal agreement in late May of 1915, the Japanese withdrew most of their troops from Jinan but left a permanent garrison and railroad police in the settlement district of the Jinan station area. Needless to say, lack of revenue due to these military maneuvers and the decline in trade of overseas exports due to World War I decreased the business profit of the Qingdao-Jinan railroad.

From 1916 onwards the Qingdao-Jinan railroad was transferred under the control of the Japanese National Railway Administration, which began to hire Japanese skilled labor and managers: in 1921 there were 1,658 Japanese compared to 4,233 Chinese employees.[11] By updating the facilities and adding new equipment the Japanese management succeeded in increasing the profits of the Qingdao-Jinan railroad substantially. However, this development did not automatically translate into more business for the JinPu railroad because—in contrast to the Japanese-controlled line—transit tax (*likin*) was levied on goods transported on the JinPu line, which Japanese merchants tried to avoid.[12]

With the Versailles peace treaty in 1919, negotiations about the return of the Shandong leasehold and the Qingdao-Jinan railroad were reopened again, but they quickly deadlocked. Only Sino-Japanese talks at the disarmament conference in Washington in 1921 brought a breakthrough. The 1922 Washington agreement settled the return of the Jiaozhou leasehold to China and the purchase of the Qingdao-Jinan railroad by the Chinese government from Japan for 40 million yen, backed by Chinese Treasury Notes.[13]

By 1923, Japan began to withdraw its troops from Shandong and from the military stations along the Qingdao-Jinan line. Once the railroad was again under

Chinese management, the Qingdao-Jinan and JinPu railroads started to discuss the linkage of their two track systems in Jinan so that goods and passenger would no longer have to interrupt their journey and move between stations in the city. It seems plausible that the Japanese management had never actively sought the unification of the two lines because it did not expect increased revenue due to the transit tax situation. From the Chinese perspective, a link between the two lines might have appeared undesirable during the years of Japanese control over Shandong, because it would have given Japan easier access to military transport into northern China and the Yangzi area. However, by 1926 both lines were finally linked and the event celebrated by the citizens of Jinan with an elaborate ceremony and festivities.[14]

Considering the complex political and socio-economic environment of Shandong province and Republican China in the early twentieth century, the JinPu railroad provides us with an excellent lens to examine the issue of how Chinese railroads came into existence in a semi-colonial historical context, how this new infrastructure and technology was received by the local population, and to what extent it improved social mobility and standards of living along the railroad line. Existing studies on Chinese railroads by Western as well as Chinese scholars have focused mainly on their role in political history, in particular on the role of foreign powers and the negotiation of their colonial interests in the late nineteenth and early twentieth centuries.[15] The impact of railroads on Chinese economic development and market integration presents another focus of historical railroad studies, mostly from a macro-economic point of view.[16] Surprisingly little has been written about the social, institutional, and cultural impact of the railroad lines on Chinese local society.

As this chapter will argue, railroad companies in China emerged as hybrid business institutions combining aspects of Western corporations with characteristics of the traditional Chinese firm. In the beginning, they were notable for their lack of standardization and high level of administrative and operational costs. However, as the case of the JinPu railroad shows, the rise of the Nationalist government under Jiang Jieshi (Chiang Kai-shek) led to attempts for improved administrative integration and stronger political control over the railroad network and its employees under the newly formed Ministry of Railroads. This centralization effort served mainly the Nationalists' political agenda. It was constantly contested by the various railway companies, which wanted to retain their relative financial and managerial autonomy.

As substantial business institutions with economic leverage and responsibility for large numbers of employees and workers, railroad companies—like many other enterprises in Republican China—had to cope with the impact of political fragmentation in the 1910s, rising labor activism, the heavy-handed interference of the Nationalist government in the late 1920s, and resistance activities among the workforce in response to the Japanese occupation and war in the late 1930s and 1940s. The complex company history of the JinPu railroad involved Chinese, German, British, and Japanese management, which all impacted in different ways the company's organizational structure, workforce, and relationship with local society and state. However, as will be argued here, due to its ability to adapt to a constantly changing political environment and with a professional management attuned more to local than national interests, the JinPu railroad gained a major institutional presence in Jinan city and Shandong province at a time when "modern" industrial enterprises and railway infrastructure had just started to develop in China.

Building the JinPu Railroad: Construction, Engineers, and Equipment

The construction and operation of the JinPu line brought new technology, management methods, and new employment opportunities for the local population. Knowledge about railroads in terms of technology, land surveys, construction methods etc., was introduced to China through translation of Western texts during the late nineteenth century before railroad engineering developed as a new profession with its own schools and training institutes in the Republican period. The earliest images and descriptions of locomotives and railroad technology can be found in publications compiled and translated by scholars hired for the translation department of the Jiangnan Arsenal, which developed into a major force in the transmission of knowledge about natural sciences and engineering in China. In the spirit of China's Self-Strengthening Movement in the 1870s, the Chinese government sponsored the building of the Jiangnan arsenal and similar institutions, but considered the building of machines as the base for creating industry in China.[17]

The founding period of the JinPu railroad company under German and British management reflects colonial hierarchies as well as an almost complete absence of technical knowledge and experience with railroad engineering among the Chinese at the turn of the twentieth century. Initially, Chinese played a negligible role as engineers and technical advisors in the construction process of the JinPu railroad and other lines as well. Railroad engineering in terms of academic training and as a profession did not emerge until the late 1910s when railroad engineering institutes were established and began to produce engineers with expertise in technology, geological sciences, and bridge and tunnel construction. The employment of foreign engineers was the general solution to this initial issue but caused considerable problems because of the language barrier between foreign engineers and Chinese foremen. Therefore railway companies competed for the employment of the few foreign-trained Chinese engineers who returned to China after completing their studies in the United States or Europe to work for foreign railroad companies.[18] For example, in 1909, after competing with the Shanghai-Nanjing line for the precious human resource, the JinPu line managed to hire Albert C. Lee, an American-trained engineer, who was the first Chinese to join the company at the management level.[19]

Before any railway construction could begin, a detailed report from German surveyors was required to decide on the course of the JinPu line, to adapt it as efficiently as possible to the landscape, and avoid costly construction of bridges or tunnels. Within Shandong province the JinPu line ran parallel to an old imperial highway, and the most difficult part of the construction was to deal with the crossing of the Huanghe (Yellow river) near Jinan.[20] Until a cast-iron bridge was completed by German engineers in 1912, ferries transported passengers across the river.[21] The first German engineers and surveyors were almost all attached to the military as part of the German colonial authorities stationed in Qingdao. They had to report to the colonial administration in Beijing and the German Ministry for Foreign Affairs back in Berlin.[22]

The British in their section of the JinPu railroad sent out detailed expeditions employing engineers, like those working for the Beijing Syndicate, who previously had spent time working in India on the colonial railway expansion. They carried out their survey in 1899 in Henan and Shanxi provinces under rules issued for the preparation of railway projects by the government of India.[23] Apart from surveying the land, other objectives of the expeditions included exploring the existence of coalfields, iron ore, and petroleum and any possibilities for extracting resources.[24] During their field trip, the surveyors were required to make notes about accommodation work (i.e. means of crossing the line by level crossing and bridges, especially in the case of villages close to the line and owning a large amount of land on the opposite side), building materials, availability of skilled and unskilled labor, the selection of suitable sites for stations and trade and statistics on any form of existing or potential traffic "such as coal or minerals, timber, pilgrims etc."[25] According to the guidelines under the section "relations with the public" issued by the head of the expedition, "every endeavour should be made to avoid interference with religious edifices, burial grounds or other objects which may be considered sacred."[26]

Unfortunately, documents providing first-hand evidence related to land purchases are difficult to locate. In order to avoid dealings with individual farmers as much as possible and use the backing of the Chinese officialdom, the JinPu railroad management entered arrangements with local magistrates in charge of the area surrounding the proposed track. These local magistrates became middlemen negotiating the price (within a limit given by the company) and arranging the official transaction.[27] Needless to say, this method opened the door to corruption and embezzlement. For example, as soon as Daotai Li in Tianjin in his capacity as agent for the JinPu railroad company learned about the proposed location of the railroad station in the city in 1909, he founded the Huaxing real estate company together with another official. The company bought the land near the station for 400,000 taels but registered it with the government valued as 1.3 million taels and then sold it back to the JinPu company, obtaining an exorbitant profit from the deal.[28]

Although corrupt practices, discovered by the railroad's German managers during an internal audit in 1909, led to some minor changes in land purchase policy, the reliance on Chinese government officials continued. In contrast to the assumption that local farmers were against new and foreign technology and tried to resist the "exploitative" nature of land acquisition by colonial railroad companies, archival documents indicate that purchasing land from Chinese farmers along the line was not a major problem for the JinPu railroad.[29] In order to avoid public protest and lengthy negotiations, the railroad company offered a much higher price per *mu* (0.067 hectares) than the local average. Railway companies were also aware of religious or *fengshui* concerns among the local population and dealt with the delicate matter of moving gravesites and buying grave land by offering generous remuneration. For example, in 1899 the American chief engineer in charge of surveying the railroad between Hankou and Guangzhou stated that "a payment of about $5 per grave removes all objections" on the side of the Chinese farmers.[30] The German engineers of the JinPu railroad expressed a similar opinion when stating in correspondence from 1910 that land with ancestral graves and 'holy mountains' which provided the best stones for track bed construction, became 'secular' very quickly once the right price was offered.[31]

The only major land dispute on which evidence is available involves one of the most influential families in Shandong province—and China at that—the Kong family, the direct descendants of Kongzi (Confucius), and their family estate in Qufu. According to the original plans from 1904, the JinPu line was supposed to run through Qufu and at a point close to the western wall of the Kongzi lin (Forest of Confucius). Kong Delin, the head of the Kong lineage at the time, objected to this plan vehemently and petitioned the Guangxu emperor with several proposals, claiming that the railway would violate the *fengshui* of the sacred place, "shake the tomb of the sage," "stop the sage's very pulse," and "that the spirits of the ancestors would not be able to rest in peace."[32]

However, it appears that the Kong family was not willing to sell part of their land surrounding Qufu because it was a gift from the imperial court and served as sole source of income supporting their lineage estate, providing for the ceremonial sacrifices and the livelihood of their servants and dependants.[33] Not surprisingly, after pressure from the Chinese imperial government, which for centuries had extended special patronage to the Kong family, the engineers of the JinPu railroad had to alter their plan for the route. As a result, the railway passes through the area in a curve around Qufu, and visitors to the place then and now have to get off the train at Tai'an station instead.[34]

The construction and operation of the JinPu line also introduced new employment opportunities for the local, agriculture-dependent population in Shandong living in close proximity to the line. The clearing of the terrain, preparation of the railroad bed, and construction of the tracks were completely undertaken by Chinese day laborers recruited from villages close to the section under construction. The day laborers worked in the traditional contract-labor (*baogong*) system under Chinese foremen (*gongtou*) who were in charge of recruiting and paying these construction workers.[35]

The foreign engineers on the JinPu line were formally responsible to two Chinese managing directors who supervised the British and German section, respectively. However, any disputes between the chief engineers and the managing directors about hiring or dismissal of technical staff for the line was decided by the Chinese Director-General. In addition, the Chinese side was in charge of appointing a European chief engineer, who supervised the whole line after its construction independently from the requirements of the syndicate.[36]

As company correspondence from the 1900s shows, much friction existed between the foreign chief engineers and the Chinese managing directors. One of the Westerner engineers' most frequent complaints involved irregularities in accounting, with accusations of graft and embezzlement.[37] To make the issue more complicated, methods of traditional Chinese business accounting and Western railroad accounting were not compatible before the 1920s. Until the mid-teens, the JinPu railroad company had two sets of accounts, one Chinese and one German, and from 1909 on decided to have the Chinese accounts "translated" in order to rein in corruption and financial irregularities. At the time, accounting systems used in China's industrial enterprises did not apply the concept of depreciation (*zhejiu*) to their machinery and buildings in a satisfactory way.[38] Depreciation rates were not related to the growth of the firms' productive assets which had long-term negative consequences for the companies' finances.

Lack of depreciation in the accounting system was, of course, even worse for asset-oriented enterprises like railroad companies. According to John Earl Baker, who became advisor to the Ministry of Communications in the 1910s and in 1923 authored a classic textbook for Chinese railway accountants, "no accountant becomes valuable to a railway or any other business until he knows considerable about the technical work of that business."[39] Without prior technical knowledge about railroad construction and equipment maintenance and without appropriate accounting training, Chinese accountants faced a particularly difficult task in the early years of the railroad business.

The equipment and rolling stock of the JinPu railroad consisted almost exclusively of foreign imports. In the German section, large steel companies and prominent machine manufacturers like MAN (Maschinenfabrik Augsburg-Nürnberg) in Germany supplied the initial equipment which was sent by ship to Qingdao and from there via the Qingdao-Jinan line to the JinPu headquarters.[40] The Chinese managing director in the British section was able to obtain construction material that had been purchased by foreign brokers originally to be used by other railway lines and thus came at a much lower price. The method of buying either second-hand equipment or material originally designated for other companies was not a custom unique to the railway business in China: many industrial enterprises like cotton spinning mills relied in their initial stage on this type of affordable equipment.[41] However, the British did not approve of the Chinese managing director's policy and especially criticized the fact that American manufacturers like Baldwin Locomotives or Westinghouse won contracts, thereby beating British competition as they were able to supply machinery and equipment at lower prices.

In the long run, the JinPu railroad and other railroad companies in China continued to import all rolling stock from Germany, Britain, and the United States until 1949.[42] Import substitution with Chinese engines started only after 1949 when economic and technological self-reliance became a priority of the new socialist state.

Management Organization and Work Hierarchies

The role of the JinPu railroad as one of the major white- and blue-collar employers in Jinan during the Republican period was significant. In 1925, the JinPu company listed about 1,000 workers and employees in service at the Jinan headquarters and station alone.[43] The repair workshops, a large factory compound known as the *Jinan jichang*, complete with storage facilities, employee housing, and administrative buildings, came to occupy a whole district in the new urban settlement outside and to the west of the old city walls. After 1949 this company town was transformed into the Jinan Railway Machine Factory (*Jinan tielu jiqichang*) as a state-owned enterprise.[44] The compound still exists today and as a state-owned work unit houses about 4,000 workers (compared to 6,000 in the 1950s).[45]

The physical presence of the JinPu railroad had a major impact on the urban development of Jinan, the provincial capital.[46] With the JinPu station in close proximity to the Qingdao-Jinan railroad station, the improved transportation of agricultural commodities from southern Shandong and northern China led to increased commercial traffic into eastern Shandong and long-distance shipping from Qingdao. The resulting economic and urban growth of Jinan shifted the city's character from an administrative center to a commercial, industrial, and transportation center in the early twentieth century. The railway station of the JinPu line attracted various commercial establishments, shops, and warehouses into the neighborhood.[47]

The perceived modernity of the railroad as a means of transportation and large-scale business operation also inspired urban planning and architecture and was reflected in a large number of Western-style office buildings and institutions such as the headquarters of the JinPu railroad company (*JinPu tieluju*), the JinPu Railway Hotel (*JinPu tielu binguan*), the JinPu railroad hospital etc.[48] In contrast to the old walled city, Jinan's railroad district developed into a separate city with a modern grid system of streets named according to the numerical system "Jingyi lu," "Jing'er lu" (Street No. 1, No. 2) and so on. This "modern" part of Jinan became the home to new banks, business enterprises, hospitals, schools, and foreign trading companies in the 1910s and 1920s.[49]

As a result of the 1911 revolution and the creation of the Republican nation-state, the JinPu railroad company became a national railroad, still financed by foreign capital raised on the London capital market but now under Chinese management. In terms of managerial organization, the company adopted the "departmental" system, i.e. the establishment of administrative departments in charge of traffic, mechanics, construction, accounting etc., with department heads responsible for each department.[50] This system originated with European and British railroads; Chinese railroad companies seem to have adopted their organizational structure because they had a much more visible presence in China at the time compared to American-run railroads, which used the divisional system. Although the departmental system allowed for greater centralization, it also led to conflict and fragmentation through lack of cooperation between section chiefs.[51]

The JinPu railroad yard at Jinan became the largest repair shop in Shandong province attracting labor and administrators from all over the country. According to oral history interviews conducted with former workers of the JinPu railroad in 2005, many of them were second- and third-generation railroad workers. Their families had moved to Jinan from Tianjin, Tangshan, and other places in Hebei province in the 1920s and 30s, and they still kept the residential permit (*hukou*) registered in their original native place. As the interviewed workers pointed out, career opportunities through company training, good social services from railway hospitals to schools, company housing, and the reputation of railway companies as reliable institutional employers played as much a role in attracting them as skilled workers as did railway companies for their colleagues in Europe or North America.[52]

Many of the first-generation skilled workers had previous work experience with machinery in arsenals, coal mines, or as blacksmiths and came to Shandong to join the JinPu railroad in the 1910s. Similar to industrial labor in the spinning mills of the early Republican period, native place identity determined group organization among the workers in the workshops and hiring processes through foremen working on behalf of the JinPu railway management. Like in the West, engine drivers occupied the top of the work hierarchy in terms of wages and prestige. According to data from 1931, engine drivers on the JinPu line earned almost four times as much as the fireman and almost three times as much as the foreman in charge of the train service.[53]

Under the supervision of the Ministry of Transportation and Communication (*jiaotong bu*), three major railroad engineering schools (the so-called *jiaotong daxue*) were founded in Shanghai, Tangshan, and Beijing which began to produce graduates for potential employment in railroad companies from the late 1910s onward.[54] As employment records of the JinPu line and other railroads show, many of these graduates began their careers in smaller railway companies moving on to larger ones, while others obtained administrative positions with the government.[55] Until 1927, the financial and personnel control of the ministry over the JinPu line was relatively weak because the government only monitored the profit situation in terms of creditors' rights and loan histories. This only changed when the Nationalist government set up a separate Ministry of Railways in 1928, which exercised full administrative powers over all national railways and supervisory powers over the few and small private and province-run railroads.

As part of the increasingly centralized bureaucracy of the nationalist government, railroad companies like the JinPu line became perfect examples of the government's standardization efforts in terms of railroad finances, personnel, and politics. Publications by the Ministry of Railroads set standards for uniforms and the wearing of railway insignia, indicating an attempt to improve institutional discipline and efficiency together with greater public display of government authority in the realm of railway administration.[56]

At the same time a wide range of literature published by the Ministry of Railroads as well as by individual railroad companies targeted railway employees with the intent to improve their professional knowledge and ethical behavior. In the case of the JinPu railroad, these magazines and pamphlets not only circulated professional news and information concerning railway employees' tasks at work and their day-to-day activities in social clubs etc., but also reinforced their moral dedication to the railway company as a modern business institution and corporate employer with a strictly hierarchical organization.[57]

The government-controlled railroad bureaucracy used these publications to advertise its efforts for political and economic centralization and stabilization. Railroad employees and workers were encouraged not only to become a better workforce but also to become better citizens of the Republican state through improved professional training, hygiene, and moral education.[58]

Like many other railroads, the JinPu line had it its own magazine called *JinPu zhi sheng* (JinPu Railway Echo), published by the railroad's special branch of the Nationalist party which circulated the government's political agenda, especially during the New Life Movement of the 1930s.[59] However, as former JinPu railroad workers stated, these publications never reached the workers in the railroad yard and on the shop floor but were reserved for the white collar employees and engineers of the company.[60]

From their post-1949 perspective, the workers identified the management of the JinPu railroad in the pre-1937 period as completely dominated by the Guomindang, which led to serious consequences for their relationship with the company management after 1945. From the beginning of the Japanese invasion in 1937, many of the JinPu managers moved with the Nationalist government into the safety of the interior provinces of unoccupied China. However, once the war ended in 1945, they returned to Jinan and reclaimed their old positions in the JinPu railroad company, which did not endear them to the workers whom they had abandoned to work under Japanese occupation.

Unionism and Labor on the JinPu Railroad

In sharp contrast to other railroads in China, unionism and labor activism did not have a strong presence among the JinPu railroad's workforce.[61] Like in other major cities, the first strikes in Jinan came about in two Japanese-owned factories and one Chinese-owned spinning mill in 1921–22 which were either resolved or put down by the management and strike-breakers fairly quickly. The years 1922–23 saw briefly intense labor-organizing activities among workers of the JinPu line, which were subsequently suppressed by the Shandong provincial administration because it feared the consequences of social and economic interruption, and in particular hostile responses by foreign powers to the situation.[62]

Evidence so far suggests that serious politicization of the JinPu railroad workers only took place after 1945. As a report from 1934 states, union organization among the workforce of the JinPu line was still slow and membership numbers low. As former workers of the JinPu railroad in interviews confirmed, the number of Communist members among them working in the repair shops and maintenance yards between 1937 and 1945 was very small. In the pre-1945 period, the unskilled dockworkers at the Pukou crossing on the northern bank of the Yangzi river represented the largest number of railroad-affiliated members in the union with 1,800 organized members. They exceeded by far the number of unionized railroad employees and skilled workers in the JinPu railroad company.[63]

Articles in professional magazines like the *Tielu zhigong zhoubao* (Railroad Employees' Weekly) from 1933 to 1934 discussing unionization in other railroad lines in China suggest that these lines experienced a low response among their workers too. The extremely complex work hierarchy in railway companies and the high percentage of skilled workers are part of the reason why labor unions did not easily evolve in the pre-war railroad company environment.[64] These findings confirm Elizabeth Perry's interpretation of labor activism and class consciousness in Shanghai's factories during the 1920s and 1930s.[65]

It is necessary to point out that the term worker (*gongren*) in the railroad context referred to highly skilled workers who all had gone through at least a two-year apprenticeship in the machine workshops and repair shops, and some of them were even sent on to railroad technical colleges by the JinPu management to improve their skills.[66] In terms of social organization, these skilled workers bonded with each other on the shop floor according to their native-place origins, and with so many workers originally hailing from Tianjin, Tangshan, and other places in Hebei province, the Hebei *bang* (group) and their northern accent dominated the shop floor.

The absence or small number of skilled workers and employees hailing from Shandong on JinPu shop floors is quite stunning. For example, according to an employee record published in 1937, the materials' workshop on the JinPu compound had 30 workers on the payroll, with nine men from Zhejiang, six from Hebei and four from Guangdong, but not a single one from Shandong.[67] The situation in the machine shop was similar.

Apart from native-place groups, ritual-based brotherhoods played a powerful role in the dynamics among the company's workforce, which former JinPu railroad workers in interviews now classify as *hei shehui* (underworld society) according to the official post-1949 narrative.[68] The leaders of these brotherhoods ruled with absolute power over their sections in the railroad yard and acted as mediators and negotiators in job-related disputes and social situations. Workers had to pay their respect and present them with gifts at occasions like the New Year celebration. Personnel files of the YueHan railroad from the Guangzhou archives show that this phenomenon was not limited to the shop floor of the JinPu railroad. In 1948, newly hired members of the railroad's police force had to sign a formal document stating that the railroad company did not permit them to join a gang (*banghui*).[69]

One reason for this drastic measure might have been rampant smuggling of opium by railroad employees and workers along the YueHan line and across the border into Hong Kong via the Canton-Kowloon line. The YueHan administration obviously feared cooperation between smugglers and policemen who might belong to the same gang and work on the same side, against the interests of the government and the railroad company.[70]

Freight and Passenger Transportation on the JinPu Railroad

Considering the improved commercial and passenger traffic along the Shandong corridor, how did people use railroads in Shandong for travel? Although we have only scattered information about ticket prices and passenger numbers for the few lines operating in the first decade of the twentieth century, data from these railroad companies in the 1910s and 1920s give us an idea of ticket affordability and passenger volume.

The JinPu railroad, which was opened for traffic in 1910 and was fully completed in 1912, transported 1.57 million passengers in 1916 and with a slight increase 1.63 million passengers in 1917.[71] The Qingdao-Jinan railroad, completed in 1904, counted 828,735 passengers in 1908, a number that decreased over the next two years and then rose to 909,065 in 1911.[72] If we compare the Qingdao-Jinan railroad's annual revenue from freight with revenue from passenger transportation, it is clear that revenue from freight transportation was much higher: in 1908 the freight revenue was three times higher than that from passenger transportation, in 1910 almost five times, and in 1911 almost four times.[73] Income data for the JinPu line confirm this trend. In 1916 and 1917 the railroad company's revenue from freight transportation amounted to 2.5 times the revenue derived from passenger transportation.[74]

Freight transportation was economically far more important for the business portfolio of the first Chinese railroad companies than passenger transport. Before the late 1920s, when rail tourism and long-distance travel in comfortable sleeper cars with dining facilities created a larger share of the business revenue, most passengers traveled short distances between railroad stations along the JinPu and Qingdao-Jinan lines, and the transport of fourth class passengers in open gondola cars was a familiar practice.[75]

One reason for the more basic services on railroads before the 1910s can be found in the relatively slow construction and complicated management of railroads with foreign involvement such as the JinPu line, the Canton-Hankou line, or the Shanghai-Hangzhou-Ningbo line. Section of tracks were often opened for traffic years before the completion of the whole line, which allowed short-distance travel for the local population on finished track sections but made long-distance travel or connection with other train lines still difficult.[76]

Passenger tickets were sold for first class (*toudeng*), second class (*erdeng*), and third class (*sandeng*) on regular trains (*tongche*), with additional tickets required for the transportation of bulky luggage and personal goods. Despite the foreign involvement, there were no separate train carriages for foreigners, and ticket prices were the same for foreigners and Chinese. Express trains (*kuaiche*) between Shanghai and Beijing with sleeping cars charged additional fees, while mixed passenger-goods trains (*hunheche*) offered the cheapest and slowest form of transportation.[77]

The JinPu and Qingdao-Jinan railroad lines played an important role in transporting migrant labor from Shandong into Manchuria. Especially the Qingdao-Jinan railroad in the years under Japanese management advertized its special connection with Manchuria and sold so-called "through-passenger tickets" from major stations of the line to eleven major Manchurian destinations such as Dairen, Mukden, or Fushun.[78] Most of the migrant workers entering Manchuria from Qingdao via ship came from the region southeast of the JinPu and Qingdao-Jinan lines, from the coastal area near Haizhou and the mining belt on the Shandong peninsula.[79]

A German manager on the JinPu line commented in 1914 on the enormous passenger traffic of so-called coolie labor between Shandong and Manchuria in both directions, all accommodated in fourth class carriages.[80] In 1919, the JinPu railroad sold 43,000 train tickets alone which were labeled "coolie" class in a Japanese survey of that year, supposedly referring to transportation in open box cars.[81] Although the JinPu management recognized a business opportunity and in correspondence discussed offering more trains for migrant labor transportation, the company did not have enough train engines at the time to exploit this opportunity.[82]

But how cheap or expensive was it for Chinese to take the train? In 1923, a trip from Qingdao to Jinan, a distance of 256 miles, cost 14.3 yuan in first class, 7.02 yuan in second class and 4 yuan in third class.[83] In the same year the 911-mile trip from Beijing to Shanghai, using three different lines (Beijing to Tianjin via the JingFeng line, Tianjin to Pukou via the JinPu line, and Nanjing to Shanghai via the HuNing line) would have cost 52.45 yuan in first class, 33.25 yuan in second, and 16.75 yuan in third class.[84]

In order to relate these ticket prices to income levels at the time, we can refer to the wages and salaries of workers and employees of the JinPu company. According to data in personnel files, the monthly wage of an unskilled worker washing engines (*cache*) in 1922 was 12 yuan per month whereas a fireman (*sihu*) as a skilled worker earned 45 yuan per month in the same year.[85] Engine drivers (*siji*) occupied the top of the work hierarchy and with their high level of professional skill and responsibility earned a monthly wage that also reflected the years of work experience. An engine driver starting out earned 55 yuan a month, which rose to 61.5 yuan after three years of work experience, but with overtime and on-the-road expenses he could make about 100 yuan a month.[86]

Obviously, these numbers allow for preliminary and extremely general assumptions only: a first class ticket from Beijing to Shanghai would still have been a major expense for a Chinese employee with an urban professional background, as the ticket price would have amounted to about one month's salary. Traveling in second class would have amounted to one third of the monthly salary, whereas traveling third class would have been a more affordable option for members of the urban petty bourgeoisie, shopkeepers, teachers, or clerks if they saved up for the trip.

The data indicates that train travel for people from lower income groups was not inexpensive. Even if we can assume that farmers and laborers covered short distances rather than long-distance travel by train, the simple trip of 67 kilometers from Xuzhou to Lincheng in Shandong province would have cost 1.3 yuan in third class in the early 1930s. According to a detailed Japanese survey of the JinPu line in 1919, 96 percent of the 2.5 million passenger tickets sold that year were third class tickets providing 81 percent of that year's revenue from ticket sales.[87] By comparison, the total revenue of the JinPu railroad from freight transport was only 7.5 percent higher than income from passenger tickets that year, probably due to major line interruption in the north by fighting warlord troops.[88]

In short, railroad travel was neither a cheap form of transportation nor did it develop into a means of mass transportation during the Republican period. However, it did have a very important military function. This became particularly clear after 1937, when the Japanese invaded Central China.

The JinPu and Qingdao-Jinan Railroads During War and Occupation

In 1937, the Japanese invasion of China and ensuing occupation of Shandong presented new challenges to the JinPu railroad company and its management. In 1938, the Japanese actively took control of the JinPu and Qingdao-Jinan railroads and established their military authority in the railway stations along the lines; by 1945, the whole province had a total of 116 stations.[89] The JinPu railroad was of extreme strategic importance to the Japanese war effort because it provided the Japanese army with the fastest and most efficient way to transport troops, equipment, and administrative personnel between northern China and the Yangzi area.

The Japanese not only controlled the management of the actual railroad traffic but also the land adjacent to the railway tracks. They tried to enforce law and order in a heavy-handed manner. However, in the flat countryside south of Jinan, anti-

Japanese resistance fighters were successful in sabotaging supply trains for Japanese troops by repeatedly destroying tracks and strategically important bridges. For this purpose, small guides with titles like *"Zenme pohuai tielu*—How to Destroy a Railroad" were in circulation explaining the technical aspects of damaging tracks and engines with minimum effort and equipment.[90]

From post-1949 party-sponsored oral history projects we know that some of the guerilla activists were workers who were affiliated with the Chinese Communist Party (CCP) and had basic knowledge about railroad construction. However, these guerillas had not gained their experience in the JinPu railroad workshops, but in the nearby coalmines at Boshan and other traditional mining areas on the Shandong peninsula.[91] Their railroad guerilla squads (*tiedao youjidui*) were organized in seven different branches with membership ranging from 23 to 300 people, operating under the name of the "JinPu workers' destruction squad," "Lieshan mining guerilla squad," and so forth.[92]

In 1938 and 1939, the guerilla squads' success in destroying tracks, attacking Japanese supply trains, and robbing them of their goods and useful freight—weapons, explosives, and in some cases even the troops' payroll—was particularly noticeable. As one would expect, the Japanese military authorities tried their best to dissuade further attacks with punishing expeditions and strict but relatively ineffective regulations. For example, public announcements by the Japanese authorities issued in Jinan in 1940 limited the height of crops along the tracks and major roads so as to minimize the danger of ambush by guerilla fighters hiding in the fields.[93]

The popularity of these guerilla squads has been heavily exploited in the post-war narrative of the CCP about Communists as the only truly patriotic force fighting the war of resistance in Shandong with strong support from all levels of local society. To this end the extremely popular novel *Tiedao youjidui* (The Railroad Guerilla Squad) by Zhi Xia, who supposedly had first-hand experience with Shandong's guerilla fighters, was published in 1954 and later turned into a popular propaganda film.[94]

However, in reality the guerilla squads consisted predominantly of mining workers, about 5,000 in all of Shandong around 1940, whereas the numbers of workers in the squads associated with the JinPu railroad company itself—only about 60 members—was relatively small.[95] The company's highly skilled workforce enjoyed much better working conditions than miners and workers in other industrial enterprises. Therefore CCP activists found it more difficult to infiltrate the workforce and harder to convince the skilled workers to sabotage their own work in the name of anti-Japanese resistance.

Even with all the interruptions due to the war, it is quite remarkable that the JinPu railroad was still able to transport 4.2 million passengers in 1940. While resistance from the local population who either cooperated or openly sympathized with the guerilla fighters predictably and repeatedly generated cruel counter-measures from the Japanese military authorities, the Japanese took a different approach in their management of the JinPu workforce. The Japanese managers and engineers realized the need to run the railroad as smoothly as possible in order to provide military supplies for the troops of the occupation army in Shandong, Hebei, and North China in general. At the same time, the Japanese managers were aware of the need for highly skilled Chinese workers in the railroad yards and thus they tried to co-opt rather than alienate the workforce by improving the working conditions on the shop floor.

Some of the improvements were quite substantial. As former JinPu railroad workers stated in interviews, under Japanese management from 1938 on they began to receive a free lunch at work and had more regulated working hours than in the pre-1937 period.[96] Skilled workers employed in the JinPu maintenance workshop in the early 1940s had to work for 21 days a month with a ten-hour shift per day. The importance of this schedule lies not so much in the rest and recreation that the free days offered them but in the fact that it allowed them to engage in black market activities. The workers used the free train tickets they were entitled to as members of the JinPu railroad company and joined the black market economy of the time as small traders (*zuo xiao maimai*).[97]

For example, they took the train from Jinan to Qingdao on the coast of the Shandong peninsula, which enjoyed better food supply than central Shandong during the wartime period. The workers purchased food there, in particular grain and fresh fish, and then resold these goods with a profit margin on the black market in Jinan.[98] The fact that the workers belonged to the JinPu railroad's workforce also made them and their baggage less suspicious to Japanese railroad guards patrolling at the stations and on the trains.

The Japanese management of the JinPu railroad also offered other incentives related to job training and benefits. It allowed the workers to return home for New Year with free train tickets and made special efforts to train apprentices for the workshops as cooperative members of the workforce. For example, as former JinPu workers report, the Japanese management sent them to railroad training institutes in Shanxi and Hebei in the second year of their apprenticeship where they received specialized professional training for free. It appears that railroad workers with specific skills and technical expertise in jobs crucial to the support of the Japanese war effort did not suffer from harassment and exploitation as much as unskilled workers in confiscated commercial industrial enterprises such as cotton mills and silk filatures under Japanese management.[99]

After the end of World War II, the JinPu and Qingdao-Jinan railroads became a crucial means of transportation in the repatriation of Japanese army and civilian personnel who left for Japan from Shandong ports like Qingdao. However, very soon the train lines became strategic targets during the Chinese civil war. From 1946 onward the northern rail connection between Xuzhou and Tianjin remained permanently closed as Communists troops occupied Dezhou city north of Jinan. Nationalist troops succeeded in keeping the train corridor between Jinan and Qingdao open until the spring of 1947, even though by then the area north and south of the corridor in Shandong was already under Communist control. Once Communist troops managed to break through the corridor and disrupt the Qingdao-Jinan line in 1948, the Guomindang troops were trapped and cut off from their supplies shipped through Qingdao.

Meanwhile, the southern part of the JinPu line from Pukou to Xuzhou remained open until 1948, but with only one express train from Jinan to Pukou and one slow train from Jinan to Xuzhou per day.[100] Needless to say, the lack of railway transportation had a devastating effect on Jinan's commerce and food supplies until the end of the civil war in 1949.[101]

Conclusions

The JinPu railroad company created new infrastructure necessary for economic growth and social mobility in Shandong, resulting in increased commercialized agriculture within the province and economic integration with neighboring provinces, including Manchuria. As a national railroad, the relationship between the JinPu company and the politically fragmented government between 1912 and 1927 was weak. Its departmental organization reinforced a relatively high degree of autonomy within the railroad network. Government officials from the Ministry of Transportation and Communication interfered relatively little with the day-to-day business of the JinPu railroad company in terms of hiring practices and business strategies. However, once the JinPu railroad came under the administrative control of the Railroad Ministry and thus under direct control of the Nanjing government in 1928, it was much closer supervised and regulated. In addition, party branch offices of the Guomindang found a home in all the larger railroad compounds and headquarters along the JinPu line.

The JinPu railroad was of great economic and strategic importance to the Japanese during their presence on the Shandong peninsula between 1914 and 1923; their detailed 1919 survey compiled by the railroad office of the Qingdao Japanese Military Authority remains the most comprehensive analysis of the JinPu railroad in all its managerial and financial aspects prior to the national Railroad Ministry's surveys of the late 1920s and 1930s. Compared to Manchuria, Japanese management of the Qingdao-Jinan railroad between 1914 and 1923 never achieved the same degree of control as the South Manchuria Railway in the Northeast. However, after 1937, the Japanese military made extensive use of the Shandong railways to carry out its invasion of North China, a strategy that the Chinese Communists also studied and followed with great success during the late 1940s.

Expanding the railroad network in post-1949 China became synonymous with establishing and cementing the physical and ideological presence of the newly established socialist nation-state. During the Republican period, the Chinese state had a strong presence in national railroad companies not only because of the centralized administration and integration of the line into a nation-wide network, but also because of almost self-sufficient railroad compounds with a strong Guomindang presence attempting to influence employees, railroad engineers, and technical staff in their professional and political development.

It is probably not a coincidence that after 1949 railroad companies like the JinPu line were easily turned by the new Communist government into socialist work units (*danwei*). To a large degree, the railway comparies merely exchanged one political authority and ideology for another. In an ironic twist, administrative efficiency and discipline, praised as signs of modernity and progress in railroad companies during the Republican period, were after 1949 propagated as socialist virtues necessary to build the new economy and state through the expansion of the railroad infrastructure network in China.

Notes

1. Part of the research for this essay was made possible by an ARHC/NEH research grant from the American Council of Learned Societies for fieldwork in China in 2005.

2. Yang Yonggang, *Zhongguo jindai tielu shi* (The History of Modern Railroads in China) (Shanghai: Shanghai shudian chubanshe, 1997).

3. See, for example, Cheng, Lin. *The Chinese Railways: A Historical Survey* (Shanghai: China United Press, 1935); Jin Jiafeng (ed.), *Zhongguo jiaotong zhi fazhan ji qi quxiang* (The Development of Transportation in China and its Trend) (Nanjing: Zhongzhong shuju, 1937).

4. Cheng, *The Chinese Railways*, 82; Percy Horace Kent, *Railway Enterprise in China: An Account of Its Origin and Development* (London: E. Arnold, 1907), 152–53; There was a 5.85 percent true interest rate on the 1908 loan. Huenemann, *The Dragon and the Iron Horse*, 120.

5. Anon, *Investment Values of Chinese Railway Bonds* (Paris: La Librarie Française, 1923), 45.

6. On the history of Jinan see David D. Buck, *Urban Change in China: Politics and Development in Tsinan, Shantung, 1890–1949* (Madison: University of Wisconsin Press, 1978), and Zhang Runwu and Xue Li, *Tushuo Jinan lao jianzhu: jindai juan* (Pictures and Stories of Old Buildings in Jinan: the Modern Era) (Jinan: Jinan Chubanshe, 2001); on Shandong's economic development see Zhuang Weimin, *Jindai Shandong shichang jingji de bianqian* (The Transformation of the Market Economy in Modern Shandong) (Beijing: Zhonghua shuju, 2000), and Kenneth Pomeranz, *The Making of a Hinterland: State, Society, and Economy in Inland North China, 1853–1937* (Berkeley: University of California Press, 1993).

7. David Buck offers a detailed and insightful analysis of the shifting politics in Shandong. He uses the term "Manchurianization" in *Urban Change in China*, 114.

8. Ibid., 84.

9. Ibid., 85.

10. Ibid., 87.

11. Ibid., 111.

12. Ibid., 113.

13. Cheng, *The Chinese Railways*, 71.

14. See photographs held in the Shandong Provincial Archives (hereafter SDSDAG): Historical photograph collection, unnumbered, no date, 1920s.

15. See Chi-Keung Leung, *Railway Patterns and National Goals* (Chicago: University of Chicago, 1980); Cheng, *The Chinese Railway*; Mongton Chih Hsu, *Railway Problems in China*, (New York: Columbia University, 1915); En-Han Lee, *China's Quest for Railroad Autonomy, 1904–1911: A Study of the Chinese Railway Rights Recovery Movement*, (Singapore: Singapore University Press, 1977).

16. See Zhang Ruide, *Ping-Han tielu yu Huabei de jingji fazhan (1905–1937)* (The Beijing Hankou Railroad and the Economic Development of North China, 1905–1937) (Taipei: Zhongyang yanjiuyuan jindaishi yanjiusuo, 1998), and Zhang Ruide, *Zhongguo jindai tielu shiye guanli de yanjiu: zhengzhi cengmian de fenxi (1876–1937)* (Study of the Industrial Management of Modern Chinese Railroads: A Political Analysis, 1870–1937) (Taipei: Zhongyang yanjiuyuan jindaishi yanjiusuo, 1991); Huenemann, *The Dragon and the Iron Horse*; Ernest P. Liang, *China: Railways and Agricultural Development, 1875–1935* (Chicago: University of Chicago, 1982).

17. Benjamin Elman, *On Their Own Terms: Science in China, 1550–1900* (Cambridge, MA: Harvard University Press, 2005), 360. Due to the focus on applied science, publications like *The Engineer and Machinist's Drawing Book*, published originally in 1855, were translated by the head of the arsenal's new school, John Fryer, with the help of Xu Jianyin and published in 1872. John Fryer, together with Xu Shou, was also the creator of China's first scientific journal *Gezhi Huibian* (Compendium for Investigating Things and Expanding Knowledge), also known under its English title as *The Chinese Scientific and Industrial Magazine* with the first issue published in 1876. The journal circulated in the treaty ports and mainly featured articles on the natural sciences and technology in Europe and the United States. Ibid., 310–19.

18. The father of the writer Han Suyin, who was trained in Belgium and then worked for the railroad in Henan as railway inspector, living in houses provided by the railway administration and moving with his family from post to post, would be a typical example for such a career. See Han Suyin, *Destination Chungking* (Boston: Little, Brown and Company, 1942), 10.

19. "Records relating to German railroad construction in China, 1898–1916," Baker Library manuscript collections, Mss: 705 (hereafter quoted as Baker Library MC 705), Box. 4, Vol. 12, 1909.

20. Buck, *Urban Change in China*, 46.

21. See photographs held in the SDSDAG: Historical photograph collection, unnumbered, no date, 1920s.

22. Baker Library MC 705, Box 1, Vol. 1, 1898.

23. James G.H. Glass, *Report on the Concessions of the Pekin Syndicate, Limited, in the Provinces of Shansi and Honan, China, with Estimates of Cost of Railways and Other Works Necessary for Their Development* (London: N.p., 1899), 43.

24. Ibid., 1.

25. Ibid., 46

26. Ibid., 47.

27. Baker Library MC 705, Box 4, Vol. 12, 1909.

28. Baker Library MC 705, Box 4, Vol. 12, June 1909.

29. Baker Library MC 705, Box 4, Vol. 13, Feb. 1913, statement of chief engineer Dorpmüller.

30. Wm. Barclay Parsons, *Report on the Survey and Prospects of a Railway between Hankow and Canton* (New York, 1899), quote 40. Similar statements by the German engineer Dorpmüller in 1913 are found in Baker Library MC 705, Box 4, Vol. 13, Feb. 1913.

31. Baker Library MC 705, Box 4, Vol. 13, 21 February 1910, 4.

32. Ke Lan, *Kong Fu de zuihou yi dai* (The Last Generation of the Thousand-year-old Kong Mansion) (Tianjin: Tianjin jiaoyu chubanshe, 1999); Kong Demao and Kong Kelan, *The House of Confucius* (London: Hodder and Stoughton, 1988), 122.

33. Ke Lan, *Kong Fu de zuihou yi dai*.

34. Qufu became one of the main tourist attractions during the Republican period and together with Mount Tai (Taishan) was actively promoted by the JinPu railroad company as travel destination. See JinPu tielu guanliju zongwuchu bianchake, *JinPu tielu lüxing zhinan* (Travel Guide for the Tianjin-Pukou Railway) (Tianjin: JinPu tielu guanliju zongwuchu bianchake, 1921). On the cultural pilgrimage of Japanese travelers to Qufu see Joshua A. Fogel, *The Cultural Dimension of Sino-Japanese Relations: Essays on the Nineteenth and Twentieth Centuries* (Armonk: M.E. Sharpe, 1995), 95–117.

35. See photographs held in the SDSDAG: Historical photograph collection, unnumbered, no date, 1920s.

36. Qingdao shubi gummin seibu tetsudosho, *Qingdao shubi gummin seibu tetsudo chosa shiryo,* Vol. 25: JinPu tetsudo chosa hokokusho (Research Material from the Political Branch of the Railway Department of the Qingdao Occupation

Forces, Vol. 25: Research Report on the JinPu Railroad) (Qingdao: Qingdao shubi gummin seibu tetsudosho, 1919).

37. Cheng, *The Chinese Railway*, 60, states that 3 million taels were lost to graft in the foreign-controlled accounts department of the JinPu railroad.

38. Köll, *From Cotton Mill to Business Empire*, 176.

39. John Earl Baker, *Chinese Railway Accounts* (Peking: Commission on the Unification of Railway Accounts, 1923).

40. Shandong sheng difang shizhi bianzuan weiyuan hui, *Shandong sheng zhi tieluzhi* (Shandong Provincial Gazetteer: Railroad Gazetteer) (Jinan: Shandong Renmin Chubanshe, 1993), 236; Jinan tieluju shizhi bianzuan lingdao xiaozu, *Jinan tieluju zhi, 1899–1985* (Jinan Railroad Bureau Gazetteer. 1899–1985) (Jinan: Shandong youyi chubanshe, 1993), 226–27.

41. See Köll, *From Cotton Mill to Business Empire*, chapter 3.

42. Shanghai Municipal Archives: Q 55-2-493, 1936–38.

43. *Tielu zhigong jiaoyu xungan* (Magazine for the Education of Railroad Employees), Vol. 9, 23, 1925.

44. Jinan tieluju shizhi bianzuan lingdao xiaozu, *Jinan tieluju zhi, 1899–1985* (Jinan: Shandong youyi chubanshe, 1993).

45. Interviews at the Jinan tielu jiqichang, 30 July 2003.

46. For a detailed discussion of Jinan's urban history see Buck, *Urban Change in China*.

47. Zhang Runwu and Xue Li, *Tushuo Jinan lao jianzhu* (Jinan: Jinan chubanshe, 2001), 6–11; Luo Tengxiao, *Jinan daguan* (The Grand Sights of Jinan) (Jinan: Jinan daguan chubanshe, 1934); Jinan shi shizhi bianzuan weiyuanhui, *Jinan shizhi* (Gazetteer of Jinan City), Vol. 2 (Beijing: Zhonghua shuju, 1999).

48. Zhang Runwu and Xue Li, *Tushuo Jinan lao jianzhu*, 126–28; Toa Dobunkai, *Shina shobetsu zenshi, Vol. 4: Shandong sho* (Complete Gazetteers of China's Provinces: Vol. 4: Shandong Province) (Tokyo: Toa Dobunkai, 1918), 436–76.

49. Maps in Zhang Runwu and Xue Li, *Tushuo Jinan lao jianzhu*, 2–11, and Buck, *Urban Change in China*, 100.

50. Qingdao shubi gummin seibu tetsudosho, *Qingdao shubi gunnin seibu tetsudo chosa shiryo Vol. 25: JinPu tetsudo chosa hokokusho*, 27–46.

51. Chandler, *The Visible Hand*, 106–7.

52. Walter Licht, *Working for the Railroad* (Princeton: Princeton University Press, 1983); Lothar Gall and Manfred Pohl (ed.), *Die Eisenbahn in Deutschland* (München: H.C. Beck, 1999); interviews at the Jinan tielu jiqichang, July 30, 2003 and July 10 and 15, 2005.

53. Tiedaobu yewusi laogongke, *Gongren renshu ji gongzi tongji* (Statistics on the Number of Workers and Wages) (N.p.: Tiedaobu yewusi laogongke, 1931), 12–13.

54. Jin Jiafeng, *Zhongguo jiaotong zhi fazhan ji qi quexiang* (Nanjing: Zhengzhong shuju, 1937).

55. *Jiaotong daxue biyesheng jiaochalu* (Survey of Graduates of Jiaotong University) (N.p.: Jiaotong daxue, 1932); Shanghai Jiaotong daxue, *Jiaotong daxue 40 zhou jiniankan* (Memorial Volume for the 40th Anniversary of Jiaotong

University) (Shanghai: n.p., 1936), 21–29; *Tielu yuekan: JinPu xian* (Railway Monthly: the JinPu Line) (Nanjing: 1932–34); *Tielu zazhi* (Railway Magazine) (Nanjing: Guomin zhengfu tiedaobu mishuting yanjiushi, 1935).

56. Jiaotong tiedaobu jiaotongshi biancuan weiyuanhui, *Jiaotong shi luzheng bian* (History of Transportation, Chapter on Railway Policies) Vol. 1 (Nanjing: n.p., 1935).

57. See for example *Tielu zhigong jiaoyu xungan* (Magazine for the Education of Railway Employees), 1925–28.

58. Huang Yifeng, *Tielu zhiye zhidao* (Guide for Railroad Employment) (Shanghai: Shangwu yinshuguan, 1936) is just one example of the many handbooks published to educate railroad employees in terms of professional knowledge and ethical values.

59. *Jinpu zhi sheng* (The T.P.R. Echo), 1928–1936.

60. Interviews at the Jinan tielu jiqichang 10 and 15 July 2005.

61. See for example *Tielu zhigong jiaoyu xungan*, Vol. 11, 1925, 6–10.

62. Shandong dang'anguan, Shandong shehui kexueyuan lishi yanjiusuo (ed.), *Shandong geming lishi dang'an ziliao xuanbian* (Collection of archival materials on the revolutionary history of Shandong), Vol. 1 (1923–28), (Jinan: Shandong renmin chubanshe, 1984–1987).

63. Shandong dang'anguan. Shandong shehui kexueyuan lishi yanjiusuo (ed.), *Shandong geming lishi dang'an ziliao xuanbian* (Collection of archival materials on the revolutionary history of Shandong), Vol. 1 (1923–28); "JinPu lu gonghui gaikuang" ("The Situation of the JinPu Railroad's Union"), 8–13.

64. Elisabeth Köll, "Work Hierarchies and Standards of Living Among Railway Workers," unpublished manuscript.

65. Elizabeth J. Perry, *Shanghai on Strike: The Politics of Chinese Labor* (Stanford: Stanford University Press, 1993).

66. Interviews at the Jinan tielu jiqichang, 19 June 2005.

67. Shandong dang'anguan. Shandong shehui kexueyuan lishi yanjiusuo (ed.), *Shandong geming lishi dang'an ziliao xuanbian* (Collection of archival materials on the revolutionary history of Shandong), Vol. 1 (1923–28).

68. Interviews at the Jinan tielu jiqichang, 19 June 2005.

69. Guangdong Provincial Archives (hereafter abbreviated as GDSDAG): 40-1-174; 1948. The file contains over one hundred of these documents.

70. GDSDAG: 40-1-508, 1946–49, 142–43.

71. Qingdao shubi gummin seibu tetsudosho, *Qingdao shubi gummin seibu tetsudobu chosa shiryo Vol. 25: JinPu tetsudo chosa hokokusho*, 194.

72. Wu Xiangxiang and Liu Shaotang, *Lu an shanhou yuebao tekan: tielu* (Special Issue of the Monthly Magazine on the Reconstruction of the Shandong Case: Railroads) (N.p.: 1923, reprint Taipei: Zhuanji wenxue chubanshe, 1971), 28.

73. Ibid., 21.

74. Qingdao shubi gummin seibu tetsudosho,*Qingdao shubi gummin seibu tetsudobu chosa shiryo Vol. 25: JinPu tetsudo chosa hokokusho*, 192.

75. Wm. Barclay Parsons, *An American Engineer in China* (New York: McClure, Phillips and Co., 1900), 277–79; *The Far Eastern Review*, April 1923, 253–62.

76. See Cheng, *The Chinese Railways.*

77. JinPu tielu guanlijiu zongwuchu bianchake, *JinPu tielu lüxing zhinan* inserted time and ticket price tables, no page number.

78. *The Far Eastern Review*, December 1922, 72.

79. Xie Xueshi, *Mantie yu zhongguo laogong* (The South Manchurian Railroad and Chinese Labor) (Beijing: Shehui kexue wenxian chubanshe, 2003), 248–49; see also Thomas Gottschang and Diana Lary, *Swallows and Settlers: The Great Migration from North China to Manchuria* (Ann Arbor: Center for Chinese Studies, University of Michigan, 2000).

80. Baker Library MC 705, Box 5, Vol. 15, Jan. 1914.

81. Qingdao shubi gummin seibu tetsudosho, *Qingdao shubi gummin seibu tetsudobu chosa shiryo Vol. 25: JinPu tetsudo chosa hokokusho,* 138.

82. Ibid.

83. Wu Xiangxiang and Liu Shaotang. *Lu an shanhou yuebao tekan: tielu*, 37.

84. Prices calculated from Ibid., table on 37.

85. GDSDAG: 40-1-722, 1940–1949, 130.

86. Ibid., 123. Odoric Wou, *Mobilizing the Masses: Building Revolution in Henan* (Stanford: Stanford University Press, 1994) establishes relatively similar wage and salary patterns for railroad workers in Henan province during the early 1920s.

87. Qingdao shubi gummin seibu tetsudosho, *Qingdao shubi gummin seibu tetsudobu chosa shiryo Vol. 25: JinPu tetsudo chosa hokokusho,* 137–38.

88. Ibid., 139–140.

89. Lü Weijun, *Shandong quyu xiandaihua yanjiu, 1840–1949* (Research on the Modernization of the Shandong Region, 1840–1949) (Jinan: Jilu shushe, 2002); Buck, *Urban Change in China*, 139.

90. Junshi weiyanhui junlingbu diyiting disanchu, *Pohuai gong (tie) lu banfa* (Methods of Sabotaging (Rail)roads) (Junshi weiyanhui junlingbu diyiting disanchu, 1939).

91. Shandong sheng zonggonghui, *Shandong gongren yundongshi* (History of the Workers' Movement in Shandong) (Jinan: Shandong renmin chubanshe, 1988), 232–50.

92. Ibid., 233–35.

93. SDSDAG: J102-14–22, 1940.

94. Zhi Xia, *Tiedao youjidui* (The Railroad Guerilla Squad) (Shanghai: Shanghai renmin chubanshe, 1977 [1954]); see the author's postscript on page 605.

95. Shandong sheng zonggonghui, *Shandong gongren yundongshi*, 250.

96. Interviews at the Jinan tielu jiqichang, 15 July 2005.

97. Japanese soldiers were also engaged in opium smuggling, transporting the drug via the JinPu line from North China to the Shanghai narcotics market. See Frederic Wakeman, "Occupied Shanghai: The Struggle between Chinese and Western medicine" in Diana Lary and Ezra Vogel (eds.), *China at War: Regions of China, 1937–1945* (Stanford: Stanford University Press, 2007), 272.

98. Interviews at the Jinan tielu jiqichang, 15 July 2005.

99. Parks Coble, *Chinese Capitalists in Japan's New Order: The Occupied Lower Yangzi, 1937–1945.* (Berkeley: University of California Press, 2003) and Köll, *From Cotton Mill to Business Empire*, Chapter 8, discusses shop floor conditions

and the interaction between workers and management during the Japanese occupation.

100. Buck, *Urban Change in China,* 196–97.

101. Lü Weijun, *Shandong quyu xiandaihua yanjiu, 1840–1949.*

7

Railways in Communist Strategy and Operations in Manchuria, 1945–48

Harold M. Tanner

Beginning in mid-August 1945, the Chinese Communist Party transferred units of its armies from backward rural areas of northern China to the major cities of Manchuria, and soon afterwards challenged the Nationalists for control. The general narrative of events in Northeast China from 1945 to 198 is well known.[1] But less understood is how the civil war in Manchuria revolved around that region's 14,000 kilometers of railway lines, which in 1931 represented over 50 percent of the total railways in the Republic of China.[2] Railways shaped the field of battle in Manchuria, determining how both Communist and Guomindang commanders deployed their forces, the routes along which they chose to advance, and the strategic points that that they fought to control.

Shaping the Battlefield

The Soviet Union's declaration of war against Japan on 8 August 1945 and its rapid occupation of the key cities and major rail lines of "Manchukuo" presented the Chinese Communist Party with a new opportunity. The Communists had been preparing to make the transition from war against Japan to a nation-wide civil war against the Nationalist government of the Republic of China, and had sent troops to south China to open up new base areas. In terms of military doctrine, they were preparing to move from guerilla warfare to standard maneuver warfare carried out by trained professional army units.

Now, with the Soviet Union in the Northeast and Japan's surrender on 14 August, the Communist Party's Central Committee quickly re-adjusted its plans. Instead of developing base areas in south China, they would "defend to the south, advance to the north." Troops originally in or on the way to south China were ordered to return to the north to help establish a foothold in Manchuria, a region in which neither the Communist Party nor the Nationalist government had any presence.[3]

As Communist troops moved into Manchuria in August 1945, the Communist Party's Central Committee and Military Affairs Commission ordered them not to occupy the main cities and rail lines. Instead, they were to deploy to positions from which they could attack rail lines and cities.[4] The Party Center wanted its forces widely dispersed across the Manchurian countryside, with a platoon or company in every county.[5] The goal was not to occupy and control all of Manchuria, but rather to expand Communist forces by integrating former "Manchukuo" units and to build base areas. The Party Center wanted enough troops in South Manchuria to give them a toehold in that strategic industrial area, but special emphasis was to be placed on building base areas in the regions that backed onto Korea, the Soviet Union, Mongolia, and existing Communist base areas in northern China, where the close proximity of Soviet forces offered them protection.

In mid-October 1945, the Communist Party leadership changed both its strategic goals and its prescribed pattern of troop deployment for the Northeast. Instead of merely gaining a foothold in the south, building base areas in the north, and positioning its troops for a future attack on railway lines and major cities, the Party now aimed to control all of Manchuria. Three factors led the Party to adopt this new strategy: 1) conditions on the ground, 2) the state of the Manchurian railways, and 3) the status of talks between the Soviet Union and the Nationalists—talks that centered around the issue of control over the Manchurian railways and Manchuria's industrial base.

Conditions on the ground were challenging. The Central Committee's Northeast Bureau, a group of leaders dispatched to Manchuria to plan and execute operations there, found that many of their forces had come to Manchuria hurriedly and without adequate clothing, supplies, weapons, or ammunition. Communist leaders had falsely assumed that they could draw on resources available in Manchuria to re-supply and re-equip these troop units as they arrived.

Manchuria was rich in resources: agricultural and industrial goods, stockpiles of leftover Japanese and "Manchukuo" weapons and supplies, and the railway lines. However, Manchuria's resources were not evenly distributed: they were concentrated along the railways and in the major cities of the more industrialized, wealthier areas of South Manchuria. The countryside and those parts of North Manchuria backing on to Korea and the Soviet Union, where the Communists had hoped to build base areas, were resource-poor.

As a result, Northeast Bureau leader Peng Zhen (1902–1997) was unable to carry out the Central Committee's orders. Instead of dispersing troops widely, the Northeast Bureau chose to concentrate forces in South Manchuria along the major rail lines and in or near large cities. This deployment was determined by how the railway system influenced the distribution of resources, and also by the state of the railways themselves.

The war and its aftermath had not been kind to the railroads. As the "Manchukuo" regime fell, the railway administration fell along with it. Some lines remained functional. Soviet troops, for example, entered Harbin by rail and shipped tanks and other materiel south from Changchun to Dalian on flatcars. The Harbin-Changchun line was re-opened and running one or two freight trains a day by late August.[6] But substantial parts of the South Manchuria and China Eastern railways were still severely damaged. In some cases, retreating Japanese troops had sabotaged the railways in an attempt to slow the Soviet advance. In other cases, Manchukuo troops or local, independent forces destroyed rail lines in order to keep the Communist Party out. Many of the rural and border regions where the Central Committee wanted to establish base areas were inaccessible because the branch lines were not functioning or because there were no railway connections in the more remote regions. As they deployed their troops in the Northeast, the Communists could not always rely on the railways. Often, they had to march on foot.[7]

Despite the problems of transportation and supply, the Communists had transferred 150,000 soldiers to Manchuria during the months of August and September 1945.[8] Inside Manchuria, units of the former "Manchukuo" army were incorporated into the Communist forces, often with little training or indoctrination. In all, the Communists may have had between 200,000 and 250,000 men under arms in Manchuria by early October 1945.[9]

Soviet policy was driven primarily by Joseph Stalin's (1878–1953) understanding of Soviet strategic interests. Stalin had already acknowledged the Republic of China's sovereignty over Manchuria in a treaty of peace and friendship signed on 14 August 1945. But the Soviet government used this treaty to preserve privileges for itself, in particular rights to the railways and a dominant role in the industrial economy. A Sino-Soviet railroad agreement, signed on the same day, acknowledged Chinese ownership of the Manchurian railways, but provided for a system of joint management by a Soviet-Chinese railway administration.[10]

While he recognized and worked with Jiang Jieshi's government, Stalin was also concerned that too great an extension of Jiang's power into the Northeast would bring unwanted American influence into the region. To prevent that from happening, the Soviet Union supported the Chinese Communist forces in Manchuria when and to the extent that such support would advance Soviet interests. In the autumn of 1945, Stalin decided that support for the Chinese Communist forces would minimize Nationalist and, ultimately, American, involvement in Manchuria.

The Communist Party responded with enthusiasm. On 19 October, the Party Center issued a directive signaling a change in strategy: "Our Party's policy is to concentrate our forces along the Jinzhou-Yingkou-Shenyang line, with secondary forces along the Zhuanghe-Andong line. . . ."[11] On 28 October, the Party Center instructed the Northeast Bureau: "Our Party must resolutely mobilize all its forces, control the Northeast, protect north China and central China, smash their offensive in the next six months, then force Jiang to the negotiating table and make him accept the autonomous status of northern China and the Northeast. Only then can there be a transition to peace: otherwise, peace is impossible."[12] The Soviet Union supported this more aggressive strategy: on 25 October 1945, Soviet officials told the Northeast Bureau: "If a bit of caution was needed in the past, now is the time to take the initiative and act boldly."[13]

The Party Center's goal was to gain a monopoly on control of the Northeast. In order to do so, Communist units were no longer to be dispersed broadly; instead, they were to be concentrated in South Manchuria, so as to prevent any Nationalist troops from entering the Northeast.[14] The Soviet Union assisted: for example, Soviet officers became more generous about releasing captured Japanese arms, ammunition, and other military supplies to the Communists. They also allowed Chinese Communist units to take control of land routes from north China to Manchuria, including key stretches of railway such as the line from Shanhaiguan to Jinzhou, which was under Communist control by November 1945.[15] Chinese Communist deployment around and along the major cities and rail lines of South Manchuria had originally been determined by easy access to resources close to the railroads. Now, control of railways and cities—"points and lines"—had become essential parts of the Communist strategy of controlling all of Manchuria.

Fighting over "Points and Lines"

The decision to hold major cities and railways required the Communist forces in Manchuria to use standard base and maneuver warfare to defend territory. This was no easy task for a poorly-armed force that was more used to guerilla warfare. Only with the support of the Soviet Union would the Communists be able to keep the Nationalists out. Military weakness and reliance on Soviet support made the Communist position in Manchuria in the autumn of 1945 doubly vulnerable. In the fight to gain control over the area, Jiang Jieshi, his government, and his army exploited both the diplomatic and military weaknesses of the Communists.

On the diplomatic front, Jiang sent representatives to negotiate with the Soviets about the transfer of power in the Northeast. China and the Soviet Union had already signed agreements to return the Northeast to Jiang's government and on joint management of the Manchurian railways. Now, Jiang hoped to use economic concessions to build a stronger relationship with the Soviets—one that would transform the agreements made with the Soviet Union into realities on the ground in which the Chinese Nationalist government, and not the Chinese Communists, would take control of the Northeast.[16]

Stalin hoped that negotiations with Jiang's government would give the Soviet Union a strong presence in Manchuria and would tie the Guomindang regime more closely to the Soviet Union. From mid-November onwards, the Soviets increased their level of cooperation with Jiang's government and army. At the same time, they decreased their level of support for the Chinese Communists. On 19 November, the Soviet commander in the Northeast notified Communist forces that they were to leave the major cities and railway lines so that the Soviet Union could turn these over to the Nationalists, as stipulated by treaty.[17] The Party Center instructed the Northeast Bureau: "Since they [the Soviets] have made this decision, we have to follow it."[18]

These negotiations were accompanied by a military advance into Manchuria. From August through October, Chinese Communist sabotage of north-south railway lines in China proper, and Soviet control of the Manchurian ports of Dalian and Lüshun (Port Arthur), had delayed the advance of Nationalist government troops toward the Northeast.[19] Unable to land troops in Dalian, and facing resistance and sabotage along the north-south railways, Jiang Jieshi called on the United States for assistance. The Americans helped Jiang to secure railways and cities in North China and to move troops both to North China and Manchuria.[20] Jiang's negotiations with the Soviets, too, helped to open the door of Manchuria. On 10 November, the Soviet Union announced that it would allow the GMD to airlift troops to the major cities five days before Soviet forces were to withdraw.

Jiang's diplomatic and military assault on the Communist position soon achieved results. On 16 November 1945, Nationalist forces captured the Communist-held city of Shanhaiguan, the strategic point of entry for road and rail routes from North China to Manchuria. With the government armies on the offensive, Lin Biao's troops fought one unsuccessful defensive engagement after another along railway lines of southern Manchuria, losing ground all through November. The Communist armies were out-manned, out-gunned, and lacked training and discipline. Some had been fighting without rest since being hastily transferred into Manchuria in September and October. Former Manchukuo units that had been incorporated into the Communist ranks were poorly indoctrinated; many abandoned the field or defected.

The Communist Party also lacked popular support. There had been no time to build base areas or cultivate support among the people of the Northeast, many of whom looked forward to the arrival of Nationalist troops. As the Nationalists advanced from Shanhaiguan along the Bei-Ning railway, local officials behind Communist lines used the telephone system that linked railway stations to contact Nationalist units and tell them about Communist deployments.[21]

With the Communist position deteriorating, the Party Center again revised its policies. Admitting that it was impossible to achieve complete control over the Northeast and that the Soviet Union's treaty obligations required it to turn the cities and main railway lines over to the ROC government, the Party now ordered the Northeast Bureau to withdraw its forces from the cities and main railways, and instead to "occupy the flanks," that is, move to the small and medium-size cities, the branch railway lines, and the countryside.[22]

As they withdrew, the Communist forces carried out selective sabotage on railways. On 20 November 1945, the Party Center instructed the Northeast Bureau not to destroy railway lines, factories, and other capital equipment as they withdrew from the cities. For the most part, these should be left in place, both in order not to alienate people unnecessarily and because these facilities would eventually be useful to the Communists in the future. Railways could, however, be sabotaged when the military situation required it. For example, the Party Center recommended that if the Soviet Union would not allow the Communist forces to retain control over the Shanhaiguan to Jinzhou section of the Bei-Ning railroad, then the Northeast Bureau should consider digging the railway bed up thoroughly—but only if the Soviets did not object.[23]

Even in late November 1945, the Communist Party hoped that the Soviet Union would allow them to retain a strong presence in some of the major cities and control over important transportation links such as the rail line from Shanhaiguan to Jinzhou. It was not to be: on 28 November, the Party Center advised the Northeast Bureau: "Due to treaty restrictions, the Soviet Union will transfer authority over major cities along the Changchun railway line to Jiang Jieshi. . . ."[24] During the short time in which they had established a presence in the major cities, the Communists had, with Soviet help, taken over the administration of many of the railway lines. Now, Communist railway administration officials withdrew, and Guomindang officials moved into their places.[25]

The Communist Redeployment and the Nationalist Victory at Siping

The Communist retreat from major cities and railway lines did not represent a reversion to a purely rural guerilla war strategy. Railways still played a major role in Communist strategic thinking during late 1945. While surrendering the main lines and major cities to the enemy, the Communists retained control over branch lines in order to deprive the enemy of access to smaller and medium cities and rural areas, and to scarce resources including agricultural products and coal. In the long run, Communist commander Lin Biao and Northeast Bureau chief Peng Zhen were still interested in taking major cities and rail lines if they could.[26] Any such plans, however, would have to await the development of two new, closely related situations: 1) the Soviet Union's imminent withdrawal of troops from Manchuria, and 2) the American attempt to negotiate a cease-fire and coalition government between the Nationalist and Communist parties.

The Soviet Union had delayed its withdrawal from Manchuria three times. The Nationalist government, they argued, was not ready to maintain order. Furthermore, problems with the rail lines, bitter winter weather, and shortages of coal and rolling stock would make it impossible for the Nationalist armies to move into the Northeast in a timely manner.[27] Moscow's delaying tactics were stopped, however, soon after the Nationalist government recognized Outer Mongolia's independence from China during January 1946, which had been an essential Chinese concession in the Sino-Soviet treaty signed during August 1945.

On 8 March 1946, the Soviets began to leave their positions. Although they formally transferred authority to civil and military representatives of the Nationalist government, the Soviets conducted their withdrawal in ways that were designed to assist the Communists. Soviet units often withdrew without giving Jiang's government any warning. They put obstacles in the way of Nationalist troop movements, withholding rolling stock and, in one instance, declaring that Government troops in southern Manchuria could not proceed north because of the danger of spreading epidemic diseases.[28] At the same time, the Soviets assisted Communist forces, for example, by making passenger cars available to move Communist troops from Soviet-occupied Harbin south to Changchun.[29]

All this helped the Communists to achieve their goal: ". . . to use our utmost strength to control the two cities of Changchun and Harbin and the China Eastern Railway, to oppose the Jiang army's advance on Changchun, Harbin, and the China Eastern Railway, no matter what the sacrifice, and to regard south and east Manchuria as supplementary areas."[30] The Communists acted quickly, taking Changchun, Harbin, Siping, and other cities and towns from the token Guomindang forces to which the Soviets had transferred sovereignty.[31]

During fall 1945, the Communist attempt to defend major cities and railways in South Manchuria and prevent Jiang Jieshi's armies from gaining even an inch of ground had failed. The Communists had lost the major cities and rail lines and withdrawn to the flanks, where they were to build base areas in the countryside and in the small and medium cities. Why was the Central Committee now ordering Lin Biao to take and defend Harbin, Changchun, and the China Eastern Railway?

One possible answer lies in the Central Committee's attitude toward the American mediator, General George Marshall. General Marshall arrived in China in December 1945. President Truman had assigned him to negotiate a cease-fire and coalition government between the Nationalist and Communist parties.[32] Marshall's efforts led to a cease-fire agreement in January 1946, which quickly fell apart, partly because Jiang Jieshi insisted that the agreement did not apply to Manchuria. Marshall nonetheless continued his work: the Truman administration was determined prevent the outbreak of a full-scale civil war.

By March 1946, the Communist negotiators, led by Zhou Enlai, were very optimistic that Marshall might be able to force Jiang to agree to a cease-fire.[33] Zhou, Mao, and the Central Committee were determined that they should control as much Manchurian territory as possible in order to be in a strong position at the negotiating table. For example, some areas—the major portion of the Changchun railway from Shenyang to Harbin and a number of smaller Communist-held cities—might be traded for concessions elsewhere.[34] In the meantime, everything had to be held. But if a cease-fire was (as they thought) imminent, the Communists would not have to fight extended battles to defend their newly acquired urban territories.

Railways played an important role in the Communists' plans for defending territory in the Northeast against government attack. In late March and early April 1946, the Party Center issued repeated instructions promoting sabotage of the rail lines, which Nationalist forces would use in their advance north from Shenyang. The Northeast Bureau was advised to establish special railway destruction command centers. On 16 April, the Center reminded the Northeast Bureau that just blowing up a few bridges does not stop railway traffic: the enemy can put temporary bridges in place in a few hours. It takes a lot of work, the Central Committee emphasized, to destroy a railway completely. You need hundreds of thousands of workers to dig up the railway bed thoroughly for miles, blow up the water towers, and carry the rails away and bury them.[35]

Even after all of their efforts, the Communists could not permanently cut the railway and Nationalist forces soon moved north from Shenyang along the railway.[36] Jiang Jieshi, too, wanted to control as much of the Northeast and its major cities and railways as he could before he would agree to a ceasefire. With the Nationalists determined to advance, and the Communists equally determined to defend, a major decisive battle was inevitable. It came in April 1946 at the railway junction town of Siping.

Siping lies south of Changchun on the main north-south railway. Branch lines from the east and from the west both converge there. The rail lines and the lay of the surrounding land make Siping a key point for any army advancing on Changchun from the south. The Communist Party Center, with an eye to holding on to Changchun until a cease-fire could be negotiated, ordered Lin Biao to defend the city whatever the cost.[37] Lin and several of the generals on the ground had serious reservations about the wisdom of fighting a protracted defense of the city.[38] Nonetheless, they prepared for what they thought would be an intense, but short battle, which began on 18 April.

It soon became apparent that Mao and Zhou had miscalculated. Jiang was not the American stooge that they thought him to be. He would not agree to a ceasefire until he had defeated the Communists at Siping. As a result, the defense of Siping lasted until 19 May, when Lin's battered forces withdrew from the city. This defeat forced the Communist forces to retreat to northern Manchuria.

Railways and the Communist Rear Area

The defeat at Siping marked the end of the Communist Party's hopes of controlling major cities and railways south of the Songhua River. Communist forces tore up railway track north of Siping as they retreated, but Changchun was still indefensible.[39] Lin Biao abandoned Changchun and drew his main force back to Harbin, on the north bank of the Songhua. A small contingent of Communist troops remained in South Manchuria along the Korean border. In retrospect, the Communist Party Center suggested that failure to cut the railway north of Shenyang was one of the factors leading to the defeat.[40]

On 6 June 1946, a fifteen-day cease-fire went into effect. The cease-fire, which Marshall had finally succeeded in convincing both parties to agree to, was extended to 30 June. It marked the end of significant combat in Manchuria until October. Both the Communist and Nationalist forces needed time to rest, re-organize their troops, and make plans for the next stage of the civil war.[41] For the Communists, this meant consolidating their position north of the Songhua River.

As they worked to build their base area in North Manchuria, the Communist leaders were keenly aware of the importance of the railways. The rail lines from Harbin on north were far less developed than in the area south of the Songhua. Nonetheless, there were still several important railways that would be valuable assets. Lines linked Harbin to the other major cities of Heilongjiang province. Railways also provided connections to Communist base areas in North China and Inner Mongolia, to the Soviet Union, to Korea, and, via Korea, to the South Manchuria Base Area and (by boat from Korea) to the Soviet-controlled Manchurian port of Dalian.[42]

In order to use these assets, the Communists would need to control and repair them. Most of the North Manchurian railways had been severely damaged. Large areas of the countryside and some rail lines were under the control of local bands of armed men. Some of these forces were local militias, and posed no significant threat to the Communists. Others were loosely aligned with the Guomindang, while still others were simply bandits.

Suppression of these local military forces and restoration of rail traffic were among the top priorities of the Communist leadership in the North Manchuria Base

Area in the spring and summer of 1946. Operations against "bandit" forces were well within the capabilities of the Communist armies, whose organization, training, numbers, weapons, and supplies were far superior to anything the fragmented local militias had at their disposal. In June and July, Communist units re-opened the railway lines from Harbin to Jiamusi and from Mudanjiang to Suifenhe, both of which had been cut by "bandit" forces.[43]

As the Communists gained control over the rail lines and adjacent territory in the North Manchuria Base Area, they established a "Northeast Railway Administrative Bureau." Rail lines were repaired. In some cases, Communist engineers dismantled less valuable rail lines in order to use the parts to repair the more important ones.[44] The Soviet Union and North Korea both assisted in the task of restoring the railways of the North Manchurian Base Area to running order. Soviet technicians helped in the work and trained Chinese railway soldiers.[45] North Korea supplied locomotives, spare parts, bridge-building materials, and petroleum products.[46] Spare parts were shipped from the Soviet Union via Dalian and North Korea.

One of the challenges was to get enough locomotives. According to one source, hundreds of locomotives in various states of disrepair lay abandoned at stations and along sidetracks. Communist train crews recovered and repaired 36 locomotives in 1946 and another 232 in 1947. One of these, a locomotive manufactured in Dalian in 1941 and abandoned outside of Harbin after the Japanese surrender was named after Mao Zedong. Another repaired locomotive was named after Zhu De, the general who, along with Mao, had founded the People's Liberation Army. The Mao Zedong and the Zhu De were used not only to haul trains, but also for propaganda purposes, as when the two locomotives pulled ten or more train-cars of singing, drumming railway workers in the 1947 May Day celebrations in Harbin.[47]

From Defensive to Offensive, From Railway Sabotage to Railway Repair

While Lin Biao worked to build a strong base area north of the Songhua, Nationalist general Du Yuming (1903–1981) decided on a "first south, then north" strategy. He would hold the "points and lines" and restore vital railway connections. Then he would use the railways to move troops and supplies to staging areas for offensives, pushing outwards to eliminate all remaining Communist forces in South Manchuria. When South Manchuria was cleared, he would turn north.

The Communist response to the "first south, then north" strategy included railway sabotage, defensive battles, and counter-attacks. Communist guerrilla forces attacked along the Changchun railway, the Bei-Ning line and other railways behind Guomindang lines in South Manchuria.[48] Underground Communist Party members working in railway administration in Guomindang-controlled areas undermined Nationalist plans with work slow-downs and by sending locomotives out with coal cars full of slow-burning, sub-standard coal.[49] These actions hampered government military operations and kept Du from turning his attention to North Manchuria.[50] Nonetheless, Nationalist armies were able to repair the Shenyang-Hailong line and use it to deploy troops against the Communist South Manchuria Base Area.[51]

In December 1946, the Communist forces began to strike back at the Nationalists, first with a combination of defensive operations and counter-attacks, then with a series of major offensives. The major operations from late 1946 through autumn of 1948 included: 1) the Three Expeditions/Four Defenses (16 December 1946–3 April 1947); 2) the Summer Offensive (13 May–1 July 1947); 3) the Autumn Offensive (14 September–5 November 1947); and 4) the Winter Offensive (15 December 1947–15 March 1948).

Communist thinking on the role of the railways remained fundamentally the same during all these campaigns: destroy rail lines that are useful to the enemy, rebuild, maintain, and use rail lines in Communist areas. The closer the Communist leaders saw themselves to victory, the less interested they were in destroying railways, as it became clear that even railways in enemy territory would soon be theirs.[52] From December 1946 through November 1948, railways became important to Lin Biao as his forces abandoned guerilla warfare in favor of the large-scale mobile warfare techniques with which he defeated the Nationalists.

The Three Expeditions/Four Defenses campaign (December 1946–April 1947) was a series of defensive operations and counter-attacks designed to prevent Du Yuming from eliminating the Communist forces in South Manchuria. In the autumn of 1946, Du had used the railways to support a campaign that had reduced the Communist South Manchuria Base Area to four small counties in the Changbai Mountains. The Communist forces in the Changbai Mountains faced possible annihilation, but Lin cleverly used them to force Du Yuming to fight a two-front war. In the winter of 1946–47, Lin sent three expeditions south across the frozen Songhua River to strike at Guomindang positions. These operations were coordinated with the South Manchuria Base Area's defensive battles against four Nationalist offensives. The combination of defensive operations from the South Manchuria Base Area and the "three expeditions" across the Songhua forced Du Yuming to divide his resources and denied him victory on either front.

Du's reliance on rail lines and cities had become a disadvantage. Du now had to use thinly stretched troops to defend "points and lines" across Liaoning and Jilin provinces. This put him in an increasingly passive and reactive position. By the spring of 1947, all the Nationalist commanders in the Northeast could hope to do was to maintain their positions until Jiang Jieshi was able to transfer enough troops from North China to allow them to launch a new offensive.[53] By contrast, the

Communists had maintained their positions in both the north and the south and were preparing to move from the defensive to the offensive.

The Summer, Autumn, and Winter offensives (May–July 1947, September–November 1947, and December 1947–March 1948) were all fought over and around the railways and cities of the Northeast. One of the primary objectives of the Summer Offensive was to cut the rail link between Shenyang and Changchun.[54] This required isolating and attacking Guomindang forces in the key city of Siping—which in turn required attacks on branch railways feeding into Siping from the east and the west. Siping was successfully isolated, but Lin Biao's ambitious frontal assault on the city failed.[55] Operations designed to restore direct rail links between the Communist North and South Manchuria base areas were more successful.[56]

As they gained control of railway towns and lines south of the Songhua River, the Communists became more interested in keeping railroads in operating condition. On 4 June 1947, the Party Center notified all bureau heads and senior officers that: "At present our army's battle operations have completed the transition from the strategic defensive to the strategic counter-offensive. In the past, we needed to destroy railroads; now, in general, we do not have this need: on the contrary, if we do not put a stop to destruction of railways, we will be making an error. Therefore, from now on, other than partial strategic destruction for certain military purposes in the process of battle, all large-scale railway destruction activity should be halted."[57]

In the Autumn and Winter offensives, Lin Biao proceeded to further isolate the Nationalist forces in a few cities along the railway lines and to cut off their routes of retreat. In October, the Party Center specifically called for attacks on the railways between Shenyang and Jinzhou, Jinzhou and Shanhaiguan, and Shanhaiguan and Tianjin.[58] By the end of the Autumn Offensive, the Nationalist forces under General Chen Cheng (Du Yuming's replacement) had retreated to isolated strongholds in the cities of Jilin, Changchun, Siping, Shenyang, and Jinzhou, along with some smaller outlying towns along the major and some branch railway lines. The Communist armies controlled most of the rail lines and could disrupt traffic on the lines that it did not completely control, specifically the Bei-Ning line and the Shenyang-Siping-Changchun line.[59] As critics in Shenyang put it: "Chen Cheng is a real sensation! The trains from South Shenyang run to North Station!"[60]

Lin Biao quickly followed his success by launching a new offensive in December 1947. At this point, Chen's primary goal was to hold the major cities, particularly Changchun, Siping, and Shenyang, and to defend the Bei-Ning railway.[61] As the Communists attacked, their targets were, once again, the Changchun railway and the Bei-Ning line. Mao was concerned that Jiang Jieshi would try to withdraw his troops from Manchuria entirely. Therefore, he wanted Lin Biao to cut or take control of the Bei-Ning line, keep the Nationalists bottled up in their urban bases in Manchuria, and then cut them off and annihilate them one by one.[62]

When the Winter Offensive came to a conclusion in mid-March 1948, Lin Biao had cut the rail link from Shenyang to Changchun by taking Siping and had cut the Bei-Ning line between Shenyang and Jinzhou. The Guomindang main forces were now isolated in three areas: Changchun, Shenyang and a few surrounding cities, and the Jinzhou area[63] Nationalist units also continued to hold some smaller cities along the Bei-Ning line between Jinzhou and Shanhaiguan.[64] At this point, the Communist armies settled in for rest, re-organization, and training.

Close the Door and Beat the Dog: The Liao-Shen Campaign

While they sabotaged railways as a way of isolating Guomindang units in the major railway cities during the Summer, Autumn, and Winter offensives, the Communists remained aware of the need to rebuild and maintain railways in the increasingly large parts of the Northeast under their control. In January 1948, Mao reiterated the Party Center's admonition against unnecessary destruction of railways in a message to Fourth Field Army commanders: "Please consider that some railways should not be destroyed, or that there should be only strategic destruction, not complete destruction." The commanders responded that except for the Shenyang-Jinzhou section of the Bei-Ning line, no other railway lines would be sabotaged.[65]

As Communist units advanced in Manchuria, they set up railway administration bureaus.[66] The railway administration bureaus were considered to be among the more "advanced" bureaucracies in the Manchurian base area. Established to serve the needs of the military, the railway administration charged freight fees for non-military shipments. In August 1948, Communist railways administrator Chen Yun argued that professional management practices required that even military shipments should be paid for—in advance—urgent shipments excepted.[67]

One of Chen Yun's most pressing tasks was to repair the railways. Soviet advisers trained nearly 5,000 Fourth Field Army soldiers in railway technology by the spring of 1948.[68] Soviet technicians also played a major role in helping to rebuild railway lines and bridges. By the end of 1948, Soviets had worked on 15,000 kilometers of railway, including over 100 bridges.[69]

During the summer of 1948, as Mao Zedong and Lin Biao planned the Liao-Shen Campaign (12 September 1948–2 November 1948) that would completely defeat the Guomindang forces in Manchuria. The Communist Party controlled the major portion of Manchuria's operating railway lines and equipment. According to American intelligence reports, the Communists had "a fairly complete rail net throughout Manchuria, bypassing remaining Nationalist-held cities but connecting to the USSR, Korea, and Jehol [Rehe, in North China]." By contrast, operational railways in Nationalist hands were "limited."[70]

Communist control of the railways did not merely isolate the Nationalists in the cities, but it also helped the Communists in Manchuria to ship grain from the Northeast to units operating in grain-poor areas of North China.[71] The railways also enabled Lin Biao to move troops and supplies in order to carry out the kind of large-scale, extended operation that he would use to finally defeat the Guomindang forces in the Northeast: the Liao-Shen Campaign.

The Liao-Shen campaign was a series of battles against the remaining Nationalist forces, which were already isolated in three areas: 1) Changchun; 2) Shenyang; and 3) Jinzhou and a few related cities along the railway lines from Jinzhou to Shanhaiguan and from Jinzhou to the port of Qinhuangdao. These rail lines from Jinzhou were the Nationalists' only routes of escape; without them, Nationalist forces in Shenyang and Changchun were completely cut off. The government was keeping them supplied by airlift, at tremendous expense. Mao and the Party Center were determined that Lin Biao should "close the door and beat the dog"—cut the Nationalists' last routes of retreat and annihilate them.

The campaign that the Party Center envisioned was very ambitious, involving the deployment of units from the north to South Manchuria. The scale and aggressiveness of the plans worried Lin Biao. He doubted that he had the strength to mount a large-scale operation along the Bei-Ning line, and he feared that his best units and modern equipment would be trapped and destroyed.[72] Lin also worried that the railroads were crucial to the Communist Party's prosecution and timing of operations during the Liao-Shen campaign. In early August, Lin told the Party Center that bridges on a key freight route had been washed out and could not be repaired until the rain subsided. Mao dismissed Lin Biao's doubts as "hypothetical" and pushed him to act quickly.[73] By late August, Lin was willing to move: "The railway bridges that have been washed out can be repaired in about a week," he reported. "We plan to wait until after the railway bridges are repaired and then use three days to transport grain to be stored at Fuxin. . . . By around September 6, we can be opening fire on cities along the Bei-Ning line."[74]

By this time, the Communist armies were nothing like a guerilla force. In three short years, Communist forces in Manchuria had accumulated significant experience in mobile warfare, attacking and defending cities, and using railways. Their ranks had been reinforced by new recruits from the Manchurian countryside and by Nationalist officers and men, some captured, but others who had willingly defected. Total troop strength stood at 700,000 regular soldiers and 330,000 local militia.[75] These included railway soldiers and mechanized artillery units, both trained by Soviet advisers.[76]

The plan for the Liao-Shen campaign was to attack smaller cities along the Bei-Ning line between Jinzhou and Shanhaiguan, cut the railway, and seal up the Nationalist troops in the Northeast. Next, the Communists would attack Jinzhou, and wipe out the reinforcements that they expected the Nationalists to send out from Shenyang. Shenyang itself, and Changchun, would remain under siege, to be dealt with later.[77]

The Liao-Shen campaign went even more smoothly than expected. In early September, Communist units, moving quietly by rail and by foot, positioned themselves for attacks along the Bei-Ning line between Tangshan and Jinzhou. A smaller force set out, very openly, toward Changchun in order to make it appear as if the Communists' next move would be an attack on the city.[78] From 12 to 17 September, Lin's men successfully attacked Nationalist positions in several smaller cities between Jinzhou and Tangshan. This cut rail links from North China to Jinzhou, making it impossible for the Nationalist commander in Beiping to send reinforcements to Manchuria. Lin Biao then prepared to attack Jinzhou.

While Lin demolished railways between Manchuria and North China in order to cut the Nationalists' route of retreat, Jiang Jieshi's air force was trying to disrupt rail traffic from the Communist rear area in the north to the staging areas for the Liao-Shen campaign in the south. In late September, with Communist armies advancing on areas around Jinzhou, Nationalist airplanes bombed and strafed supply trains and truck convoys, preventing supplies from reaching the front for days at a time. In order to evade air strikes, supply trains would be accompanied by out-runners in motor vehicles in the advance and in the rear, travel only by night, and be broken up and camouflaged by day. Still, supply trains running under these difficult conditions were essential in delivering weapons and ammunition from North Manchuria and from the Soviet Union to the front during the battle for Jinzhou.[79]

The intensity of the battle for Jinzhou was determined at least in part by Jiang Jieshi's strong belief that the city was of vital strategic importance. He ordered that it be defended to the bitter end and arranged for reinforcements to be sent from the port of Huludao and from the Shenyang garrison. After a brief flurry of nervous telegrams to the Party Center, Lin Biao went through with his plans for an assault on Jinzhou, taking the city on 15 October and cutting off and wiping out the Nationalist reinforcements that had reluctantly set out from Shenyang.[80]

With all routes of retreat and reinforcement cut off, the Nationalist forces in Changchun and Shenyang could not hold out. After a bitter siege, the commanders in Changchun, who resented Jiang Jieshi, chose to surrender the city and join the Communists on 17–19 October.[81] On 1 November the Shenyang garrison was the only Nationalist force left in Manchuria. Abandoned by their commander, the soldiers put up little resistance when attacked. Lin Biao's troops entered the city in triumph on 2 November 1948.

Conclusions

When the first Chinese Communist units entered the Northeast in August and September of 1945, they gravitated toward the railway lines and major cities to obtain scarce resources. The Communist military leadership no longer viewed railway lines and railway cities as just targets to attack and sabotage. From the beginning, Communist leaders, including Mao Zedong, Peng Zhen, Chen Yun, and others, were keenly aware of the logistical benefits to be gained from controlling railways. From autumn of 1945 to spring of 1946, when they sought to control first all, and then part of Manchuria, the Communists worked to establish railway administration bureaus. Even at their lowest point, when Du Yuming's offensive had pushed their main force to Harbin, the leaders of the Northeast Bureau worked to re-open railway lines in the North Manchuria Base Area, and used railways to maintain an indirect connection via Korea to the small South Manchuria Base Area and to ship goods to and from their North China and Inner Mongolian base areas, Korea, and the Soviet Union.

Meanwhile, Jiang Jieshi's forces had also tried to use the railways to their advantage. Their initial Nationalist strategy in the Northeast was to occupy the main railway lines and cities and, using them as its supply lines and bases, to push the area of control outward. Initial success put the Nationalist troops in a vulnerable position: over-extended and unable to adequately defend the railway lines and cities that they had taken control of, they soon became targets for Communist attack. When the rail lines were cut, Nationalist units were isolated and vulnerable. Thus, while the Communist troops were on the defensive, and for much of the time when they were on the offensive as well, they placed great importance on sabotaging the railways.

As they moved from the defensive to the strategic counter-attack and the offensive, Communist leaders placed more and more emphasis on protecting and repairing railways. Mao Zedong, the Party Center, and the Northeast Bureau ordered that railways not be destroyed unless necessary for specific strategic or tactical reasons. The more territory the Communists controlled, the more they were able to use railways for their own logistical purposes. In the final stages of the civil war, Lin Biao even had to delay the start of the Liao-Shen Campaign until the rail lines linking north to south Manchuria could be re-opened.

With the end of hostilities, Communist cadres now dominated the Manchurian railroads. In early November 1948, Chen Yun became Director of the Shenyang Special City Military Administrative Committee, which was responsible for everything from securing factories to restoring electricity to keeping traffic police on the job.[82] Even before entering Shenyang, Chen had pointed to the importance of railways in shipping grain supplies to the cities.[83] As he worked on repairing the battered Manchurian railway system, Chen Yun gained the party's backing in establishing a Ministry of Railways subordinated to the Central Military Affairs Commission.[84] The Communists were especially concerned about keeping the railways in good running order, since they played a major role in the ongoing civil war by delivering supplies to the Communist armies south of the Great Wall. Party officials soon became focused on personnel management, complained about destruction and theft of electrical equipment, and ordered public security organs to teach the masses to cherish and protect railway facilities.[85] As the next chapter will show, this was a prelude to demanding that the USSR return full control of the Manchurian railways to China.

Notes

1. Steven I. Levine, *Anvil of Victory: The Communist Revolution in Manchuria, 1945–1948* (New York: Columbia University Press, 1987), 130; Levine divides the civil war in the Northeast into four stages, which will also be used in this chapter.

2. Zhu Jianhua and Zhu Xingyi. *Guogong liangdang zhengduo dongbei jishi* (How the Communist and Nationalist parties fought for control of the northeast) (Changchun: Jilin renmin chubanshe, n.d.), 23. A British Foreign Office report of 1945 estimated 9,621 kilometers. Research Department, Foreign Office, "Note on Manchurian Railways," 13 September 1945. FO 371 46271, British National Archives.

3. "Muqian renwu he zhanlue bushu" (The current situation and strategic deployment), 19 September 1945, *Liu Shaoqi xuanji (shang)* (Selected works of Liu Shaoqi] (Vol. 1)) (Beijing: Renmin chubanshe, 1981), 371–72.

4. Chinese Communist Party Central Committee and Military Affairs Commission. "Zhonggong zhongyang, zhongyang junwei guanyu gaibian zhanlue fangzhen de zhishi—muqian fangzhen zhuozhong yu duoqu xiao chengshi ji guangda xiangcun" (Central Committee and Military Affairs Commission directive regarding a change of strategy—current strategy emphasizes taking small cities and broad expanses of countryside). Document dated 22 August 1945, in Zhongyang dang'anguan, ed. *Zhonggong zhongyang wenjian xuanji* (Selected documents of the Chinese Communist Party Central Committee) volume 15 (1945) (Beijing: Zhonggong zhongyang dangxiao chubanshe, 1991), 243–44.

5. Peng Zhen, "Dongbei jiefang zhanzheng de tou jiuge yue" (The first nine months of the war of liberation in the northeast), in Zhonggong zhongyang wenxian yanjiushi, zhongyang dang'anguan *Dang de wenxian* bianjibu, editor, *Zhonggong dangshi fengyunlu* (Vivid moments of Chinese Communist Party history) (Beijing: Renmin chubanshe, 1990), 350.

6. Zhao Qingjie, *Jiaoli dongbei: Zhanhou Zhong Su guanxi yanjiu de yige zhongyao shidian* (The struggle for the northeast: a crucial vantage point for understanding post-war Chinese-Soviet relations, August 1945–May 1946), Doctoral dissertation, Nankai University, April 2006, 27. Zhang Yucai, editor.

Zhongguo tiedao jianshe shilue (1876–1949) (A brief history of Chinese railway construction, 1876–1949) (Beijing: Zhongguo tiedao chubanshe, 1997), 435.

7. Peng Zhen, 351.

8. *Zhongguo renmin jiefangjun disi yezhanjun zhanshi bianxiezu*. (Chinese People's Liberation Army Fourth Field Army Battle History) (Beijing: Jiefangjun chubanshe, 1998 [hereafter *Zhongguo renmin jiefangjun disi*]), 44.

9. Ibid., 48.

10. Zhang Yucai, 402.

11. Peng Zhen, 352.

12. "Chinese Communist Party Central Committee. "Zhongyang guanyu quanli kongzhi dongbei juzhi Jiang jun denglu zhuolu gei dongbeiju de zhishi" (Party Center directive to the Northeast Bureau on sparing no effort to control the Northeast and check Jiang's army's attempts to land or touch down). Document dated October 28, 1945, in *Zhonggong zhongyang wenjian xuanji* 15:419–20.

13. *Chen Yun Nianpu (1905–1995)* volume 1, 430, quoted in Zhao Qingjie, 126.

14. Zhai Weijia and Cao Hong, ed. *Zhongguo xiongshi disi yezhanjun* (China's great armies: the Fourth Field Army) (Beijing: Zhonggong dangshi chubanshe, 2004), 33; Tang Yilu, *Zhongguo renmin jiefangjun*, 205.

15. Zhao Qingjie, 31–32.

16. Jiang also hoped to use the Soviets to obtain more assistance from the United States. See Odd Arne Westad, *Cold War and Revolution: Soviet-American Rivalry and the Origins of the Chinese Civil War* (New York: Columbia University Press, 1993), 96–7, 100–1, 122–23.

17. Zhao Qingjie, 36–7.

18. "Zhongyang guanyu rangchu da chengshi ji Changchun tieluxian hou kaizhan dongman, beiman gongzuo gei dongbeiju de zhishi (Central Committee directive to the Northeast Bureau regarding work in east and north Manchuria after giving up major cities and the Changchun rail line), 20 November 1945. *Zhonggong zhongyang wenjian xuanji* 15, 430–31.

19. Central Committee of the Chinese Communist Party. "Zhongyang guanyu bixu lizheng zhanling de jiaotongxian ji yanxian chengshi de zhishi (Central Committee directive regarding transportation lines and cities along transportation lines that we must make strenuous efforts to occupy), document dated 12 August 1945, in *Zhonggong zhongyang wenjian xuanji* 15, 232–33; Tang Yilu, editor. *Zhongguo renmin jiefangjun quanguo jiefang zhanzhengshi* (History of the Chinese People's Liberation Army's war of national liberation), Vol. 1 (Beijing: Junshi kexue chubanshe, 1993), 144–45; Zhai and Cao, 25; Liu Tong. *Dongbei jiefang zhanzheng jishi* (Record of events of the war of liberation in the northeast) (Beijing: Dongfang chubanshe, 1997), 51; *Zhanhou diyiqi tiedao jihua* (Post-war railroad reconstruction plan, first stage) (n.p., 1947), 1–2.

20. Levine, 39.

21. Zhai and Cao, 40.

22. Liu Shaoqi, "Yi zhuyao liliang jianli dong, bei, xi man genjudi" (Deploy the main force to build base areas in eastern, northern and western Manchuria), in *Liu Shaoqi xuanji, shang*, 373–76; Dan Xiufa and Chen Yu. "Chen Yun zai dongbei

shiqi de sixiang yu shijian yanjiu shuping" (Review of research on Chen Yun's thinking and practice in the Northeast) in Zhonggong zhongyang wenxian yanjiushi Chen Yun yanjiuzu, ed. *Chen Yun yanjiu shuping* (Review of research on Chen Yun) (Beijing: Zhongyang wenxian chubanshe, 2004), 213; Peng Zhen, 353.

23. Central Committee of the Chinese Communist Party. "Zhongyang yuanyu dongbei chechu dachengshi hou de zhongxin renwu gei dongbeiju de zhishi (Central Committee directive to the Northeast Bureau regarding core tasks in the Northeast following withdrawal from the major cities), document dated 20 November 1945, in Zhongyang dang'anguan, *Zhonggong zhongyang wenjian xuanji*, 15, 433–34.

24. Peng Zhen, 354.

25. Zhang Yucai, 402, 435, 489.

26. Lin and Peng proposed attacks on Harbin, Changchun, and Shenyang in December 1945 and January 1946. The Party Center rejected these proposals. Peng Zhen, 356–57.

27. Zhao Qingjie, 41.

28. Ibid., 135.

29. Robertson to Marshall, 17 May 1946. United States National Archives, Records of the State Department, Marshall Mission Records, Box 43, "Messages— Vol. XVI-X, May 1–July 3, 1946," folder "Messages in Vol. VII 17 May 1946–2 June 1946.

30. Central Committee of the Chinese Communist Party, "Zhongyang guanyu kongzhi Changchun, Haerbin ji zhongdonglu baowei beiman gei dongbeiju de zhishi (Party central committee directive to the northeast bureau regarding control of Changchun and Harbin and defense of the China Eastern Railway), document dated 24 March 1946, in Zhongyang dang'anguan ed., *Zhonggong zhongyang wenjian xuanji* volume 16 (1946–47) (Beijing: Zhonggong zhongyang dangxiao chubanshe, 1992), 100–101; Peng Zhen, 358.

31. Peng Zhen, 358.

32. Truman to Marshall, 15 December 1945, in Lyman P. Van Slyke, ed., *Marshall's Mission to China December 1945–January 1947: the Report and Appended Documents* Vol. II, "Appended Documents," (Arlington, Virginia: University Publications of America, 1976), 1–2.

33. Yang Kuisong, "Yi jiu si liu nian Guo Gong Siping zhi zhan ji qi muhou" (Behind the curtain of the 1946 Nationalist vs. Communist battle for Siping). *Lishi yanjiu* 4 (2004) 140–41. Wang Chaoguang, *Zhonghua minguo shi di sanbian di wu juan: cong kangzhan shengli dao neizhan baofa qianhou* (History of the Republic of China, volume 3, part 5: from the victory of the war of resistance to the outbreak of civil war) (Beijing: Zhonghua shuju, 2000), 467–68; Zhonggong zhongyang wenxian yanjiushi, Zhonggong Nanjingshi weiyuan hui, ed., *Zhou Enlai yi jiu si liu nian tanpan wenxian* (Selected documents from Zhou Enlai's 1946 negotiations) (Beijing: Zhongyang wenxian chubanshe, 1996), 124, 131–32, 155–56.

34. Central Committee of the Chinese Communist Party, "Zhongyang guanyu dongbei wenti de tanpan fangzhen gei dongbeiju he zhongyang fu Yu tanpan daibiaotuan de zhishi" (Central committee directive to the Northeast bureau and the representatives to the Chongqing negotiations regarding strategy for negotiations on

the Northeast), document dated 13 March 1946, in Zhongyang dang'anguan, editor, *Zhonggong zhongyang wenjian xuanji* 16:89–91.

35. Central Committee of the Chinese Communist Party. "Zhongyang guanyu dongbei tingzhan qian jianjue baowei zhanlue yaodi gei Lin Biao, Peng Zhen de zhishi" (Central Committee directive to Lin Biao and Peng Zhen to firmly defend important strategic points prior to the cease-fire), document dated 25 March 1946, in Zhongyang dang'anguan, editor, *Zhonggong zhongyang wenxian xuanji* 16:102–3; Zhu and Zhu, 85; Central Committee of the Chinese Communist Party, "Zhongyang guanyu dongbei zuozhan wenti de buchong zhishi" (Central Committee supplementary directive on questions of the prosecution of war in the northeast), document dated 8 April 1946 in Zhongyang dang'anguan, editor, *Zhonggong zhongyang wenxian xuanji* 16: 112–13; Central Committee of the Chinese Communist Party, "Zhongyang guanyu dui wanjun jinxing zhengzhi gongshi ji chedi pohuai tielu gei dongbeiju de zhishi" (Central committee directive to the Northeast Bureau on carrying out political assaults on the opposing army and on thoroughly destroying railroads), document dated 16 April 1946 in Ibid., 127–28; Central Committee of the Chinese Communist Party, "Guanyu junshi douzheng yu qunzhong gongzuo wenti gei dongbeiju ji Lin Biao de zhishi" (Central committee directive to the Northeast bureau and Lin Biao regarding questions of military struggle and mass work). document dated 12 April 1946, in Ibid., 118–19.

36. Junshi kexueyuan junshi lishi yanjiubu, *Zhongguo renmin jiefangjun quanshi* (hereafter Junshi kexueyuan), 28; Zhu and Zhu, 105.

37. *Zhongguo renmin jiefangjun disi,* 91–2.

38. Peng Zhen, 359. Huang Kecheng, "Cong Subei dao dongbei—xinsijun disan shi jinjun dongbei canjia dongbei jiefang zhanzheng de huigu" (From Subei to the northeast—recollections of the New Fourth Army Third Division's deployment in the Northeast to join the War of Liberation in the Northeast), *Zhongguo dangshi ziliao 16* (Reference materials on Chinese Communist Party history, Vol. 16), 74.

39. Zhang Yucai, 510, 545.

40. Peng Zhen, 360.

41. Historians differ on the significance of the Marshall ceasefire. See Harold M. Tanner, "Guerilla, Mobile and Base Warfare in Communist Military Operations in Manchuria, 1945–1947," *The Journal of Military History* 67 (October 2003), 1221.

42. Zhonggong zhongyang wenxian yanjiushi, *Chen Yun nianpu: 1905–1994* (A chronology of Chen Yun's life: 1904–1994), Vol. 1 (Beijing: Zhongyang wenxian chubanshe, 2000), 473.

43. Zhu and Zhu, 172–73; Zhai and Cao, 77.

44. "Current Reports on Railroad Destruction," 17 March 1947. United States Archives, Army Intelligence Document File, Box 2351, MIS #358537.

45. Zhao Qingjie, 155; Westad, 175; Levine, 128, 240.

46. Zhonggong zhongyang wenxian yanjiushi, editor. *Chen Yun nianpu,* 1:468.

47. "Mao Zedong hao" jicheshi bianxie xiaozu, "'Mao Zedong hao' jicheshi (chugao) (History of the locomotive 'Mao Zedong' (draft)), 10–15. Document consulted in the Reference Room of the Museum of the Liao-Shen Campaign, Jinzhou, China, June 2008.

48. *News Excerpts* Vol. 2 no. 3 (October 2, 1946). Hoover Institution Archives, China Subject Collection, Box #2; *News Excerpts* Vol. 2 no. 18 (October 22, 1946), Hoover Institution Archives, Chinese Subject Collection, Box #2.

49. "Yao Liang (Yao Tingqu) Tongzhi tanhua jilu" (Record of a conversation with comrade Yao Liang (Yao Tingqu)). Changchun defang shizhi bianzuan weiyuanhui, ed., Changchun dangshi ziliao (Materials on Changchun Party History), volume 1 (Changchun: n.p., 1987), 141–42.

50. Central Committee Military Affairs Commission. "Junwei guanyu shenru dongbei dihou kaizhan youji zhanzheng gei Huang Kecheng deng do zhishi" (Military Affairs Commission directive to Huang Kecheng et al. on penetrating deep into the enemy rear to carry out guerilla warfare), document dated 26 May 1946, in Zhongyang dang'anguan, *Zhonggong zhongyang wenjian xuanji* 16:173–74; Zhu and Zhu, 121.

51. Zhu and Zhu, 190; Zhai and Cao, 88.

52. By contrast, in spring 1947, the Nationalist Ministry of Communications did not plan any extensive repair work on the Manchurian railways: "Rail lines will be pieced together as recovered, but the recognized ability of the Communist forces to hold in a small area, permit Central Government troops to pass through, then cut the rail supply lines to their rear, makes thorough restoration impracticable." Assistant Military Attaché, Nanjing, China, "Intelligence Report," 18 March 1947. United States National Archives, Army Intelligence Document File, Box 2316, MIS #353942.

53. *Zhongguo renmin jiefangjun disi*, 185–86.

54. Zhai and Cao, 101.

55. Levine, 132.

56. Junshi kexueyuan, 122–23.

57. Central Committee of the Chinese Communist Party, "Zhongyang guanyu tingzhi polu de zhishi" (Central Committee directive on halting destruction of railways), document dated 4 June 1947, in Zhonggong dang'anguan, *Zhonggong zhongyang wenjian xuanji* 16:460–61.

58. Junshi kexueyuan, 183.

59. Westad, 173, 175; Zhai and Cao, 112; Junshi kexueyuan, 182–83.

60. Du Yuming, "Liao-Shen Zhanyi gaishu" (Brief overview of the Liao-Shen Campaign), Zhongguo renmin zhengzhi xieshang huiyi quanguo weiyuanhui wenshi ziliao yanjiu weiyuanhui "Liao-Shen zhanyi qinliji" bianshenzu, ed. *Liaoshen zhanyi qinliji: yuan Guomindang jiangling de huiyi* (Personal records of the Liao-Shen campaign: memories of former Guomindang generals) (Beijing: Wenshi ziliao chubanshe, 1985), 4.

61. Junshi kexueyuan, 221.

62. Zhonggong zhongyang wenxian yanjiushi, *Chen Yun nianpu*, 1:515–16.

63. Zhai and Cao, 121–22.

64. Map 11 "Liaoshen zhanyi qian shuangfang taishitu" (Positions of the two sides prior to the Liao-Shen campaign), in *Zhongguo renmin jiefangjun disi*.

65. Junshi kexueyuan, 223.

66. Zhang Yucai, 584.

67. Zhonggong zhongyang wenxian yanjiushi, *Chen Yun nianpu*, 1:522.

68. Zhao Qingjie, 155; Westad, 175; Levine, 128, 240.

69. Zhao Qingjie, 155.

70. General Headquarters Far East Command, Military Intelligence Section, General Staff, "Intelligence Summary" no. 2137, 21 June 1948, 2. United States National Archives, Army Intelligence Document File, box 3060, MIS # 472782.

71. Zhongyang junwei guanyu chouhua you dongbei yunshu liangshi zhi Jin-Yu-Jin-Ping ji Zhang-Sui-Bao liang xian zhi Lin Biao, Luo Ronghuan, Liu Yalou deng dian" (Central Military Commission telegram to Lin Biao, Luo Ronghuan and Liu Yalou regarding preparation and plans for shipment of grain from the northeast to the Jinzhou-Shanhaiguan-Tianjin-Beiping and the Zhanjiakou-Guisui-Baotou lines), 31 May 1948, in Zhang Zanxin, Sun Shufan and Gao Yingjie, ed. *Changchun weikunzhan* (The siege of Changchun) (Changchun: Zhonggong Changchun shiwei dangshi yanjiushi, 1999), 23–4.

72. Westad, 193–94. Lin's temerity was a cause of friction between him and Mao Zedong.

73. *Zhongguo renmin jiefangjun disi*, 303-304; Junshi kexueyuan, 250; Westad, 193.

74. Quoted in Junshi kexueyuan, 250.

75. William W. Whitson, *The Chinese High Command: A History of Communist Military Politics, 1927–71* (New York: Praeger Publishers, 1973), 312.

76. Zhao Qingjie, 155; Westad, 196.

77. *Zhongguo renmin jiefangjun,* 306.

78. Zhai and Cao, 140.

79. "Shenglidi wancheng jianju er jinji de junshi yunshu renwu—ji Qitie Angangxi 3005 ci lieche zhiqian de yingyong shiji" (Victorious completion of an emergency military transport task—a record of the heroic feats of the Qiqihaer railway's Ang'angxi train number 3005), document consulted in the Reference Room of the Museum of the Liao-Shen Campaign, Jinzhou, China, June 2008.

80. Ibid., 140–52. See also *Zhongguo renmin jiefangjun disi*, 324–26; Whitson, 314; Westad, 196.

81. *Zhongguo renmin jiefangjun disi*, 327–29.

82. Chen Yun, "Jieshou Shenyang de jingyan [Lessons from taking over Shenyang], *Chen Yun wenxuan (1926–1949)* [Chen Yun: selected writings, 1926–1949]. Beijing: Renmin chubanshe, 1984, 269–74.

83. Zhonggong zhongyang wenxian yanjiushi, *Chen Yun nianpu*, 1:532.

84. Dan Xiufa and Chen Yu, "Chen Yun zai dongbei shiqi de sixiang yu shijian yanjiu shuping," 223.

85. Zhang Wentian, "Guanyu dongbei jingji goucheng ji jingji jianshe jiben fangzhen de tigang." (Outline of the structure and basic guiding principles of the economy of the Northeast), document dated 15 September 1948, in Zhonggong zhongyang dangshi ziliao zhengji weiyuanhui, Zhongguo renmin jiefangjun Liaoshen zhanyi jinianguan jianguan weiyuanhui, ed., *Liao-Shen juezhan* (The Liao-Shen Campaign), Vol. 1 (Beijing: Renmin chubanshe, 1988), 51; Dongbei renmin zhengfu ling (Order of the Northeast people's government), dated 22 November 1949, in *Jubao* volume 2, no. 5 (2 December 1949), 1.

8
Return of the Chinese Changchun Railway to China by the USSR

Zhang Shengfa

This chapter will focus on the USSR's 1952 return of the Chinese Changchun Railway (CCR) to the People's Republic of China.[1] In addition to examining the negotiations conducted by Sino-Soviet leaders during 1949 and 1950, it will use both Russian and Chinese documentary materials to evaluate the circumstances surrounding the final handover of this railway, as well as analyzing the main reasons why the Soviet Union agreed to return the CCR to China and this decision's impact on the Sino-Soviet relations. Since the railway line historically had close links with the port cities of Lüshun (formerly Port Arthur) and Dalian (formerly Dairen), this chapter will also include information of the status of these two cities.

Early Sino-Soviet Negotiations Concerning the Chinese Changchun Railway

During World War II, the fate of the Chinese northeastern region, including the exclusive railway system, was negotiated by the United States and the Soviet Union. In February 1945 at the Yalta conference, the political conditions for the Soviet Union entering the war against Japan were discussed, and the Yalta Agreement determined that the Chinese Eastern Railroad (CER) and the South Manchuria Railroad, which provides an outlet to Dalian, should be operated by the establishment of a joint Soviet-Chinese Company.[2] During August 1945, according to the spirit of the Yalta Agreement, the Soviet and the Chinese Nationalist government signed the "Sino-Soviet Treaty of Friendship and Alliance," as well as agreements on the CER, Dalian, and Lüshun. According to these, the CER and South Manchurian Railway were merged and renamed as the CCR, placed under Sino-Soviet joint possession, and managed by a CCR company composed of Sino-Soviet representatives assigned to a Council and Board of Supervisors; after thirty years, the railway would be returned to China free of charge.[3]

However, during the increasing tensions of the Chinese civil war, which was focused primarily in Manchuria, it proved impossible to implement the joint management of the CCR. In the summer of 1946, after the outbreak of full-scale civil war between the Guomindang (GMD) and the Communist Party of China (CPC, or in some sources CCP), many sections and stations of the CCR were destroyed, and the railway operations were at a standstill. Initially, Moscow sought to cooperate with the West to protect the vested interests that the Yalta system brought to the Soviet Union.[4] However, the formal alliance between the Guomindang and the Soviet Union soon broke apart, in particular when the USSR openly supported the Chinese Communists.[5] From 1947 onwards, as a result of the outbreak of the U.S.-Soviet Cold War and the strategic counterattack of the Communists' forces in the civil war, Stalin's attitude and stance toward the Communists and the Chinese revolution changed gradually from passive indifference to active support.[6]

In 1949, in expectation of the Communists' upcoming victory, the CPC's political ties with Moscow were strengthened. During January–February 1949, Mikoyan, a politburo member of the Central Committee of All-Union Communist Party (Bolshevik), paid a visit to the Xibaipo, the Communist headquarters. The leaders of the two parties exchanged views on the issue of the Lüshun and the CCR.

According to the Soviet record, discussing with Mikoyan on 4 February 1950 about treaties with foreign countries the GMD government signed, including the 1945 Soviet-Chinese treaty: "Mao Zedong informed that in his talk with the Chinese democratic leaders, they explained that they understand the coming abolition of the traitorous treaty Chiang Kai-shek [Jiang Jieshi] signed. They are not asking for the abolition of all treaties signed by Chiang Kai-shek, because some have a patriotic meaning. For example, the following treaties belong to this kind: 1. the treaties concerning the abolition of foreigners' extraterritoriality in China [good examples include the Sino-American and Sino-British treaty signed in January 1943–Note by author]; 2. in accordance [with] the so-called eight country treaty [the 1922 Nine Power Treaty–Note by author] the rights were cancelled; 3. the Soviet-Chinese treaty on the CCR and Lüshun."[7]

Mikoyan asked Mao Zedong: "in his talk (with the democratic leaders) how he demonstrated the patriotic nature of the Sino-Soviet treaty," "responding to it, Mao Zedong said with a smile that this treaty was not signed by him, but Chiang Kai-shek." Mao Zedong added: "I explained to them that the Soviet Union has come to Lüshun in order to defend itself and China against Japanese fascism, because without help from the Soviet Union, China is too weak to be unable to defend itself. The Soviet Union not as an imperialist power but as a socialist power has come . . . in order to safeguard common interests."[8]

When asked about why the Communists opposed the U.S. base in Qingdao, China, and actually supported the Soviet base in Lüshun, Mao Zedong answered: "the U.S. imperialism in China is to carry on the oppression (of China), but the Soviet Union having its troops in Lüshun is to guard against Japanese fascism. When China become powerful and can itself resist the Japanese danger, the Soviet Union no longer need the base Lüshun."[9] According to the later Mikoyan report, he explained the Central Committee (CC) of the All-Union Communist Party (Bolshevik) and Stalin's position on this issue: "If the Chinese government is the Communist one, the Soviet Union would not need the base there."[10]

On 5 February, after receiving Mikoyan's report, Stalin in a telegram to Mao Zedong said: "With [the] coming into power by the Chinese communists, the situation will change fundamentally. The Soviet government has decided that once the peace treaty with Japan is signed and the U.S. troops withdraw from Japan, the unequal treaty would be abolished. If, however, the CPC thinks that it is better to immediately withdraw the Soviet forces from Lüshunkou, the Soviet Union would be prepared to meet the aspirations of the Chinese Communists."[11]

In their talks on 6 February, the leaders of the two parties discussed specially the 1945 Sino-Soviet agreements. Mikoyan said:

> On the problems relating the Sino-Soviet Treaty, I said, we believe that the Soviet-Chinese treaty on Lüshunkou is unequal, the signature of the treaty was to prevent the GMD from collusion with Japan and the United States against the Soviet Union and the Chinese liberation movement. I said that the treaty brought some benefits to the Chinese liberation movement, but with the CPC coming to power, China's domestic situation has undergone a fundamental change. Therefore, I added, the Soviet government decided that as long as a peace treaty with Japan was signed, it would immediately abolish the unequal treaty and withdraw the Soviet troops from Lüshunkou. However, if the CPC considers that the Soviet troops should be immediately withdrawn, the Soviet Union would meet this requirement. As for the CCR Treaty, we do not think it is an unequal treaty, this is because the Railway was mainly financed by Russia. The treaty may not fully reflect the principle of equality, however, I said, we intend to discuss and resolve this issue with the Chinese comrades in a friendly manner.[12]

Mikoyan described the positive reaction of Mao Zedong and other Chinese leaders to his speech:

> After hearing the evaluation on the treaty, [the reaction of] Mao Zedong and members of the Political Bureau appeared to be very sudden. They did not hide their surprise. After the talks, Mao

Zedong and the members of the Political Bureau almost unanimously believed that the Soviet Union should not withdraw its troops from Liaodong and abolish its base in Lüshunkou immediately, because if we do so, it could only be benefit to the United States. Mao Zedong said, 'we will keep the secret on the issue of withdrawal of the Soviet troops from Liaodong. In the future, when China smashes the reactionary political forces and people are mobilized for the expropriation of foreign capital, and with the Soviet help the country is to be in an orderly manner, we will reconsider the treaty.' Mao Zedong said, 'the Chinese peoples [are] grateful to the Soviet Union for the treaty. When we get strong, you can leave China, and by that time we will be able to sign the Soviet-Sino Mutual Assistance Treaty similar with the Soviet-Polish treaty'."[13]

It is clear from Mikoyan's report and telegram that Stalin and the other Soviet leaders deemed the 1945 Sino-Soviet agreements to be both unequal and equal: the agreement on Lüshun was unequal, while the CCR was equal. Even if the agreement on Lüshun was unequal, it was originally designed to prevent the Nationalists from allying with Japan and the United States against the Soviet Union and the Chinese Communists, so the inequality in fact benefitted the Chinese revolution.[14] On the one hand, while Stalin did not want to give up the overall special interests in China, on the other hand, Stalin was prepared to sacrifice some of the USSR's local interests in the Manchurian railways to acquire an important political ally.

Mao Zedong and the other Chinese leaders were well aware that under existing conditions, including the U.S.-Soviet Cold War and the division of the world into two opposing camps, the new China would need the Soviet support and assistance. In their view, in the early days of the new China the Soviet troops stationed in Lüshun might help prop up China's security. Therefore, from the point of view of China's security needs, it was important for the PRC to continue to endure unequal relations with the Soviet Union. Consequently, Mao Zedong not only did not demand that the Soviet Union withdraw its troops at this time, but he even expressed "gratitude" for agreement keeping the Soviet army in Lüshun. However, the Soviet leaders also left open the door for renegotiating Sino-Soviet Treaty in the near future.

From February 1949, Stalin asked repeatedly through telegrams to Kovalev, a representative of the CC of All-Union Communist Party (Bolshevik), in China: "What is the real attitude of the Chinese comrades to the agreement on the CCR? Do they think that the agreement is truly equal?"[15] During June–August 1949, Party

Secretary Liu Shaoqi secretly visited the Soviet Union. On 4 July, in the report to the All-Union Communist Party (Bolshevik) and Stalin on the Sino-Soviet Treaty in 1945, Liu Shaoqi raised the following three methods of the treatment: "1. China's new government will announce that the treaty shall remain in force without any modification. 2. According to the original spirit of the Treaty, the representatives of the governments of both countries will sign a new Sino-Soviet Treaty on Friendship and Alliance. 3. Through exchanging the notes by the representatives of the governments of both countries, the *status quo* of the Treaty will be temporarily maintained, but at the appropriate time the new treaty will be prepared to be signed." Of these "three ways, which kind shall we take as a best way?" Liu Shaoqi wrote in his report, to which Stalin replied: "This problem will be decided after Mao Zedong comes to Moscow."[16]

Opening Negotiations for the 1950 Sino-Soviet Treaty

Shortly after the founding of the People's Republic of China on 1 October 1949, Mao Zedong made a two month-long visit to the Soviet Union from December 1949 to February 1950 to discuss out-standing problems with the 1945 Sino-Soviet treaty.[17] Stalin initially refused to open negotiations on a new treaty, and it took Mao almost two weeks to change his mind.

According to the record of Mao's first talk with Stalin on 16 December 1949, Stalin had some misgivings discussing changes to the Sino-Soviet treaty and the Yalta Agreement. After a simple exchange of views on signing a peace treaty with Japan, Mao Zedong in an indirect way put forward a new treaty issue: "Since Liu Shaoqi's return to China from the Soviet Union, CC CPC has been discussing the issue of the Sino-Soviet treaty of friendship, alliance and mutual assistance." Stalin replied: "We should discuss and resolve the issue. We need to ascertain whether to declare retaining the current 1945 Sino-Soviet Treaty of Friendship and Alliance, to announce impending changes in the future, or to make these changes right now." But Stalin then made it absolutely clear to Mao that the USSR wanted to retain the treaty unchanged:

> As we all know, the Soviet-Sino treaty was concluded as a result of the Yalta Agreement, which provided for the several most important points (the question of the Kurile Islands, South Sakhalin, Port Arthur, etc.). This means that the given treaty was concluded with the consent of America and England. Keeping in mind this circumstance, we, within our inner circle, have decided not to modify any of the points of the treaty for now, since a

change in even one point could give America and England the legal grounds to raise question about modifying also the treaty's provisions concerning the Kurile Islands, South Sakhalin, etc. This is why we searched to find a way to modify the current treaty in effect while formally maintaining its provisions, in this case by formally maintaining the Soviet Union's right to station its troops at Port Arthur while, at the request of the Chinese government, actually withdrawing the Soviet Armed forces currently stationed there. Such an operation could be carried out upon China's request.

One could do the same with the KChZhD [CCR], this is, to effectively modify the corresponding points of the agreement while formally maintaining its provisions, upon China's request.

If the Chinese comrades are not satisfied with the proposition, they can present their own proposals.[18]

In order not to touch the Yalta Agreement, Stalin did not want to sign a new Soviet-Sino treaty that might be inconsistent with the Yalta Agreement, in particular since the 1945 Sino-Soviet Treaty itself was the product of the Yalta agreement. Although the Cold War had already started, neither the United States nor the USSR wanted to destroy the basic framework of the Yalta agreement. Therefore, Stalin advocated retaining the 1945 Sino-Soviet Treaty and agreements *in toto*, while actually modifying individual terms by signing separate provisions.

Mao Zedong, who had already announced his pro-Soviet policy of "leaning to one side," certainly could not dispute Stalin's wishes, even though he had come to Moscow with the clear intention of signing a new Sino-Soviet treaty recognizing the legitimacy of the new Communist government in China. Therefore, to leave Moscow without such a treaty could have a highly negative impact on Mao's position as leader of the PRC.

Mao was temporarily at a loss for words. However, he agreed to maintain the *status quo*: "the present situation with regard to KChZhD [CCR] and Port Arthur corresponds well with Chinese interests, as the Chinese forces are inadequate to effectively fight against imperialist aggression. In addition, KChZhD is a training school for the preparation of the Chinese cadres in railroad and industry." Mao then blamed himself for his ill-timed suggestion that the treaty be changed: "In discussing the treaty in China we had not taken into account the American and English positions regarding the Yalta agreement. We must act in a way that is best for the common cause. This question merits further consideration." Mao immediately added, "However, it is already becoming clear that the treaty should not be modified at the present time, nor should one rush to withdraw troops from Port Arthur."[19]

Even though Mao agreed to retain the 1945 treaty unchanged, he was clearly reluctant to put this issue of the Sino-Soviet Treaty on the shelf. This is revealed by Mao's next question to Stalin: "Should not Zhou Enlai come to Moscow to decide the treaty question?" Stalin ambiguously replied, "No, this question you must decide for yourselves. Zhou Enlai may be needed in regard to other matters."[20]

Stalin's decision not to renegotiate the treaty with Zhou Enlai left Mao with nothing to do in Moscow, which was a very embarrassing situation for Mao to be in. From 16 to 24 December, before a second talk could be scheduled, Mao remained in a bad mood and stayed almost the entire time at his government villa, with the sole exception of participating in Stalin's seventieth birthday celebration activities on 21 December.

On 22 December, the day after Stalin's birthday party, Mao asked Kovalev to suggest to Stalin that meetings be held on 23 and 24 December to resolve all outstanding issues with regard to the Sino-Soviet Treaty, the loan agreement, the trade treaty, and to the aviation agreement, etc. Once new terms had been achieved, then Zhou Enlai could be invited to come to Moscow to perform the signing procedures.[21] But, during the second meeting between Stalin and Mao on 24 December, the two leaders discussed the general affairs of the Asian Communist Parties, and the problem of the Sino-Soviet treaty was never even mentioned at all.

Although clearly upset by Stalin's poor treatment, Mao was determined to force Stalin to change his mind. On 1 January 1950, in a conversation with N. Roshchin, the Soviet ambassador to China, Mao revealed: "In recent days, he received a report from Beijing. According to the report, Myanmar and the Indian government were willing to recognize the People's Republic of China. . . . There was also information which suggested that Britain and other countries of Commonwealth of Nations would take the obvious steps to recognize the PRC." Mao also said, "During this time, He would like to meet Stalin to discuss practical issues."[22]

Mao's warning to Roshchin contained multiple meanings: First, if India and Myanmar recognized the PRC, and then convinced England to do likewise, then this implied that China's relations with the West were warming, which was something the Soviet Union most likely wanted to prevent. Second, if the United Kingdom recognized China, while the United States did not so, it showed that the position of America and England were inconsistent, so that signing a new Sino-Soviet treaty would not necessarily result in the United States and Britain trying to overturn Yalta. Third, a new Sino-Soviet Treaty would be the best way to counter Western attempts to split apart China and the USSR.[23]

Meanwhile, it was absolutely true that the Western countries were trying their best to drive a wedge between China and the Soviet Union. Since Mao rarely appeared in public after his short visit at Stalin's birthday party, the Western media were reporting that Mao Zedong had been placed under house arrest by Stalin.[24] Although this was only a rumor, the press reports were correct in asserting that Mao's decision to remain in his villa indicated increasing Sino-Soviet tensions. In order to display unbroken solidarity between China and the Soviet Union, and to prevent the West from attempting to undermine these relations, Stalin may have decided that a new treaty of alliance was the best way to eliminate these rumors.

Thus, Stalin decided to change his original position on the Sino-Soviet Treaty. On 1 January 1950, Kovalev was ordered by Stalin to visit Mao to report that Stalin had approved Mao's planned interview with reporters of the TASS Agency announcing that Mao's visit to the Soviet Union would include resolving problems with the existing Sino-Soviet Treaty and other issues.[25] In this backhanded way, Stalin communicated to Mao that his position on a new Sino-Soviet Treaty had changed. Mao was naturally very pleased that his implied threat to move closer to the West had forced Stalin to back down.

The Status of the Manchurian Railways in the 1950 Sino-Soviet Treaty

On 2 January 1950, Molotov and Mikoyan came to Mao's residence, and consulted with him about the problem of the Sino-Soviet Treaty. Mao Zedong reiterated China's three proposals that the two countries should sign a new Sino-Soviet Treaty, delay negotiations, or sign a statement clarifying the main points of their relations. Molotov said he agreed with the first one, which is what Mao clearly wished, to which Mao asked: "Does a new treaty replace the old one?" Molotov gave a definite answer: "Yes." To this, Mao responded that he would order Zhou Enlai to come to the Soviet Union to negotiate and sign the treaty.[26]

On 6 January, in a talk with Vyshinsky, the Soviet foreign minister, Mao reiterated that China and the Soviet Union should sign a new treaty: "The new treaty, which would be signed between us, will reflect the completely new type of relationship between the PRC and the Soviet Union after the victory of (the Chinese) people's revolution. It is absolutely necessary to reconsider the existing treaty, because two important components (Japan and the GMD) have already undergone major changes: Japan is no longer an armed force, and the GMD has already collapsed. Besides, as we all know, among the Chinese people some people are discontented by the existing Sino-Soviet Treaty. Therefore, it is in interest of both sides to sign a new Sino-Soviet Treaty of Friendship and Alliance."[27]

Vyshinsky replied: "In my view, it seems that the new treaty is a complex matter, because the signing of a new treaty or reviewing of the existing treaty, and any changes in the treaty will be used as excuses for the review and revision of other parts of the Treaty by Americans and the British. This change would have damaged the interests of the Soviet Union and China. This is what we do not want, and [should] not be allowed to happen." Mao replied: "There is no doubt that when we are determining the prospects of signing the treaty, this must be considered."[28]

It also appears that the Soviets were worried that the new treaty might have a negative impact on Soviet special rights and privileges in China. In early January, Kovalev submitted his report on the CCR to Stalin.[29] Kovalev believed that Chinese were not sincere when they said that they continued to support the terms of the 1945 Treaty: "Mao Zedong, Liu Shaoqi, Zhou Enlai, and Gao Gang have many times stated that the treaty on the Chinese Changchun Railway is just and good, totally satisfying the interests of the Chinese people." But, assuming a more critical tone, he wrote:

> However, on the eve of Zhou Enlai's departure for Moscow, acting on his instructions, the minister railway of China, Deng Daiyuan, through the chief of the General Board of Railways of Manchuria, Yu Guangsheng, asked the manager of the Chinese Changchun Railway, comrade Zhuravlev, on what basis the Chinese Changchun Railway would work in the future; answering comrade Zhuravlev's question about their own thoughts on this matter, Yu Guangsheng conveyed the opinion of Deng Daiyuan that it would be desirable not to single out the Chinese Changchun Railway from the railway system of Manchuria. Probably for this reason, the Chinese side until now has not nominated its leading representatives for the joint management of the railway (in accordance with the 1945 treaty). Nor, in connection with this, has any [financial] accounting for the activities of the Chinese Changchun Railway [in its operation, apart] from the [other] Manchurian railways been introduced. Since its restoration, the Chinese Changchun Railway has in fact been managed by the Chinese, who are also in command of the railway's finances, while Soviet railway personnel, headed by the manager of the railway, all in all 277 people . . . have found themselves in the positions of adviser-consultants.

Kovalev further wrote: "Such behavior by Zhou Enlai can be explained by nothing else than pressure on the government of China from the right wing of the national bourgeoisie, which has pro-American inclinations, [which] considers the treaty on the Chinese Changchun Railway of 1945 unequal, and hopes for the railway's transfer as the exclusive property of China and for the Soviet side's exclusion from the territory of Manchuria."[30]

Kovalev further warned Stalin: "For my own part, [I] consider that it is not in the interests of the Soviet Union to permit a change in the conditions of the 1945 treaty on the Chinese Changchun Railway, and that the order for its use as defined by this treaty should be preserved." To this end, he suggested that the Soviet Union should take the following actions:

(1) To reiterate the treaty conditions on the management and use of the Chinese Changchun Railway as settled in 1945.

(2) To require the Chinese side to immediately nominate its representatives to the Executive Board of the Society of the Chinese Changchun Railway, to the Audit Committee of the society, and to the Management Department of the railway.

(3) To create a Soviet-Chinese commission to draft the constitution of the board of the Railroad and identify the railway's property.

(4) To introduce separate [financial] accounting on the operations of the railway within the Limits of the treaty boundaries because the absence of such accounting every day brings loses to the economic interests of the USSR.

(5) To put the port of Dalian and the Dal'dok plant under the single, already operating Society of the Chinese Changchun Railway without creating a separate society for it.[31]

Kovalev's report showed that the differences between two nations on the problem of the CCR were profound. Most important among them was that the Soviet Union really did not want to give up its special privileges in the CCR. It took Stalin's personal intervention to make this crucial decision.

Stalin's Decision to Abandon Soviet Privileges in China

On 20 January 1950, the Chinese premier and foreign minister Zhou Enlai came to Moscow to take part in negotiations on the conclusion of the Sino-Soviet treaty and supplemental agreements. Dealing with the Soviet rights and interests in China's northeast, including the CCR, was one of the most sensitive and important problems in the negotiations between the two countries. In the talks on 22 January, the leaders of the two countries explained their basic standpoints on the problems regarding the treaty and agreements.

About the Sino-Soviet treaty and agreements in 1945, Stalin said, "We believe that these agreements need to be changed, though earlier we had thought that they could be left intact. The existing agreements, including the treaty, should be changed because war against Japan figures at the very heart of the treaty. Since the war is over and Japan has been crushed, the situation has been altered, and now the treaty has become an anachronism." Mao Zedong replied: "It is necessary to fundamentally distinguish our future treaty from the existing one," and "the new treaty should include the problems of political, economic, cultural and military cooperation. Of most importance will be the problem of economic cooperation." Stalin agreed with Mao Zedong. Therefore, both sides entrusted Vyshinsky and Zhou Enlai with drawing up the treaty draft.[32]

About the CCR, the Chinese side presented its own requests in a tactful way. Mao stated, "perhaps we might accept as the guiding principle the idea of making practical changes concerning the CCR (KChZhD) and the Lüshunkou (Port Arthur) agreements, while legally continuing them in their present state." Stalin asked: "That is, you agree to declare the legal continuation of the current agreement, while, in effect, allowing appropriate changes to take place." Mao answered, "We must consider the interests of both sides, China and the Soviet Union." Mao then said: "The basic idea is that the new treaty should note that joint exploitation and joint management will continue in the future. However, in the case of management, China should play a major role. Furthermore, it is necessary to examine the question of shortening the duration of the agreement and to determine the amount of investment by each side."[33]

On the question of the railway management, Molotov argued: "The conditions governing the cooperation and joint management of an enterprise by two interested countries usually provide for equal participation by both sides, as well as for alternation in the appointment of replacements for management positions. In the old agreement the management of the railroad belonged to the Soviet side; however, in the future we think it necessary to alternate in the creation of management functions. Let's say that such an alternation could take place every two-three years." Zhou Enlai replied: "Our comrades believe that the existing management of the CCR and the office of the director ought to be abolished and a railroad administration commission be set up in their place; and that the offices of the commission chairman and of the director should be replaced by Chinese cadres. However, given comrade Molotov's proposals, this question requires more thought." Stalin made his views known: "If we are talking about joint administration, then it is important that the replacement for the managing position be alternated. That would be more logical. As for the duration of the agreement, we would not be against shortening it."[34]

Zhou Enlai immediately asked: "Should we not change the ratio of capital investment by each side, by increasing the level of Chinese investment to 51 percent, instead of the current requirement for parity?" Molotov expressed his opposition: "This would go against the existing provision for parity." To this Stalin added: "Since we already have joint administration, then we might as well have equal participation." Finally, Mao Zedong compromised: "The question needs to be further examined, keeping in mind the interests of both sides."[35]

This discussion revealed that while the Soviet side agreed to shorten the duration of the agreement and reached agreement with the Chinese side on the direction of joint management and operation, it had differences with the Chinese side on the ratio of capital investment and the distribution of leadership positions. The Chinese side demanded that it predominate in the ratio of capital investment and the managing positions so as to emphasize its sovereignty over the CCR. Finally, both sides agreed to shorten the duration of the agreement.

As for Lüshun, as Mao Zedong previously suggested, the Lüshun agreement legally continued, while, in fact, the two sides made appropriate changes to it. Stalin admitted that the agreement on Lüshun was unequal.[36] However, Stalin attempted to argue that this unequal agreement had a positive side: "As you know, we made the current agreement during the war against Japan. We did not know that Chiang Kai-shek would be toppled. We acted under the premise that the presence of our troops in Lüshunkou would be in the interests of the Soviet Union and democracy in China." Because the People's Liberation Army did obtain benefits from the presence of the Soviet troops in China's northeast and the CPC received actual assistance from the Soviet Union, Mao Zedong said without thinking, "This matter is clear."[37]

Later, Stalin presented two solutions: "declare that the agreement on Lüshunkou shall remain in force until a peace treaty with Japan is signed, after which the Soviet troops would be withdrawn from Lüshunkou . . . declare that the current agreement shall remain in place, while in effect withdrawing troops from Lüshunkou." He said that the Soviet side would agree with either of these solutions.[38]

Mao replied: "We agree with the opinion of Comrade Stalin and believe that the agreement on Lüshunkou must remain in force until a peace treaty is signed with Japan, after which the agreement shall become invalid and the Soviet troops will leave. However, we would like for Lüshunkou to be a place for military collaboration, where we could train our military naval forces."[39] Accordingly, the compromise Stalin and Mao reached was that after a peace treaty with Japan was signed, the agreement on Lüshun would be abolished, and the Soviet troops would leave. This compromise at least temporarily satisfied Stalin's desire, since the bases would not be dismantled, and the Soviet troops would remain.

With regard to Dalian, Stalin said: "We have no intention of securing any Soviet rights in Dalian." However, at the same time, he pointed out that if Dalian remained a free port, "it is a house with open gates." Mao understood what Stalin meant: "We believe that the Lüshunkou could serve as a base for our military collaboration, while Dalian could serve as a base for Sino-Soviet economic collaboration. In Dalian there is a whole array of enterprises that we are in no position to exploit without Soviet assistance. We should develop a closer economic collaboration there."[40]

The talks between Stalin and Mao determined the basic direction and framework for the future negotiations. After these talks, both sides better understood the other side's positions. Subsequently, in the process of negotiations on the specific treaty and agreements, the conflicts of interest of both sides were exposed.

Finalizing the Sino-Soviet Treaty

By the terms of the "Sino-Soviet Treaty of Friendship, Alliance and Mutual Assistance" and the agreement on the CCR, Lüshun, and Dalian signed by Stalin and Mao during February 1950, the CCR was to be jointly managed and operated by the two countries. On 1 May 1950, the CCR Company jointly organized by China and the Soviet Union began operations. However, according to the various provisions of this treaty and subsidiary agreements, the USSR actually retained full use of the CCR and the naval base in Lüshun.

Even as early as 5 January 1950, article VII of the Sino-Soviet treaty draft drawn up by the Soviet Union stipulated: "High Contracting Parties recognize that the Agreements between the Soviet Union and the Chinese Republic, which were concluded on 14 August 1945, on the CCR, on Port Arthur, and on the harbor of Dairen, are in effect."[41] This recognized the unequal terms of the 1945 treaty, so the Soviet government later revised its draft several times. On 22 January 1950, the Central Committee of the All-Union Communist Party (Bolshevik) approved a new Soviet treaty draft. This draft separated the CCR, Lüshun, and Dalian issues from the Sino-Soviet Treaty draft, turning them into two separate protocols. The Soviet draft of a Protocol concerning the Agreement on the CCR stipulated: "The validity of the Soviet-Chinese Agreement on the Chinese Changchun Railway, done in Moscow on 14 August 1945, is confirmed for the period indicated in this Agreement, while a few supplementary provisions can be added, at the recommendation of each of the parties, in the interests of guaranteeing the successful operation of the Railway."[42] That was to say, there was still a thirty-year period set in the 1945 agreement.

On 23 January, the Soviet side submitted the treaty draft to the Chinese side in the talks. Late at night on 24 January, the Chinese side presented its own treaty draft to the Soviet side.[43] On 26 January, Zhou Enlai gave the Chinese draft of the agreement on Lüshun, Dalian, and the CCR to the Soviet Foreign Minister Vyshinsky. The major contents of the Chinese draft were as follows: "According to the new cooperative situation between China and the Soviet Union formed at present, the Soviet government states that the Soviet Union gives up its right to lease Lüshunkou as a naval base, and gives up all its rights and interests to Dalian and the CCR, meanwhile states that all above-mentioned rights and obligations are returned to the People's Republic of China (Article I)." "Both contracting parties agree that the Soviet government immediately transfer without compensation to the PRC the CCR and all property belonging to the Railway after the conclusion of a peace treaty with Japan. Pending the transfer, the current Sino-Soviet joint administration of the CCR shall remain unchanged. However, after this Agreement becomes effective, posts will be periodically alternated between representatives of China and the Soviet Union. . . . If the signature of a peace treaty with Japan is hindered for some reason, and the validity of this agreement exceeds a three-year period and the relevant treaty is not concluded, then the Soviet government should immediately transfer without compensation the CCR and all property belonging to the Railway to the PRC (Article IV)."[44]

The Chinese draft, which abolished almost all Soviet special rights and interests in China's northeast, did not please the Soviet leaders. However, this bold draft was basically accepted by Stalin. On 29 January 1950, the Soviets transmitted to the Chinese side the Soviet draft, which amended the Chinese agreements and its protocols on Lüshun, Dalian, and the CCR. The content of the Soviet draft was generally similar with the Chinese draft, only without renouncing the Soviet rights and interests in Lüshun, Dalian, and the CCR, and without mentioning the Chinese would take over the property of the Lüshun areas leased by the Soviet Union. In addition, the Soviet draft suggested that the issue of the port of Dalian be handled after concluding a peace treaty with Japan.[45]

The USSR did not want to discard completely its privileges. It attached a draft protocol infringing on China's sovereignty and dignity. This protocol provided that Soviet troops and military goods could be transported unhindered on the CCR, and the transportation of the Soviet military goods in Chinese territory would be free of customs duties or other taxes.[46] This protocol created new tensions. On 31 January, Zhou Enlai modified the Soviet protocol. Under this amendment, the Chinese troops and its military supplies could be transported from China's northeast to Xinjiang by passing freely through the Soviet Union.[47] Due to strong opposition from the Soviet Union, the Chinese addition had to be abandoned.

On 10 February, when the two sides had reached an agreement on almost all issues, Molotov submitted the additional draft of the treaty to the Chinese delegation. The draft stated that in the interests of the defense of both countries, no right to concessions will be granted to foreigners and no actions will be allowed by industrial, financial, trade, or other companies or by institutions, companies, or organizations in which capital from third countries or citizens of these states participate either directly or indirectly either on the territory of the Far East region or of the central Asian republics of the USSR or on the territory of Manchuria or Xinjiang.[48] The Soviet request for an exclusive sphere of interest in these areas indicated that the Soviet Union would not allow any third party to emerge in China.[49]

On 14 February, the fifth anniversary of the Yalta anniversary, China and the Soviet Union finally signed the Treaty of Friendship, Alliance and Mutual Assistance, and separate agreements on the CCR, Lüshun, and Dalian. Under the Treaty, China and the Soviet Union formally established a political alliance, "in the interests of consolidating peace . . . both contracting parties will consult with each other in regard to all important international problems affecting the common interests of China and the Soviet Union."[50]

According to the Agreement on the CCR, Lüshun, and Dalian: "Both Contracting parties agree that the Soviet government transfer without compensation to the government of the PRC all its rights to joint management of the Chinese Changchun Railway with all property belonging to the Railway. The Transfer shall be effected immediately after the conclusion of a peace treaty with Japan, but not later than the end of 1952." The posts, such as manager of the Railway and chairman of the Board, etc. will be periodically alternated between representatives of China and the Soviet Union; not later than the end of 1952, the Soviet troops shall be withdrawn from the naval base Lüshun, and the installations in this area shall be handed over to China. In the event of aggression, both countries may jointly use the naval base at Lüshun for the purpose of conducting joint military operations against the aggressors; the question of Dalian harbor shall be further considered after the conclusion of a peace treaty with Japan, but the administration of Dalian shall be in the hands of the government of the PRC."[51]

When the treaty discussing the CCR, Lüshun, and Dalian had finally been settled, Stalin had abandoned almost all Soviet special rights and interests in China. This was Mao's most important achievement during the trip to the Soviet Union. The end result was the final return of the CCR to China.

Return of the Railway to China and Its Impact on the Sino-Soviet Relations

After the signing of the CCR agreement, the actual process of the CCR's return to China proceeded as scheduled, although because of the Korean War certain basing rights were extended through 1955. During August–September 1952, Chinese Premier Zhou Enlai led a delegation to the Soviet Union, and conducted talks with Stalin and other Soviet leaders on bilateral relations and issues of the Korean War.

The Korean War, which broke out in June 1950, was the extension on the Korean Peninsula of the U.S-Soviet competition and confrontation in Europe. Initially, Stalin believed that North Korean army would be able to achieve a rapid victory. Later, the Korean situation dramatically changed as a result of the U.S. military intervention and North Korea was on the verge of destruction. However, in October 1950, China decided to send troops to help North Korea turn the tide.

By May 1951, the Korean War was stalemated. Stalin instructed Malik, the Soviet representative in the United Nations, to contact the American representative and in July, the armistice negotiations were opened at Kaesong near the 38th Parallel. Although Stalin had no hope of achieving victory, it was very clear to him that the Korean War would consume American military and economic strength, create tensions between the United States and its allies, undermine the political prestige of the United States, and thus restrict and weaken indirectly the American position in Europe. Accordingly, Stalin encouraged China and North Korea to take a tough stance in the truce negotiation.

During August 1952, in his talks with Premier Zhou Enlai, Stalin promised to strengthen military assistance to China and support China's position of "repatriation of all prisoners" that Beijing maintained in the negotiations. Stalin thought that the Korean War marred the vigor of the United States and exposed the weaknesses of the United States. Stalin also said, "Chinese comrades must understand that if the United States does not lose the war, China would never reoccupy Taiwan."[52]

It was during this visit that China and the Soviet Union exchanged a note on extending the duration for the Soviet use of the military base in Lüshun. On 15 September 1952, the two countries issued a communiqué on the talks that stated: "In the process of negotiations, the two sides agreed to proceed with various measures so that the Soviet government could transfer all its rights to joint management of the CCR with all the property belonging to the Railway to the government of the PRC before the end of 1952."[53] The communiqué on the transfer of the CCR published at the same time stated that both governments had carried out the measures set up in their 1952 agreement, and to this end had agreed to set up the Sino-Soviet Joint Commission. The committee "should complete the transfer of the CCR to the PRC before December 31, 1952."[54]

On 31 December 1952, a ceremony handing over the CCR was held in Harbin, the capital of Heilongjiang province. Grunichev, a director general of management bureau of the CCR Company read the order abolishing the Sino-Soviet common management of the CCR. Lu Ping, a director general of the newly established Harbin Railway Management Bureau, read the order about the establishment of the Harbin Railway Management Bureau. In this way, the CCR was finally returned to China after Sino-Soviet joint administration of two years and eight months, but in fact thirty-three years after the 1919 Karakhan Manifesto and twenty-eight years after the USSR's promise to return the railway to China, as stated in the 31 May 1924 Sino-Soviet Treaty.

On the same day, China and the Soviet Union published the communiqué on the handover of the CCR from the Soviet government to the Chinese government. The communiqué explained: "The CCR property that the Soviet government transferred to the People's Republic of China without charge included: the basic trunk line of the railway from Manzhouli station to Suifenhe station as well as from Harbin to Dalian and Lüshunkou, along with the lands working for the line, railway buildings and equipments, vehicles—locomotives, wagons and carriage compartments, internal-combustion engine vehicles, repair factories of locomotives and compartments, power plants, telephone and telegraph offices, communication equipments and communication lines, railway branches, technical business buildings and residential buildings, economic organizations, subsidiary enterprises and other enterprises and organs, as well as the property redeemed, recovered and built newly during the Sino-Soviet joint management period."[55]

In line with the final protocol of the Sino-Soviet Joint Committee on 31 December 1952, Sino-Soviet joint management of the CCR was declared to be ended at 18:00 Beijing time on 31 December 1952. At that point, the CCR Council, the CCR Board of Supervisors, and the CCR Audit Bureau stopped work.[56] The total cost of the fixed assets and liquid funds of the CCR, which was transferred free of charge to China, reached 22.8 trillion yuan (or 2.28 billion new yuan).[57]

According to the 1952 balance sheet, CCR assets transferred included: 3,282.7 km railway lines, 10,200 trucks, 880 locomotives, 1.85 million square miles of houses, 121 medical and health agencies (including hospitals, polyclinics, clinics, and epidemic prevention stations), 69 schools, 25 cultural centers and clubs, and 322 "Red Corners" (entertainment rooms). Other items transferred included communication, signal, and liaison devices, together with all communication equipments, telephone offices, and motor repair plants; Harbin and Dalian locomotive vehicle repair factories; coal mines in the region Muling and Zharnuor; forestry enterprises—tree farms and lumber plants; commercial and public food enterprises—shops and public dining-rooms; the technical business buildings of the

CCR railroad company council, management bureau, substations, and business units.[58]

The return of the CCR to China enhanced development of the railroad industry and economy, in particular in the Northeast region. What was even more important was that the handover of this railway removed the fetters imposed on China by the Yalta Agreement and the Sino-Soviet agreements in 1945, obtaining territorial integrity, full Chinese sovereignty, and reviving the national self-esteem and self-confidence of the Chinese people. So, the transfer of the CCR from the Soviet Union won high praise for the Chinese government. Chairman Mao sent a telegram to Stalin expressing his gratitude.[59]

Conclusions

The handover of the CCR to China indeed weakened the USSR's influence over China, and especially weakened its near monopoly over China's economy. From the early 1950s, the Soviet Union provided China with large-scale economic assistance. According to the Sino-Soviet loan agreement in February 1950, the Soviet Union would offer China 300 million U.S. dollars in loans as payment for the machinery and other equipment that the Soviet Union agreed to deliver to China.[60] In the same year, the Soviet Union helped China with the first group of 50 major projects through using this loan. Later, from 1953 to 1954, the projects were increased by 91 and 15 respectively, to a total of 156.[61] Thus, the Soviet leverage over China's economy was enormous, and the CCR's return to China undermined the USSR's ability to influence China's economy.

Chinese statistics indicated that from 1950 to 1953 there were altogether 1,093 Soviet experts who had successively traveled to China to help its economic development.[62] According to other statistical railway data, 1,565 Soviet experts in various fields worked in the CCR: "Most experts are engineers and the technicians on each kind of service in the railway transportation, but there were also engineers in the coal industry and forestry, commercial and public diet staffs, doctors and teachers, as well as artistic and sports staffs."[63] Although the definition of "expert" was broad, there was no doubt that they had a tremendous influence on the CCR and its attached enterprises. In addition, in the process of jointly managing the CCR, there were some disputes between the representatives of both sides because the Soviets tried to turn the CCR into an economic entity independent from Chinese sovereignty, and did not observe China's uniform vehicle scheduling system.[64] The handover of the CCR eliminated much economic friction between the two countries.

Equally important, as the CCR was integrated in the national railroad system, China's railway administration was no longer guided by the USSR. The CPC's eighth conference decided that: "It is necessary to study the foreign experience according to the Chinese reality and prevent verbatim copy[ing] and dogmatism," and China's Ministry of Railways "examined and summed up certain dogmatism shortcomings which were reflected in the process of learning Soviet railway experience and promotion the CCR's experience." The Ministry of Railways proposed that from 1957 onward learning and promoting "the CCR's experience" would no longer be the only working policy governing nationwide railways.[65]

Finally, the handover gradually undermined the Soviet immigrant community in Northeastern China. Historically, the CER/CCR had been managed by Russian and Soviet citizens. This turned the railway and its adjacent areas into a workers' "paradise" where they lived and worked. In northeastern China there emerged a large Russian and Soviet immigrant society. During the mid-1950s, when the Soviet Union launched a campaign of reclaiming virgin land, the Soviet government started mobilizing the Soviet immigrants in China's Northeast to return to the Soviet Union. On 23 April 1954, the Soviet embassy in Beijing informed the Chinese government that the Soviet government would recall all Soviet immigrants in China group by group to join the construction of the Soviet Union, and hoped that the Chinese government would assist USSR in this regard.

In 1954, a total of 5,842 Soviet immigrants went back home. In 1955, 8,090 Soviet immigrants were repatriated. From 1956 to 1959, 2,522 Soviet immigrants were repatriated continuously. From 1954 to 1959, the total of repatriated Soviet immigrants and Russians without nationality reached 17,586, while a total of 6,672 people left for various capitalist countries.[66] Over more than twenty years from 1963 to 1985, the number of the Soviet immigrants in Heilongjiang province was gradually reduced. In 1964, the number of Soviet immigrants was 475. In 1975, the number was decreased to 107. In 1979, there were 66. In 1985, the number was only 39.[67] These numbers dramatically reveal how Manchuria was once again becoming an integral part of China, rather than a Russian puppet state dominated by Moscow by means of its majority control over Manchuria's railways and ports.

Notes

1. The Chinese Changchun Railway (the CCR) is the later name of the Chinese Eastern Railway (CER). In August 1945, according to the Sino-Soviet agreement, the CER and South Manchuria Railway were merged, and it was called the Chinese Changchun Railway. In December 1952, after the handover of the CCR to China, the rail line was respectively renamed as Binzhou (Harbin-Manzhouli), Bin-Sui (Harbin-Suifenhe), and the Hadassah (Harbin-Dalian) railways.

2. *Foreign Relations of the United States* (hereafter *FRUS*), "The Conferences at Malta and Yalta, 1945" (Washington, DC: G.P.O., 1976), 984.

3. *Zhongwai jiuyuezhang huibian* (Collection of Old Treaties and agreements between China and foreign countries, Vol. III, (Beijing: Sanlian Bookstore, 1962), 1328–40.

4. Zhang Shengfa, "The Establishment of the Yalta System and the Setting Up of the Soviet Sphere of Influence," *Historical Research*, 2000, No. 1.

5. Zhang Shengfa, "The Contention of great powers for Northeast China and the historical evolution of the ownership of the CER," *Eluosi Dong-Ou Zhongya Yanjiu* (*Russian, East European and Central Asian Studies*), 2007, No. 5, 64–72.

6. Zhang Shengfa, "From passive indifference to active suppor: on Stalin's Attitude towards Chinese Revolution 1945–1949," *World History*, No. 6, 1999.

7. Archive of the President, Russian Federation (hereafer APRF), fond 39, opis 1, delo 39, listy 62–63, *Sovetsko-kitayskie otnosheniya*, T. 5, Kn. 2, Moskva, Pamyatniki istoricheskoy mysli (The Soviet-Sino Relations, Vol. 5, part 2, Moscow, Monument of historical thought, 2005), 71–72.

8. APRF, fond 39, opis 1, delo 39, listy 62–63; *Sovetsko-kitayskie otnosheniya*, T. 5, Kn. 2, 72.

9. APRF, fond 39, opis 1, delo 39, listy 63; *Sovetsko-kitayskie otnosheniya*, T. 5, Kn. 2, 72.

10. A.I. Mikoyan's Report about his conversations with the leaders the CPC in 1949, 22 September 1960, *Sovetsko-kitayskie otnosheniya*, T. 5, Kn. 2, 340.

11. *Sovetsko-kitayskie otnosheniya*, T. 5, Kn. 2, 340–41.

12. APRF, fond 39, opis 1, delo 39, listy 78–79, *Sovetsko-kitayskie otnosheniya*, T. 5, Kn. 2, 82.

13. APRF, fond 39, opis 1, delo 39, listy 79, *Sovetsko-kitayskie otnosheniya*, T. 5, Kn. 2, 82.

14. See Bruce A. Elleman, "Soviet sea denial and the KMT-CCP Civil War in Manchuria, 1945–1949," in Elleman and Paine, *Naval Coalition Warfare*, 119–29.

15. I.V. Kovalev, "Dialog Stalina s MaoTszedunom (Okonchanie)," *Problemy Dal'nego Vostoka*, 1992, Nos 1–3, 86.

16. APRF, fond 45, opis 1, delo 328, listy 11–50, quoted in A. Ledovskii, "Vizit v Moskvu delegatsii kommunisticheskoy partii Kitay v iyune-avguste 1949 g.," (The visit of the CPC delegation to Moscow in June 1949) *Problemy Dal'nego Vostoka*, 1996, No. 4, 80–81.

17. On 10 November 1949, Premier Zhou Enlai told Roshchin that Mao's visit in the Soviet Union was to discuss the Sino-Soviet Treaty issues. Archive of Foreign Policy, Russian Federation (hereafter AFPRF), fond 0100, opis 42, delo 19, Papka 288, listy 81–85, quoted in B. Kulik, "Kitayskaya Narodnaya Respublika v period stanovleniya, 1949–1952, [Okonchanie]," *Problemy Dal'nego Vostoka*, 1994, No. 6, 76.

18. APRF, fond 45, opis 1,delo 329, listy 10–11; *Sovetsko-kitayskie otnosheniya*, T. 5, Kn. 2, Moskva, Pamyatniki istoricheskoy mysli (The Soviet-Sino Relations, Vol. 5, part 2, Moscow, Monument of historical thought, 2005), 108; Woodrow Wilson International Center for Scholars, *Cold War international history project*, issue 6–7, Washington DC, winter 1995/1996, 5.

19. APRF, fond 45, opis 1, delo 329, listy 11–12; *Sovetsko-kitayskie otnosheniya*, T. 5, Kn. 2, 230; *Cold War international history project*, issue 6–7, 5.

20. Ibid.; *Sovetsko-kitayskie otnosheniya*, T. 5, Kn. 2, 231; *Cold War international history project*, issue 6–7, 5.

21. I.V. Kovalev, "Dialog Stalina s MaoTszedunom (Okonchanie)," 89.

22. AFPRF, fond 0100, opis 43, papka 302, delo 10, list 1, 2; *Sovetsko-kitayskie otnosheniya*, T. 5, Kn. 2, 249, 250.

23. Later, on 31 March 1956, in his conversation with P.F.Yudin, the Soviet ambassador in Beijing, Mao Zedong said, "Stalin's position changed, and perhaps this was help which the Englishmen and the Indians gave us in this regard." Quoted in "Mao Tszedun o kitayskoy politike Kominterna i Stashina," *Problemy Dal'nego Vostoka*, 1994, No. 5, 106.

24. Pei Jianzhang, *Zhonghua renmin gongheguo waijiaoshi* (The Diplomatic History of the People's Republic of China), (Beijing: the World Knowledge Publishing House,1994), Vol. 1, 1949–1956, 20.

25. Ibid., 19; *Jianguo yilai maozedong wen gao, diyice* (Mao Zedong's Manuscripts Since the founding of the PRC, Vol. 1), (Beijing: Central Literature Publishing, 1987), 206.

26. *Mao Zedong's Manuscripts Since the founding of the PRC*, Vol. 1, 212; Shi Zhe: *Zai lishi juren shenbian* (Together with the Giant of the history), (Beijing: The Central Literature Publishing House, 1995, 2nd edition), 439–40.

27. APRF, fond 3, opis 65, delo 349, listy 92–93; *Sovetsko-kitayskie otnosheniya*, T. 5, Kn. 2, 259.

28. Ibid.

29. Henzig asserted that this report "reached Stalin after 10 and clearly before January 20." See Henzig, *The Soviet Union and Communist China 1945–1950*, 333.

30. Documents from Kovalev's personal archive, quoted in N.Goncharov, et al, *Uncertain partners*, 248–249.

31. Ibid.

32. APRF, fond 45, opis 1, delo 329, listy 40-42; *Sovetsko-kitayskie otnosheniya*, T. 5, Kn. 2, 267–68. According to the Wang Dongxin's Diary, Mao Zedong said, "the problems of the CCR, Lüshun and Dalian can be included in another agreement." (*Wang Dongxin Riji* [Wang Dongxin's Diary], [Beijing: China Social Sciences Publishing House, 1993]), 194.

33. APRF, fond 45, opis 1, delo 329, listy 44-46; *Sovetsko-kitayskie otnosheniya*, T. 5, Kn. 2, 268, 269–70; *Cold War international history project*, issue 6–7, winter 1995/1996, 7–9.

34. Ibid.

35. Ibid.

36. APRF, fond 45, opis 1, delo 329, listy 43; *Sovetsko-kitayskie otnosheniya*, T. 5, Kn. 2, 268; *Cold War international history project*, issue 6–7, winter 1995/1996, 7–8.

37. APRF, fond 45, opis 1, delo 329, listy 42-44; *Sovetsko-kitayskie otnosheniya*, T. 5, Kn. 2, 268–69; *Cold War international history project*, issue 6–7, winter 1995/1996, 8.

38. Ibid.

39. Ibid.

40. APRF, fond 45, opis 1, delo 329, listy 44; *Sovetsko-kitayskie otnosheniya*, T. 5, Kn. 2, 269; *Cold War international history project*, issue 6–7, winter 1995/1996, 8.

41. AFPRF, fond 07, opis 23a, papka 18, delo 235, listy 12–15; Quoted in Heinzig, *The Soviet Union and Communist China 1945–1950*, 403.

42. The Soviet draft of a Protocol concerning the Agreement on Port Arthur and Dairen presented at the same time stated: "1) in accordance with the changed conditions in China and with the readiness expressed by the Soviet Union, the Agreements concluded between the USSR and China on August 14, 1945, on Port Arthur and the harbor of Dairen shall be subjected to renewed examination following the conclusion of a peace treaty with Japan; 2) The Soviet military units currently located in Port Arthur and Dairen will be totally withdrawn to the territory of the USSR in the course of a period of 2 to 3 years after the present treaty becomes effective, whereby the troop withdrawal shall begin in 1950."AFPRF, fond 07, opis 23a, papka 18, delo 235, listy 49–50. Quoted in Heinzig, *The Soviet Union and communist China 1945–1950*, 408.

43. *Wangdonxin Riji*, 194.

44. The stipulation on the Lüshun issue in the Chinese Draft is as follows: "Both Contracting Parties agree that the Soviet troops be withdrawn from the jointly utilized naval base Port Arthur immediately after the conclusion of a peace treaty with Japan. For the period pending the withdrawal of the Soviet troops, the governments of China and the Soviet Union will appoint an equal number of military representatives to form a joint Chinese-Soviet military Commission which will be alternately presided over by each side and which will be in charge of military affairs in the area of Port Arthur. . . . Since certain reasons block the signature of a peace treaty with Japan, and the this Agreement becoming effective have exceeded three years and the corresponding agreement is not concluded again, the Soviet troops will immediately withdraw from the area of Port Arthur. . . . In the event of either of the Contracting Parties becoming the victim of aggression on the part of Japan or any state that may collaborate with Japan, and as a result thereof becoming involved in hostilities, China and the Soviet Union may, on the proposal of the government of the PRC and with the agreement of the government of the USSR, jointly use the naval base Port Arthur for the purpose of conducting joint military operations against the aggressors." The stipulation on Dalian issue in the Chinese Draft is as follows: "Both Contracting Parties agree that all the property in the areas of Dalian and Lüshunkou now temporarily administrated by or leased to the Soviet Union shall be taken over by the government of the PRC." AFPRF, fond 07, opis 23a, papka 20, delo 248, listy 38–55.

45. AFPRF, fond 07, opis 23a, papka 18, delo 235, listy 77–79.

46. AFPRF, fond 07, opis 23a, papka 18, delo 235, listy 80; Quoted in Heinzig, *The Soviet Union and Communist China 1945–1950*, 357.

47. APRF, fond 3, opis 65, delo 369, list 3, 16; *Sovetsko-kitayskie otnosheniya*, T. 5, Kn. 2, 273–78.

48. APRF, fond 45, opis 1, delo 334, list 53; *Sovetsko-kitayskie otnosheniya*, T. 5, Kn. 2, 292–93.

49. Subsequently, Mao Zedong complained in his talks with Yudin: "According to Stalin's initiative, the Northeast and Xinjiang in fact became the sphere of influence of the Soviet Union. Stalin maintained that in these areas were only allowed the Chinese people and the Soviet citizens to live." Quoted in "Mao Tszedun o kitayskoy politike Kominterna i Stashina," 106.

50. For the Chinese version of the Treaty, see Chinese Institute of International Relations, ed., *Xiandai guoji guanxishi cankao ziliao* (Reference Materials Relating to Modern International Relations), Vol. 1: *1950–1953* (Beijing: People's Education Press, 1960), 9–11; for the Russian version of the Treaty, see *Sovetsko-kitayskie otnosheniya*, T. 5, Kn. 2, 296–304.

51. For the Chinese version of the Agreement, see *Xiandai guoji guanxishi cankao ziliao: 1950–1953*, 11–13; for the Soviet version of the Agreement, see *Sovetsko-kitayskie otnosheniya*, T. 5, Kn. 2, 305–7.

52. APRF, fond 45, opis 5, delo 329, listy 65–66, 68; Also see A.Ledovskii, "Stenogrammy peregovorov Stalina s Chzhou Enlayava v guste-sentyabre 1952g," *Novaya i noveyshaya istoriya*, 1997, No. 2, 75.

53. *Zhonghua renmin gongheguo duiwaiguanxi wenjianji*, dierji, 1951–1953 (Documents of Foreign Relations of the People's Republic of China), Vol. 2, 1951–1953 (Beijing: World Knowledge Publishing House, 1958), 88.

54. Ibid., 89. At the same day, in a note to the Soviet Foreign Minister A.Vyshinsky, Chinese Premier and Foreign Minister Zhou Enlai stated: "Since Japan rejected the conclusion of a comprehensive peace treaty and did not sign a peace treaty with China and Soviet Union, posing the threat to the cause of peace and facilitating the recurrence of aggression from Japan, therefore, in order to safeguard the interest of peace, and in accordance with the Sino-Soviet Alliance and Mutual Assistance Treaty, the Chinese Government proposes that the Soviet government agree to extend the deadline of withdrawal from Chinese Lüshunkou naval base used by two countries until a peace treaty between the People's Republic of China and Japan and between the Soviet Union and Japan would be concluded." Also at the same day, in his replying note A.Vyshinsky agreed with Chinese request. *Zhonghua renmin gongheguo duiwaiguanxi wenjianji*, dierji, 1951–1953, 89–91. The Final Protocol, which was signed by the Sino-Soviet Joint Military Commission in Lüshunkou on 24 May 1955, determined that the Soviet troops would fully withdraw from Lüshunkou before 31 May 1955 (*The People's Daily*, 25 May 1955). On the issue of the real date of full withdrawal of the Soviet troops, there are some different interpretations. According to Sheng Zhihua, from 25 to 27 May 1955, the Soviet military authorities and about 120,000 army, navy, and air force personnel evacuated the Lüshun region in batches (Sheng Zhihua, "Khrushchev and return of base of Lüshunkou to China by Soviet Union," in Sheng Zhihua and Li Danhui, *Research on a number of issues about postwar Sino-Soviet relations* (Beijing: the People's Publishing House, 2006), 185–86; According to *Diplomatic History of the People's Republic of China*, withdrawing the Soviet troops was completed on 31 May 1955, *Zhonghua renmin gongheguo waijiaoshi*, Vol. 1:1949–1956, 39; But, according to a chronology appearing on a website sponsored by WorldStatesmen.org, Lüshun was not formally re-incorporated by

China until 11 October 1955, almost exactly sixty years after the tsarist treaty with China was signed (http://www.worldstatesmen.org/China_Foreign_colonies.html).)

55. Ibid, 116–17.

56. *Zhongguo waijiaobu dang'an* (Archive of Chinese Foreign Ministry), 109-00175-01, 36.

57. Ibid., 35; According to the figure given by Ablova, the Soviet property transfer to China was worth of 600 million U.S. dollars. N.E. Ablova, *Istoriya KVCD i rosiiskai amigarazii v kitae,* 378.

58. "Zhongchangteilu yijiuwuernian daijiepinghenbiao ji shengchancai-wugongzuo juesuan shuomingxshu" (The balance sheet of loan and final account specification on production and financial work of the CCR in 1952), Archive of Harbin, 10–12.

59. *Zhonghua renmin gongheguo duiwaiguanxi wenjianji,* dierji, 1951–1953, 118.

60. *Sovetsko-kitayskie otnosheniya,* 1917–1957, sbornik dokumentov (Soviet-Chinese relations, 1917–1957, collection of documents, M., Izd-vovo stochnoy literatury, 1959), 222–24.

61. Pei Jianzhang, *Zhonghua renmin gongheguo waijiaoshi* Vol. 1:1949–1956, 39–40.

62. Chinese Academy of Social Sciences and Central Archive, ed., *Zhonghua renmin gongheguo jingji dang'an ziliao xuanbian (Economical Reference material Collections of People's Republic of China, 1953–1957:* volume of investment in the fixed assets and architecture industry (Beijing: Chinese Price Publishing house, 1998), 387.

63. "Zhongchangteilu yijiuwuernian daijiepinghenbiao ji shengchancai-wugongzuo juesuan shuomingxshu," 18.

64. Pei Jianzhang, *Zhonghua renmin gongheguo waijiaoshi* Vol. 1: 1949–1956, 42.

65. See Li Wenyao, "Tui Guang 'zhongchang tielu jingyang' shimo" ("Story about promoting 'experience in the CCR"), *People's Railway,* 18 August 2006, http://www.rmtd.com.cn/Article/2006/200608/2006-08-16/20060816094335.html)

66. *Heilongjiangshengzhi,* Vol. 69, 169–70.

67. Ibid., 123.

Epilogue

Rivers of Steel: Manchuria's Railways as a Natural Extension of the Sea Lines of Communication

Bruce A. Elleman

A river can act as a foreign invasion route, a conduit moving people and produce, or as a barrier defending a nation-state. A "river of steel," like the Manchurian railways discussed in this volume, can serve similarly diverse functions. Depending on the circumstances, the railways running through Manchuria were used to assert military dominance, promote immigration and trade, and to facilitate the establishment of a strong nation-state. For this reason, the history of the Manchurian railways is intricate, and yet key to understanding the late nineteenth and early twentieth century development of Northeast Asia.

During the sixty-year span examined in this book, the Manchurian railways were a constant source of imperialist conflict. From the mid-1890s onward, control over Manchuria was hotly contested by Qing China, Japan, Russia, the Republic of China, and the Soviet Union, and ultimately by various political factions within China, including the Communists supported by the USSR and the Nationalists supported by the United States. From their creation, the Manchurian railways were seen as being synonymous with foreign intervention and aggression. Foreign powers used them on many occasions to invade northeast China, including the Russo-Japanese War, the Sino-Soviet Conflict in 1929, and the Second Sino-Japanese War leading up to and including World War II.

Since their construction in the late 1890s, the Chinese Eastern Railway and the South Manchuria Railway lines have also played an instrumental economic role in China's growth and modernization. Just as maritime "sea lines of communication" have played a vital role in supporting China's vibrant coastal growth rates, the "rivers of steel" running through Manchuria and into Central China were the "land lines of communication" that held the promise of bringing modernization to many as-yet undeveloped rural areas of northeast China. More important, as Stanley K.

Hornbeck, the Chief of the Division of Far Eastern Affairs, Department of State, stated, the Manchurian railways were the final "link in the one and only direct railway route from Europe, across Siberia, to the Asiatic ports of the Pacific Ocean."[1] The railway terminus, in the neighboring cities of Port Arthur and Dalian, became the prime focus of these economic efforts, forming the essential trade juncture between the land and sea lines of communication.

Warring Chinese factions also attempted to use the Manchurian railways to establish their hegemony over China. After World War II, civil war in Manchuria spread along China's railway system to the south, eventually resulting in the Communist victory in 1949. Only in the mid-1950s were all the railways in Manchuria finally under complete Chinese control. This transition from foreign concession to an integral part of the Chinese nation symbolized the People's Republic of China's unification of Manchuria with China proper. Over time, the PRC broke away from the formerly unequal alliance with the Soviet Union. Only with the collapse of the USSR in 1991, have the railways in Manchuria once again reverted to their more benign function, serving as an essential land line between Europe and Asia as well as within China itself.

*　　　　*　　　　*

The city and harbor of Port Arthur, called Lüshun by the Chinese and Ryojun by the Japanese, are located on the southern tip of the Liaodong peninsula in Manchuria. Throughout most of the last decade of the nineteenth century and all of the first half of the twentieth century, non-Chinese occupied Port Arthur continuously. Russia and Japan constantly fought for control, with the city occupied by Japan from 1894 to 1895, Russia from 1897 to 1905, Japan from 1905 to 1945 and, finally, after the end of World War II, the Soviet Union once again from 1945 to 1955.

Because Port Arthur provided year-round sea access to Manchuria, it was one of the most fiercely contested of the foreign Treaty Ports of Northeast Asia. Positioned on the Yellow Sea, Port Arthur offered a "gateway" into Manchuria, as well as an important military and naval base for any action directed against northern China, Manchuria, or Korea. During the Sino-Japanese War of 1894–95, for example, the Japanese army, in a pincer movement that included attacking Northeast China through Korea, also landed an amphibious force to take possession of Port Arthur; ten years later, in 1904, the Japanese largely repeated this strategy against the Russians. During the final days of World War II, however, the tables turned when Soviet forces pushed the Japanese out and occupied Port Arthur.

After agreeing to send troops against Japan at Yalta, the Soviet government negotiated post-war terms with China's Nationalist government. Their August 1945 "friendship" treaty, gave the Soviet Union the right to "erect at its own expense such installations as are necessary for the defense of the naval base," and up to a thirty-year time limit could also maintain the Soviet "army, navy and air forces" within the boundaries of Port Arthur. This allowed the USSR to intervene actively on the side of the Chinese communists in the on-going Chinese civil war. In fact, Soviet "sea denial" helped insure that Nationalist troops could not arrive by ship, thus denying the Nationalist army and navy a two-front strategy; this foreign intervention helped focus the major battles of the Chinese civil war on the Manchurian railways, and especially on the single train line linking China to Manchuria.[2]

Following the Communist victory in 1949, instead of leaving China the Soviet troops remained in Port Arthur through 1952, at which time their promised evacuation was delayed yet again by "American imperialism" and Washington's efforts to defeat the "world peace force headed by the Soviet Union" during the Korean War.[3] In 1952, the "Sino-Soviet Joint Communiqué on the Withdrawal of Soviet Armed Forces from Port Arthur" was signed, stating that all Soviet forces would withdraw from Port Arthur by 31 May 1955, on the thirty-first anniversary of the signing of the Sino-Soviet treaty opening supposedly "equal" diplomatic relations.[4]

Moscow also agreed to transfer "the installations in the area of the Port Arthur naval base to the Government of the People's Republic of China." China naturally expected that this would include the heavy artillery protecting Port Arthur from attack. But, as Khrushchev wrote in his memoirs, Zhou Enlai expected the weapons to be handed over for free. He told Zhou: "Excuse me, but I would like you to understand me correctly. These are very expensive weapons, we would be selling them at reduced prices. We would like these weapons to be transferred to you on the terms that we are proposing. We have not yet recovered from the terribly destructive war with Germany. Our economy was ruined and our people are living poorly. This is why we would ask you not to insist on your request, but to agree to our proposal."[5] Earlier published versions of this exchange are somewhat less diplomatic, with Khrushchev concluding: "That's where the matter rested. The Chinese didn't raise the subject again."[6]

Stripping Port Arthur of its main defensive weapons left China vulnerable to foreign attack, and contributed to souring Sino-Soviet relations. At the same time as the artillery in Port Arthur was being dismantled, the PRC was engaged in fighting the Nationalists far to the south during the first Taiwan Strait Crisis. Interestingly, the PRC backed down in this conflict, and on 1 May 1955, the People's Liberation Army (PLA) stopped shelling the Nationalist-held islands of Quemoy and Matsu. One can only speculate on the impact that the Soviet demilitarization of Port Arthur must have had on the Chinese Communists' decision to halt their southern offensive against Taiwan.

The final withdrawal of all Soviet troops from Port Arthur was an important military watershed in Chinese history. For the previous sixty years, China had been incapable militarily of standing up to the foreign powers that sought to dominate Manchuria. After the evacuation of Soviet troops from Port Arthur in 1955, however, China could and did begin to act more independently of the Soviet Union. Manchuria would never again be dominated by foreign powers.

*   *   *

Port Arthur was originally conceived as the northern equivalent to Britain's trade city of Hong Kong, far to the south. After 1898, however, Russia saw it as an ice-free alternative to Vladivostok, which was ice-bound for an average of 56 days every winter. It was hoped that cheaper freight and more rapid transit via the Trans-Siberian Railway from Europe would allow tsarist Russia to compete with Britain as economic equals. However, due in part to the enormous military costs involved with protecting the railway, the Chinese Eastern Railway while under Russian management never managed to pay for itself. Then, as a result of the Russo-Japanese War, Russia lost the southern half of its railway network, plus Port Arthur and the neighboring port city of Dalny (the Russian name for Dalian), which were the essential links with the crucial sea lanes in the Yellow Sea. The Russians retained northern Manchuria, and its economic center at Harbin. For the next forty years, the Russians and the Japanese remained in fierce economic competition.

From 1905 to 1945, Ryojun (Port Arthur) prospered under the direct control of Japan. The city became the terminus for the South Manchuria Railway, which transported the iron, coal, soybeans, rice, and timber resources of Manchuria to port. From Manchuria, these resources were exported overseas; according to some Chinese estimates, as much as 80 percent of all of the industrial output of Southern Manchuria was transported directly to Japan.[7] To handle this traffic, the port facilities at nearby Dairen (Dalian), in particular, were expanded so that they could simultaneously handle dozens of ships of up to 10,000 tons in size. Port Arthur and Dalian together soon became one of the most highly industrialized areas in northeast China. After 1931, the Japanese puppet state of Manchukuo quickly became the most industrialized region of East Asia outside of the Japanese home islands, overshadowing even the foreign enclaves near Shanghai.

In sharp contrast to Japan's successful management of Manchukuo, the post-World War II Soviet occupation resulted in the stripping away of a large portion of Manchuria's industrial wealth. Claiming that all former Japanese factories were legitimate "war booty," the Soviet government authorized the dismantling and shipping back to the USSR of an estimated two billion U.S. dollars worth of machinery and industrial goods. The Soviets confiscated not only machinery and entire factories, but even took the "pianos, sofas and fine furniture of the Japanese high-ranking officials and army officers."[8]

On 9 February 1946, the American Secretary of State, James F. Byrnes, sent a protest to the Chinese and Soviet governments denouncing the removal of industrial goods and machinery from Manchuria. He suggested that "an inter-Allied Reparations Commission" be set up to determine the "final allocation of Japanese external assets among the various claimant nations," but the Soviet government ignored this recommendation. In November 1946, the U.S. Pauley Mission further reported that the USSR had confiscated "by far the larger part of all functioning power generating and transforming equipment, electric motors, experimental plants, laboratories, and hospitals." Besides the value of this machinery "irreparable damage" had been inflicted on the valuable mines throughout Manchuria when the Soviets removed "vital generating equipment and pumps." The value of the confiscated property was estimated to be 50 percent of the total industrial capacity of Manchuria, which crippled the productivity of China's most industrialized and economically advanced region.[9]

In addition to this confiscated property, the Soviet Union used its military occupation of Manchuria to "exact excessive economic concessions from the Chinese government."[10] These concessions were structured as jointly operated companies, which included "specified coal mines, power plants, iron and steel industries, chemical industries and cement industries." By using Japanese printing presses to print money, the Soviet Union soon doubled the amount of Manchurian currency in circulation and, with its newly-minted bills, bought Japanese factories and property at reduced prices.[11]

After the 1949 creation of the PRC, the Soviet Union promised to turn over the "war booty" that had been taken out of Manchuria and also to help build up China's economy by sending advisors and technical equipment. In 1950, the industrial output of Manchuria was still only 30 percent of the 1945 output, when Manchuria was under Japanese control.[12] The 1950 Soviet "loan" of three hundred million U.S. dollars was insufficient to counter China's massive economic problems, and represented a small fraction of what had been taken away as war booty. A list of the factories returned in 1951 included only a single cement works and three sawmills out of a total of twenty-one plants. As one historian commented wryly at the time: "The fact that five breweries have passed from Russian into Chinese hands will not alter the balance of power in the Far East."[13]

In spite of these problems, the Cold War atmosphere of the early 1950s threw the Soviet Union and China together in an uneasy economic partnership. Over the next few years the People's Republic of China signed over 110 trade treaties and agreements with the Soviet Union and various Eastern European countries, but only 20 to 30 treaties with all of the other countries of the world combined. By 1957, fully 50 percent of China's foreign trade was with the USSR.[14]

Only a small fraction of the two billion U.S. dollars worth of equipment taken out of Manchuria was ever returned to China. In October 1954, the Soviet government did finally agree to sell its stock in four of the joint Sino-Soviet companies, including a mining firm and a petroleum firm in Xinjiang, a shipbuilding company in Dalian, and a civil aviation company. But, according to some estimates China had to pay almost one billion U.S. dollars in restitution.

As a result of the Soviet Union's economic policies, by the mid-1950s China's debt owed to the USSR was well into the billions of U.S. dollars. To many Chinese, it must have appeared as if they were buying back from the Soviet government industries that really should have been China's already. Afterall, the USSR had only entered the war against Japan at the last minute, while China was fighting constantly for many years. In addition, the Japanese had used Chinese labor and resources to create the factories, and the Soviets had then bought them at reduced prices after World War II with inflated currency.

Then, as a result of increasing Sino-Soviet tensions "the Soviets sought to punish China by withdrawing advisors, halting aid, walking off with blueprints to unfinished industrial installations, and leaving the country a debt burden that had to be repaid."[15] Some scholars have argued that Mao, in order to pay off China's foreign debt to the USSR, adopted shortsighted economic policies, such as the 1958 Great Leap Forward, that produced a nationwide famine.[16]

*   *   *

The final return of the Manchurian railway concessions in 1952 symbolized the long-awaited national reunification of most of the contiguous territory of China proper.[17] After almost sixty years of constant imperialist intrusions, known to many foreigners as the "scramble for concessions," but to Chinese as "guafen" or "cut up like a melon," China was finally able to reclaim its lost territory in Manchuria. The Changchun Railway's return was an important step, transferred to China without payment in December 1952, with all additional railway property returned within the year, and then followed in 1955 by the transfer of Port Arthur and Dalian.

During May 1955, the naval facilities at Port Arthur were handed over to China in the midst of fanfare and daily Chinese press coverage. Soong Ching-ling, Sun Yat-sen's widow and the president of the thirty-nine million member Sino-Soviet Friendship Association, called this "An Historic Event" and applauded the Soviet Union for "preventing the rebirth of Japanese imperialism and the resumption of aggression on the part of Japan or any other state that would unite in any form with Japan in acts of aggression." Perhaps hoping to hide from foreign observers that Port Arthur's artillery had been removed, Soong praised the Soviet willingness to transfer "without compensation all facilities, which have been completely restored and further developed." This proved "the high value the Soviet Union places on the fraternal alliance of our two countries and peoples."[18]

On 25 May 1955, the Chinese delegation to the Sino-Soviet Military Commission gave a farewell dinner to the high-ranking Soviet and Chinese officials in Port Arthur and Dalian where it was announced that the Sino-Soviet Joint Communiqué had been signed and that the Soviet troops were now officially withdrawn from Port Arthur. By 26 May, all of the Soviet soldiers had departed, and some 20,000 citizens gathered at the Port Arthur railway station to bid farewell to the Soviet High Command. But many Russians continued to reside in Manchuria, some even bearing special Soviet passports with "City of Dalny, People's Republic of China" listed as their birthplace.[19]

To China's leaders, the final return of Port Arthur and Dalian represented Chinese independence from Soviet political influence. To foreign observers, China's relations with the Soviet Union in 1955 may have appeared to be friendly, but there were still serious underlying tensions. Territorial frictions over Manchuria's border with the USSR, sovereignty disputes over Outer Mongolia, and political disputes over Xinjiang remained unresolved.[20] Full control over Manchuria gave the PRC leadership more latitude to resolve these other issues.

Many experts who have studied the Sino-Soviet split begin their discussion in 1956, with Khrushchev's opening of the de-Stalinization campaign. However, the conditions that made a schism likely clearly existed before 1956, and are linked with the post-war Soviet occupation of Port Arthur and Dalian, as well as Moscow's control over much of Manchuria's industrial base, including the railways. The return of Port Arthur can thus be represented as either the high-point in Sino-Soviet relations, in so far as it outwardly reflected a growing sense of friendship and cooperation between the USSR and China, but also as the beginning of the end of their unequal relationship, since for the very first time since the dawn of the twentieth century China was not occupied by foreign militaries. In the wake of Port Arthur's and Dalian's return, therefore, divisions between China and the USSR increased through the rest of the 1950s, leading to an open rift by 1960.

*   *   *

After the railway's return in 1952, Beijing was faced with the difficult task of reasserting control. In 1953, tensions erupted into "the first significant purge of senior Party officials," when the Manchurian official Gao Gang was purged for allegedly allowing "Russian influence to rise in Manchuria."[21] As a result of such actions, the railways in Manchuria were for the first time centralized into one united system with the railway lines in China proper, the very Qing policy that had resulted in the 10 October 1911 revolution, in the creation of the Republic of China, and the abdication of the Manchus in 1912.

Meanwhile, the PRC's first Five-Year Plan more than doubled China's railway mileage, and by 1957 for the first time the inland provinces of Xinjiang, Qinghai, and Sichuan were linked to Central China by rail.[22] The railway network supported the government's task of assimilating the Han majority and non-Han minorities into a new sense of Chinese nationhood. The 1954 constitution divided China into provinces, autonomous regions, and special municipalities, and guaranteed smaller nationality groups living in these autonomous regions—including Uighurs, Tibetans, Manchus, and Koreans—that they could retain their language, culture, and customs. But, the building of railways allowed for a rapid influx of Han immigrants into areas that had traditionally been inhabited by minorities. To many minorities, therefore, railway construction signified the beginning of the end of their independence, in a process that critics of the PRC's nationality policies have called "internal colonialism."[23]

Government-sponsored programs relocating Han immigrants into minority regions increased during the ten-year-long Cultural Revolution from 1966 to 1976. In Manchuria, for example, the rapid increase of Han immigrants to the Yanbian Korean autonomous region meant that the percentage of Koreans living there fell from 70.1 percent in 1955 to 42.2 percent by the mid-1970s.[24] The expansion of railways into minority areas has continued to this day with the 1 July 2006 inauguration of the Qinghai-Xizang railway to Lhasa, Tibet, a plan originally proposed by Mao Zedong in 1958.[25]

Railways not only had an enormous impact on Beijing's ability to administer and absorb its far-flung "colonial" regions, but also to transport and garrison troops there. The major battles in the 1969 Sino-Soviet border conflict occurred along Manchuria's borders, with pitched battles on Zhenbao (Damansky in Russian) Island during March 1969. Although the PLA did not win these battles, it did not lose them either: "China had shown that it was unwilling to bow before Soviet military power, and by so doing had directly challenged the 'Brezhnev' doctrine that claimed that the Soviet Union had the right to intervene in other socialist countries."[26]

As Sino-Soviet tensions increased during the 1960s, the railways were also used to transport Han civilians to settle on the Manchurian side of the border. Beijing adopted a policy of "frontier-supporting households," whereby Han immigrants were transported by trains "to the strategic Sino-Soviet borders to increase their local population and, thereby, facilitate and strengthen border defense in case of an eventual war with the Soviet Union."[27] The use of forced civilian migrations followed in line with Leon Trotsky's 1926 suggestion to increase Russian immigration to Siberia, a policy largely adopted by Stalin in the early 1930s.[28]

Fearful of the rapidly expanding Russian population, Japan later adopted similar state-sponsored migration policies during the mid-1930s in Manchukuo.[29]

A final impact of the railway system was arguably political. During the Cultural Revolution, when Mao and his followers attempted to reassert complete control over the Chinese government, Red Guards supporting Mao converged on Beijing. The prime means of transport were the railways. By "late fall of 1966 millions of students were moving about the country, taking over the railroads without paying for either their tickets of their accommodations."[30] One can certainly disagree with the goals of the Cultural Revolution, and many scholars have, but it cannot be disputed that the centralized PRC's railway network allowed for a new unity of national effort by the Chinese people.

*   *   *

After the decade-long turmoil of the Cultural Revolution, and throughout most of the Cold War, China's trade and transportation between Manchuria and the neighboring Soviet territories was severely limited, and the borders remained highly militarized. As a result of the normalization of relations with the United States and Japan during the 1970s, sea lines of communication became increasingly important, and China's most spectacular growth rates occurred along its eastern seaboard. The relative isolation of Manchuria changed rapidly following the 1989 end of the Cold War and the subsequent collapse of the Soviet empire in 1991. In the modern era, Manchuria and its railways once again offer a potential transnational bridge linking China with Siberia, Mongolia, and Korea.

This is especially true with regard to energy. In the 1970s, China was already concerned about insufficient energy resources. The Ten-Year Plan (1976–85) focused on building six new trunk railways to transport oil and promoted the discovery of "ten new Daqings," the most important oil-producing center in Manchuria, to increase China's production of petroleum from 100 million to 400 million tons per year. In fact, China's domestic petroleum output peaked in the early 1980s, and it became imperative to look outside of China for new sources of energy.[31] Part of the answer includes oil purchases from Russia. Until one or more of the proposed pipelines are built, the Manchurian railway system will remain the primary way of moving Siberian crude to markets in East Asia.

Several pipelines are being discussed. Transneft, Russia's state-owned oil pipeline monopoly, has announced plans to construct a major pipeline to Nakhodka, near Vladivostok, where the oil would then be loaded onto tankers and shipped to various Asian buyers. The massive project—begun in 2006 but not scheduled to be completed for many years—has been estimated to cost $11 billion.[32] A second proposed pipeline to China and South Korea would skirt Mongolia, pass through

Manchuria, and terminate in Daqing, near the Chinese coast; a non-binding Sino-Russian agreement signed in 2003 promised China approximately 700 million tons of oil through a second Siberian pipeline to Daqing.[33] Finally, the Russian natural gas corporation, Gazprom, has signed a memorandum of understanding in 2006 with the Chinese government to build two natural gas pipelines from Siberia into China by 2011.[34] While China has been active in constructing its section of the pipeline, Russia has continued to delay starting its section from the town of Angarsk to the Sino-Russian border, choosing instead to focus on what it sees as the more profitable route to Nakhodka.[35]

As planned pipeline construction falls behind schedule, oil imports via the Manchurian railroads have grown to help meet China's demand for energy. In 2005, China imported 200,000 barrels per day via Manchurian rail. According to China's Ministry of Railways that figure ballooned to 300,000 barrels per day in 2006, a startling 50 percent increase.[36] In 2005, Russia supplied 7.6 million tons of oil to China by rail, and during 2006, nearly four million tons of oil passed through the frontier at Zabaykalsk-Manzhouli while a similar amount came via Naushki on the Russian-Mongolian border.[37]

The Russian Railways Company (RZD) has recently sought ways to make shipments into China more attractive to firms like LUKoil. One report identified a 17 percent reduction in freight tariffs in 2006 to entice oil companies other than Rosneft to export to China via railway, with further reductions possible if volume targets are hit.[38] On 17 February 2009, it was reported that Russia would continue to provide China with over 300,000 barrels of oil per day in return for a $25 billion Chinese line-of-credit.[39] If one considers that China imported about 180 million tons of foreign oil in 2008, this figure of 15 million tons equals about 8 percent of the PRC's oil imports. While hardly sufficient to cover more than three to four weeks of China's total energy needs, this oil trade could prove crucial in an emergency.[40] In the near term, however, these figures suggest the continuing dominance of China's sea lines over landlines for delivering energy supplies.

*   *   *

Manchuria's relatively short 115-year railway history is complex, with numerous actors. It is a story of competing imperialisms—both foreign and domestic—as well as a story of competing nationalisms among political groups—such as Communist versus Nationalist—and among ethnic groups—including Han versus non-Han minorities. As this book has shown, the network of railways running through Manchuria was time after time used by foreign powers to dominate China. Although condemned by most Chinese, this process did gradually help turn Manchuria into China's most highly industrialized region. When Mao and his followers reclaimed

Manchuria, and took control over these important industrial assets, they were able to use them to catapult themselves into power throughout all of mainland China.

Since 1991, the Manchurian railways have gone back to what they were intended to be from the very beginning: an economic bridge linking Europe and Asia. China's enormous growth rates in recent years have focused intense interest on Siberian oil and gas supplies. Today, Manchurian railways are providing a cheap and reliable commercial route linking Western Siberian's oil fields with China's thriving economy. Until the planned Sino-Russian oil and gas pipelines are completed, the Manchurian railways will remain the primary over-land mode for transporting much of these essential oil supplies to China.

Looking into the future, the flow of resources from Siberia to China might someday be reversed. Could, for example, Northeast China become a springboard for Chinese penetration of and acquisition of the Russian Far East or Eastern Siberia—China's version of "Manifest Destiny"?[41] Is China destined to expand to the north, because of demographics and Russian weakness, as many Russian analysts fear? Will the phenomenon of Russian "railway imperialism" be reversed, in China's favor? If this happens, then Manchuria's "rivers of steel" may once again begin to play a central role not just in China's, but in all of Northeast Asia's, future development.

Notes

1. Japanese Foreign Ministry Archives (Gaimusyo), File F 192.5-4-7.

2. See Bruce A. Elleman, "Soviet sea denial and the KMT-CCP Civil War in Manchuria, 1945–1949," in Bruce A. Elleman and S.C.M. Paine, eds., *Naval Coalition Warfare: From the Napoleonic War to Operation Iraqi Freedom* (London: Routledge, 2008), 119–29.

3. China News Agency, *Renmin Ribao,* 17 September 1952.

4. While more difficult to prove, this was also the 100th anniversary of the Qing forces defeating the Taiping's Northern Expedition on 31 May 1855, which has often been seen as the dominance of the North, in this case the USSR, over the South—China.

5. Nikita Sergeevich Khrushchev, Sergei Khrushchev, *Memoirs of Nikita Khrushchev: Statesman, 1953–1964* (University Park, PA: Pennsylvania State Press, 2007), 434.

6. Nikita Khrushchev, *'Khrushchev Remembers* (London: Andre Deutsch, 1974), 247.

7. *People's China,* 16 June 1955, 17.

8. Wu Xiu-quan, "Sino-Soviet Relations in the Early 1950's," *Beijing Review,* Vol. 26, No. 47, 21 November 1983, 19.

9. *The China White Paper August 1949* (Stanford: Stanford University, 1967), 597–602.

10. Henry Wei, *China and Soviet Russia* (Princeton: D. Van Nostrand Company Inc., 1950), 194.

11. *China White Paper*, 598–602.

12. Alfred D. Low, *The Sino-Soviet Dispute* (London: Associated University Presses, 1976), 58.

13. Max Beloff, "Manchuria as Prize," *The Spectator,* 2 March 1951, 270.

14. See Bruce Elleman, "The Nationalists' Blockade of the PRC, 1949–58," in Elleman and Paine, *Naval Blockades and Seapower: Strategies and counter-strategies, 1805–2005* (London: Routledge, 2006), 142.

15. This openly left-wing essay, for all of its problems, does focus attention on China's foreign debt problems: Raymond Lotta, "Socialism is much better than Capitalism, and Communism will be a far better world," *Revolution*, No. 33, 5 February 2006, at http://revcom.us/a/033/socialism-communism-better-capitalism-pt9.htm

16. See Lawrence C. Reardon, *The Reluctant Dragon: Crisis Cycles in Chinese Foreign Economic Policy* (Seattle: University of Washington Press, 2002), 103–4.

17. Hong Kong and Macao, both offshore islands, were to follow almost fifty years later, while Taiwan remains separate to this day, as does Mongolia.

18. China News Agency, *Renmin Ribao,* 1 April 1955.

19. http://www.daochinasite.com/eng/places/dl1.shtml

20. See Bruce A. Elleman, "The Final Consolidation of the USSR's Sphere of Interest in Outer Mongolia," in Stephen Kotkin and Bruce A. Elleman, eds., *Mongolia in the Twentieth Century: Landlocked Cosmopolitan* (Armonk, NY: M.E. Sharpe, 1999), 123–36.

21. Lucian W. Pye, *China: An Introduction*. Third Edition (Boston: Little, Brown and Company, 1984), 238; reportedly Gao Gang committed suicide rather than face the charges laid against him.

22. Roderick MacFarquhar and John K. Fairbank, eds., *The Cambridge History of China:* Volume 14, *The People's Republic, Part I: The Emergence of Revolutionary China, 1949–1965* (New York: Cambridge University Press, 1987), 176.

23. Dru C. Gladney, *Dislocating China: Reflections on Muslims, Minorities, and Other Subaltern Subjects* (Chicago: The University of Chicago Press, 2004), 360.

24. Bernard Vincent Olivier, *The Implementation of China's Nationality Policy in The Northeastern Provinces* (San Francisco: Mellen Research University Press, 1993), 161.

25. Tibetans, who oppose the railway line, fear that Han immigrants will soon swamp their small numbers, and are "concerned that this influx of the Chinese migrants has another motive—changing the demographics inside Tibet, and impacting the Tibetan [independence] movement." Prerna Sun, "China cashes in on Tibet's economy," 11 February 2009, www.ndtv.com.

26. Bruce A. Elleman, *Modern Chinese Warfare, 1795–1989* (London: Routledge, 2001), 279–80.

27. Olivier, 161.

28. See Elleman, *Moscow and the Emergence of Communist Power in China*, 28, 206–11.

29. See Bruce A. Elleman, "Japanese Immigration to Manchukuo and Its Impact on the USSR," with Sarah C. M. Paine, *Working Papers in International Studies,* Hoover Institution, Stanford University (January 1995).

30. Pye, 301.

31. Roderick MacFarquhar and John K. Fairbank, eds., *The Cambridge History of China:* Vol. 14, *The People's Republic, Part 2: Revolutions within the Chinese Revolution, 1966–1982* (New York: Cambridge University Press, 1991), 495–96.

32. http://www.upstreamonline.com/live/article144640.ece

33. Walter B. Parker, "Circumpolar Oil and Gas Prospects: The Role of the Commons," dlc.dlib.indiana.edu/archive/00001193/00/Parker,Walter.pdf

34. David Lague, "China seeks oil security with stake in Russia firm," *International Herald Tribune,* 20 July 2006.

35. John Helmer, "Putin's hands on the oil pumps" 26 August 2004, http://www.atimes.com/atimes/Central_Asia/FH26Ag01.html

36. http://www.eia.doe.gov/emeu/cabs/Russia/Oil_exports.html

37. Sergei Blagov, "Russia Ups Oil Exports to China by Rail," Jamestown Foundation, http://www.jamestown.org/edm/article.php?article_id=2371314

38. Ibid.

39. Lucian Kim, "Russia Agrees to $25 Billion Oil-for-Loans Deal With China," 17 February 2009, Bloomberg press.

40. For example, if a crisis over Taiwan were to lead to an oil embargo, or perhaps even a naval blockade of the Malacca Strait, oil transported overland from Siberia would be one of the PRC's only remaining secure sources. See Bruce A. Elleman, *Waves of Hope: The U.S. Navy's Response to the Tsunami in Northern Indonesia.* Newport Paper 28 (Newport, RI: Naval War College Press, 2007), 104–5.

41. In 2002, President Vladimir Putin warned, "If people here [Far East] will not regenerate their region and economy, they will all speak the Asian language." Frederick W. Stakelbeck, Jr., "China's manifest destiny," *American Thinker,* 1 June 2005, http://www.americanthinker.com/2005/06/chinas_manifest_destiny.html

Selected Bibliography

Anderson, Benedict, *Imagined Communities* (New York: Verso, 1991).

Andō Hikotarō, (ed.), *Mantetsu: Nihon teikokushugi to Chūgoku*, (Waseda study group, Tokyo: Ochanomizu shobō, 1965).

Andō Yoshio, (ed.), *Nihon keizai seisaku shiron, II* (Tokyo: Tokyo daigaku shuppankai, 1976).

Anon, *Investment Values of Chinese Railway Bonds* (Paris: La Librarie Française, 1923).

Arnold, Julean, *China: A Commercial and Industrial Handbook* (Washington, D.C., 1952).

Baker, John Earl, *Chinese Railway Accounts* (Peking: Commission on the Unification of Railway Accounts, 1923).

Bannō Junji, *Kindai Nihon no gaikō to seiji* (Tokyo: Kenbun shuppan, 1985).

Barnhart, Michael A., *Japan Prepares for Total War* (Ithaca: Cornell University Press, 1987).

Benson, Lee, *Merchants, Farmers and Railroads: Railroad Regulation and New York Politics, 1850–1887* (New York: Russell and Russell, 1969).

Betts, Raymond, *Uncertain Dimensions: Western Overseas Empires in the Twentieth Century* (Minneapolis: University of Minnesota Press, 1985).

Beveridge, Albert J., *The Russian Advance* (New York: Harper and Brothers, 1904).

Buck, David D., *Urban Change in China: Politics and Development in Tsinan, Shantung, 1890–1949* (Madison: University of Wisconsin Press, 1978).

Carr, E.H., *The Russian Revolution from Lenin to Stalin, 1917–1929* (London, 1979).

Chandler, Alfred D. Jr., and Daems, Herman, (eds), *Managerial Hierarchies: Comparative Perspectives on the Rise of the Modern Industrial Enterprise* (Cambridge: Harvard University Press, 1980).

————, *The Visible Hand: The Managerial Revolution in American Business* (Cambridge: Belknap Press, 1977).

Chang, Chung-li, *The Income of the Chinese Gentry* (Seattle, 1962).

Changchun defang shizhi bianzuan weiyuanhui, (ed.), *Changchun dangshi ziliao* (Materials on Changchun Party History), 1 (Changchun: n.p., 1987).

Chen Hui, *Zhong-guo tie-lu wen-ti* (China's Railroad Problems) (Shanghai, 1936).

Chen Yun, *Chen Yun wenxuan (1926–1949)* (Chen Yun: selected writings, 1926–1949) (Beijing: Renmin chubanshe, 1984).

Cheng Lin, *The Chinese Railways: A Historical Survey* (Shanghai: China United Press, 1935).

China White Paper, The, August 1949 (Stanford: Stanford University, 1967).

Chinese Academy of Social Sciences and Central Archive, (ed.), *Zhonghua renmin gongheguo jingji dangan ziliao xuanbian, 1953–1957 (Economical Reference material Collections of People's Republic of China,1953–1957)* (Beijing: Chinese Price Publishing House, 1998).

Chinese Eastern Railway Printing Office, *North Manchuria and the Chinese Eastern Railway* (Reprint of an original volume published in English in Harbin, 1924) (New York: Garland Publishing, 1982).

Chinese Institute of International Relations, (ed.), *Xiandai guoji guanxishi cankao ziliao* (Reference Materials Relating to Modern International Relations), Vol. 1: *1950–1953* (Beijing: People's Education Press, 1960).

Christopher, J.W., *Conflict in the Far East: American Diplomacy in China from 1928–1933* (New York, 1970).

Coble, Parks, *Chinese Capitalists in Japan's New Order: The Occupied Lower Yangzi, 1937–1945.* (Berkeley: University of California Press, 2003).

Cordonnier, E.L.V., *The Japanese in Manchuria 1904*, trans. Capt. C.F. Atkinson Vol. 1 (London: Hugh Rees, 1912).

David, Clarence B., and Wilburn, Kenneth E. Jr., (eds.), *Railway Imperialism* (New York: Greenwood Press, 1991).

De Siebert, Benno Aleksandrovich, and Schreiner, George Abel, (eds.), *Entente Diplomacy and the World* (New York, Knickerbocker Press, 1921).

Degras, Jane, *Soviet Documents on Foreign Policy* (New York: Oxford University Press, 1952).

Department of State, *Papers Relating to the Foreign Relations of the United States*, 1929, Vol. II (Washington: Government Printing Office, 1943).

Dushen'kin, V., *ot soldata do marshala* (Moscow: 1964).

Duus, Peter, Myers, Ramon H., and Peattie, Mark R., (eds.), *The Japanese Informal Empire in China, 1895–1937* (Princeton, NJ: Princeton University Press, 1989).

Elleman, Bruce A., *Modern Chinese Warfare, 1795–1989* (London: Routledge, 2001).

————, *Wilson and China: A Revised History of the 1919 Shandong Question* (Armonk, New York: M.E. Sharpe, 2002).

————, and Paine, S.C.M., eds., *Naval Blockades and Seapower: Strategies and Counter-strategies, 1805–2005* (London: Routledge, 2006).

————, and Paine, S.C.M., eds., *Naval Coalition Warfare: From the Napoleonic War to Operation Iraqi Freedom* (London: Routledge, 2008).

————, *Moscow and the Emergence of Communist Power in China, 1925–30: The Nanchang Uprising and the Birth of the Red Army* (London: Routledge Press, 2009).

Elman, Benjamin, *From Philosophy to Philology: Intellectual and Social Aspects of Change in Late Imperial China* (Cambridge: Harvard University Press, 1984).

————, *On Their Own Terms: Science in China*, 1550–1900, (Cambridge: Harvard University Press, 2005).

Ericson, Steven J., *The Sound of the Whistle: Railroads and the State in Meiji Japan* (Cambridge: Harvard, 1996).

Esherick, Joseph W., *The Origins of the Boxer Uprising* (Berkeley: University of California Press, 1987).
————, *Reform and Revolution in China: The 1911 Revolution in Hunan and Hubei* (Berkeley: University of California Press, 1976).
Floud, Roderick, and Johnson, Paul, (eds.) *The Cambridge History of Modern Britain: Industrialisation, 1700–1860* (Cambridge: Cambridge University Press, 2004).
Fogel, Joshua (trans.) *Life Along the South Manchurian Railway: The Memoirs of Itō Takeo* (Armonk: M.E. Sharpe, 1988).
————, *The Cultural Dimension of Sino-Japanese Relations: Essays on the Nineteenth and Twentieth Centuries* (Armonk: M.E. Sharpe, 1995).
Fogel, Robert W., *Railroads and American Economic Growth: Essays in Econometric History* (Baltimore, Johns Hopkins Press, 1964).
Fuller, William C., *Civil-Military Conflict in Imperial Russia 1881–1914* (Princeton: Princeton University Press, 1985).
————, *Strategy and Power in Russia 1600–1914* (New York: The Free Press, 1992).
Gaimushō, *Nihon gaikō nenpyō narabini shuyō bunsho, I* (2 vols., Tokyo: Hara shobō, 1965–66).
Gall, Lothar, and Pohl, Manfred, (ed.), *Die Eisenbahn in Deutschland* (Munchen: Beck, 1999).
Gatrell, Peter, *Government, Industry and Rearmament in Russia, 1900–1914: The Last Argument of Tsarism* (Cambridge: Cambridge University Press, 1994).
Gerschenkron, Alexander, *Economic Backwardness in Historical Perspectives: A Book of Essays* (Cambridge, MA, 1962).
Geyer, Dietrich, *Russian Imperialism*, Bruce Little, trans. (New Haven: Yale University Press, 1987).
Gladney, Dru C., *Dislocating China: Reflections on Muslims, Minorities, and Other Subaltern Subjects* (Chicago: The University of Chicago Press, 2004).
Glass, James G.H., *Report on the Concessions of the Pekin Syndicate, Limited, in the Provinces of Shansi and Honan, China, with Estimates of Cost of Railways and Other Works Necessary for Their Development* (London: n.p., 1899).
Glinka, G.V., (ed.), *Atlas Aziatskoi Rossii* (Atlas of Asiatic Russia) (St. Petersburg: Izdanie Pereselencheskogo upravleniia, 1914).
————, *Aziatskaia Rossiia* (Asiatic Russia), Vol. 2 (1914. Reprint. Cambridge, MA: Oriental Research Partners, 1974).
Gottschang, Thomas, and Lary, Diana, *Swallows and Settlers: The Great Migration from North China to Manchuria* (Ann Arbor: Center for Chinese Studies, University of Michigan, 2000).
Gourvish, T.R., *Railways and the British Economy, 1830–1914* (London: Macmillan, 1980).
Great Britain, Naval Intelligence Division, *China Proper, Vol. III, Economic Geography, Ports and Communications* (London, 1945).
Gregory, Paul R., *Russian National Income 1885–1913* (Cambridge: Cambridge University Press, 1982).

Gurko, Vladimir Iosifivich, *Features and Figures of the Past,* J.E. Wallace Sterling, et. al, eds. Laura Matveev, trans. (Stanford: Stanford University Press, 1939).

Han Suyin, *Destination Chungking* (Boston: Little, Brown and Company, 1942).

Harada Katsumasa, *Mantetsu* (Tokyo: Iwanami shoten, 1981).

Headrick, Daniel, *The Tools of Empire: Technology and European Imperialism in the Nineteenth Century* (New York: Oxford University Press, 1981).

Henzig, D., *The Soviet Union and communist China 1945–1950: The arduous road to the alliance* (Armonk: M.E. Sharpe, 2004).

Holborn, Hajo, *A History of Modern Germany, 1840–1945* (Princeton: Princeton University Press, 1969).

Hoshino Tokuji, *Economic History of Manchuria* (Seoul: Bank of Chōsen, 1920).

Hou Chi-ming, *Foreign Investment and Economic Development in China 1840–1937* (Cambridge: Harvard University Press, 1965).

Hsu Shuhsi, *China and Her Political Entity* (New York: Oxford University Press, 1926).

Hsu, Immanuel Chung-yueh, *The Rise of Modern China,* 3rd. ed. (Hong Kong: Oxford University Press, 1983).

Hsu, Mongton Chih, *Railway Problems in China,* (New York: Columbia University, 1915).

Huang Yan and Wang Taofu, (eds.), *Qing ji wai jiao shi liao* (Historical materials on international relations from the Qing period) (1932, Reprint; Peking: Shu mu wen xian chu ban she, 1987).

Huang Yifeng, *Tielu zhiye zhidao* (Shanghai: Shangwu yinshuguan, 1936).

Huenemann, Ralph W., *The Economic Development of Manchuria in the First Half of the Twentieth Century* (Cambridge, MA: Harvard University Press, 1969).

————, *The Dragon and the Iron Horse: The Economics of Railroads in China, 1876–1937* (Cambridge, MA: Harvard University Press, 1984).

Hummel, Arthur W., (ed.), *Eminent Chinese of the Ch'ing Period (1644–1912)* (1943. Reprint. Taipei: Ch'eng Wen Publishing Co., 1970).

Hunt, Michael, *Frontier Defense and the Open Door* (New Haven, CT: Yale University Press, 1973).

Inoue Yūichi, *Higashi Ajia tetsudō kokusai kankei shi* (Tokyo: Keiō tsūshin, 1991).

Jelavich, Charles and Barbara, (eds.), *Russia in the Far East 1876–1880* (Leiden: E.J. Brill, 1959).

Jianguo yilai maozedong wen gao, diyice (Mao Zedong's Manuscripts Since the founding of the PRC), Vol. 1 (Beijing: Central Literature Publishing, 1987).

Jiao-tong tie-dao bu Jiao-tong shi bian-zhuan wei-yuan-hui, (ed.), *Jiao-tong shi lu-zheng pian* (A History of Communication) (Nanjing, 1935).

Jiao-tong tie-dao bu jiao-tong shi bian-zhuan wei-yuan-hui, (ed.), *Jiao-tong shi zong-wu pian* (A History of Communication, General Affairs Section) (Nanjing, 1935).

Jiaotong tiedaobu, *Jiaotong shi luzheng bian,* Vol. 1 (n.p., 1935).

Jin Jiafeng (ed.), *Zhongguo jiaotong zhi fazhan ji qi quxiang* (Nanjing: Zhongzhong shuju, 1937).

Jin Shixuan, *Tie-lu yun-shu xue* (Railroad Transportation) (Chengdu, 1945).

Jinan tieluju shizhi biancuan lingdao xiaozu, *Jinan tieluju zhi, 1899–1985* (Jinan: Shandong youyi chubanshe, 1993).

Johnson, Arthur, and Supple, Barry, *Boston Capitalists and Western Railroads* (Cambridge: Harvard University Press, 1967).

Johnson, Chalmers, *MITI and the Japanese Miracle* (Stanford: Stanford University Press, 1981).

Junshi weiyanhui junlingbu diyiting disanchu, *Pohuai gong (tie) lu banfa,* (Junshi weiyanhui junlingbu diyiting disanchu, 1939).

Kadono Choryuro, *Development of Railways in Manchuria* (Tokyo: Japanese Council, Institute of Pacific Relations, 1936).

Kaneko Fumio, *Kindai Nihon ni okeru tai-Man tōshi no kenkyū* (Tokyo: Kondō shuppansha, 1991).

Kantō totokufu minseibu, *Manshū sangyō chōsa shiryō*, 8 unnumbered volumes, volume on commerce and manufacturing (Tokyo: Kokkōsha, 1906).

Ke Lan, *Kong Fu de zuihou yi dai* (n.p., 1999).

Kent, Percy Horace, *Railway Enterprise in China: An Account of Its Origin and Development* (London: E. Arnold, 1907).

Kerr, Austin, *Railroad Politics, 1914–1920: Rates, Wages and Efficiency* (Pittsburgh: University of Pittsburgh Press, 1968).

Khrushchev, Nikita, *Khrushchev Remembers* (London: Andre Deutsch, 1974).

————, and Khrushchev, Sergei, *Memoirs of Nikita Khrushchev: Statesman, 1953–1964* (University Park, PA: Pennsylvania State Press, 2007).

King, F.H.H., (ed.), *Eastern Banking: Essays in the History of the Hongkong and Shanghai Banking Corporation* (London: The Athlone Press, 1983).

Kingman, H.L., *Effects of Chinese Nationalism upon Manchurian Railway Developments, 1925–1931* (Berkeley: 1932).

Kitaoka Shin'ichi, *Nihon rikugun to tairiku seisaku* (Tokyo: Tokyō daigaku shuppankai, 1978).

Kobayashi Hideo, (ed.), *Kindai Nihon to Mantetsu* (Tokyo: Yoshikawa kōbunkan, 2000).

Kobayashi Tatsuo and Shimada Toshihiko, (eds.), *Gendai shi shiryō 7: Manshū jihen* (Tokyo: Misuzu shobō, 1964).

Kokovtsov, Vladimir Nikolaevich, *Out of My Past: The Memoirs of Count Kokovtsov,* ed. H. H. Fisher, trans. Laura Matveev, (Stanford: Stanford University Press, 1935).

Köll, Elisabeth, *From Cotton Mill to Business Empire: The Emergence of Regional Enterprise in Modern China* (Cambridge: Harvard University Asia Center, 2003).

Kong Demao and Kong Kelan, *The House of Confucius* (London: Hodder and Stoughton, 1988).

Kotkin, Stephen, and Elleman, Bruce A., (eds.), *Mongolia in the Twentieth Century: Landlocked Cosmopolitan* (Armonk: M.E. Sharpe, 1999).

Krotkov, N.N., *Russkaia manufaktura i eia konkurenty na kitaiskom rynke* (Russian manufactures and their competition on the Chinese market) Ministerstva torgovli i promyshlenosti, otdel torgovli (Ministry of Trade and Production, Department of Trade) (St. Petersburg: Tipografiia V.F. Kirshbauma, 1914).

Kulagin, V.M., and Iakovlev, N.N., *Podvig Osoboi Dal'nevostochnoi* (Moscow: 1970).

Kurihara Ken, (ed.), *Tai-Manmō seisaku shi no ichimen* (Tokyo: Hara shobō, 1967).

Kuropatkin, Aleksei Nikolaevich, *The Russian Army and the Japanese War*, A.B. Lindsay, trans., W.D. Swinton, ed., Vol. 1 (New York: E.P. Dutton and Company, 1909).

————, *Dnevnik A.N. Kuropatkina* (Diary of A.N. Kuropatkin) (Moscow: Nizhpoligraf, 1923).

La Fargue, Thomas E., *China's First Hundred* (Pullman, 1942).

Langer, William L., *The Diplomacy of Imperialism 1890–1902*, 2nd ed. (New York: Alfred A. Knopf, 1956).

Lary, Diana, and Vogel, Ezra, (eds.), *China at War: Regions of China, 1937–1945* (Stanford: Stanford University Press, 2007).

Lattimore, Owen, *Inner Asian Frontiers of China* (New York: American Geographical Society, 1940).

Lee En-Han, *China's Quest for Railroad Autonomy, 1904–1911: A Study of the Chinese Railway-rights Recovery Movement* (Singapore: Singapore University Press, 1977).

Lensen, George Alexander, (ed.), *Revelations of a Russian Diplomat: The Memoirs of Dmitri I. Abrikossov* (Seattle, WA: University of Washington Press, 1965).

————, *Korea and Manchuria between Russia and Japan 1895–1904* (Tallahassee, FL: The Diplomatic Press, 1966).

————, *The Russo-Chinese War* (Tallahassee, FL: The Diplomatic Press, 1967).

————, *The Strange Neutrality: Soviet-Japanese Relations during the Second World War, 1941–1945* (Tallahassee, FL: The Diplomatic Press, 1972).

————, *The Damned Inheritance: The Soviet Union and the Manchurian Crisis, 1924–1935* (Tallahassee, FL: The Diplomatic Press, 1974).

————, *Balance of Intrigue,* Vol. 2 (Tallahassee, FL: University Presses of Florida, 1982).

Leong Sow-theng, *Sino-Soviet Diplomatic Relation, 1917–1926* (Canberra: Australian National University Press, 1976).

Leung, Chi-Keung, *Railway Patterns and National Goals* (Chicago: University of Chicago, 1980).

Levine, Steven I., *Anvil of Victory: The Communist Revolution in Manchuria, 1945–1948* (New York: Columbia University Press, 1987).

Liang, Ernest P., *China: Railways and Agricultural Development, 1875–1935,* (Chicago: University of Chicago, 1982).

Licht, Walter, *Working for the Railroad* (Princeton: Princeton University Press, 1983).

Lieven, Dominic C.B., *Russia and the Origins of the First World War* (New York: St. Martin's Press, 1983).

Ling, H.H., *Long-hai Yue-han Xiang-gui zhu lu hui-yi* (Reminiscences on the Building of the Long-hai, Yue-han and Xiang-gui Railroads) (Taibei, 1953).

————, *Zhong-guo tie-lu zhi* (A History of Chinese Railroads) (Taibei, 1954).

————, (ed.), *Zhan Tian-you xian-sheng nian-pu* (A Chronological Biography of Chan T'ien-yow) (Taibei, 1961).

————, and Gao Zonglu, (eds.), *Zhan Tianyou yu zhong-guo tie-lu* (Chan T'ien-yow and the Chinese Railroad) (Taibei, 1977).

Liu Tong, *Dongbei jiefang zhanzheng jishi* (Record of events of the war of liberation in the northeast) (Beijing: Dongfang chubanshe, 1997).

Low, Alfred D., *The Sino-Soviet Dispute* (London: Associated University Presses, 1976).

Lü Weijun, *Shandong quyu xiandaihua yanjiu, 1840–1949* (Jinan: Jilu shushe, 2002).

Luo Tengxiao, *Jinan daguan* (The Grand Sights of Jinan) (Jinan: Jinan daguan chubanshe, 1934).

Ma Jianzhong, *Shi-ke zhai ji-yan ji-xing* (Ma Jianzhong's Essays).

MacFarquhar, Roderick, and Fairbank, John K., eds., *The Cambridge History of China:* Volume 14, *The People's Republic, Part 1: The Emergence of Revolutionary China, 1949–1965* (New York: Cambridge University Press, 1987).

————, eds., *The Cambridge History of China:* Volume 14, *The People's Republic, Part 2: Revolutions within the Chinese Revolution, 1966–1982* (New York: Cambridge University Press, 1991).

MacMurray, John V.A., (comp.), *Treaties and Agreements with and concerning China 1894–1919,* Vol. 1 (New York: Oxford University Press, 1921).

Malozemoff, Andrew, *Russia Far Eastern Policy 1881–1904* (1958. Reprint. New York: Octagon Books, 1977).

Marks, Steven G., *Road to Power* (Ithaca: Cornell University Press, 1991).

Matsumoto Toshirō, *Shinryaku to kaihatsu: Nihon shihonshugi to Chūgoku shokuminchika* (Tokyo: Ochanomizu shobō, 1988).

Matsuoka Yōsuke denki kankō kai, *Matsuoka Yōsuke–sono hito to shōgai* (Tokyo: Kōzasha, 1974).

Matsuoka Yōsuke, *Ugoku Manmō* (Tokyo: Senshinsha, 1931).

Matsusaka, Y. Tak, *The Making of Japanese Manchuria, 1904–1932* (Cambridge, MA: Harvard Asia Center, 2001).

McCormack, Gavan, *Chang Tso-lin in Northeast China, 1911–1928* (Stanford: Stanford University Press, 1977).

McDonald, David MacLaren, *United Government and Foreign Policy in Russia, 1900–1914* (Cambridge, MA: Harvard University Press, 1992).

Menning, Bruce W., *Bayonets before Bullets* (Bloomington: Indiana University Press, 1992).

Mercer, Lloyd J., *Railroads and Land Grant Policy: A Study in Government Intervention* (New York: Academic Press, 1982).

Metzger, A, *The Internal Organization of Ch'ing Bureaucracy: Legal, Normative, and Communication Aspects* (Cambridge: Harvard University Press, 1973).

Mi Rucheng, *Di-guo zhu-yi yu Zhong-guo tie-lu (1847–1949)* (Imperialism and the Chinese Railroads) (Shanghai, 1980).

Minami Manshū tetsudō kabushikigaisha chōsaka (Kudō Takeo), *Waga kuni jinkō mondai to Manmō* (Dairen: SMR, 1928).

Minami Manshū tetsudō kabushikigaisha chōsaka (Nonaka Tokio), *Manmō yori nani o kitai subeki ka* (Dairen: SMR, 1924, 1929, 1930).

Minami Manshū tetsudō kabushikigaisha chōsaka (Ueda Kenzo), *Ryōga no sui'un* (Dairen: SMR, 1911).

Minami Manshū tetsudō kabushikigaisha, *Dai 8 kai eigyō hōkokusho* (annual stockholder report for 1910, reprints, Tokyo: Ryūkei shoseki, 1977).

Minami Manshū tetsudō kabushikigaisha, *Minami Manshū tetsudō kabushikigaisha 10 nen shi* (Dairen: Manshū nichinichi shinbunsha, 1919, abbreviated hereafter as SMR I).

Minami Manshū tetsudō kabushikigaisha-keizai chōsakai, *Manshū keizai tōsei hōsaku* (Dairen: SMR, 1935).

Mommsen, Wolfgang, (ed.), *Imperialism and After: Continuities and Discontinuities* (Boston: Allen and Unwin, 1986).

Morris, Ray, *Railroad Administration* (New York, 1930).

Morse, Hosea Ballou, *International Relations of the Chinese Empire,* Vol. 3 (Shanghai: Kelly and Walsh, Ltd., 1918).

Nagao Sakurō, *Shokuminchi tetsudō no sekai keizaiteki oyobi sekai seisakuteki kenkyū* (Tokyo: Nihon hyōronsha, 1930).

Nagura Bunji, *Nihon tekkōgyō shi no kenkyū* (Tokyo: Kondō shuppansha, 1984).

Natsume Sōseki, *Meiji hoppō chōsa tanken ki shūsei 10* (Tokyo: Yumani shobō, 1989).

Nish, Ian, *Origins of the Russo-Japanese War* (New York: Longman, 1985).

Nishimura Shigeo, *Chūgoku kindai tōhoku chiiki shi kenkyū* (Tokyo: Hōritsu bunkasha, 1984).

————, *Chō Gakurō* (Tokyo: Iwanami Shoten, 1996).

Ogata, Sadako, *Defiance in Manchuria: The Making of Japanese Foreign Policy, 1931–1932* (Berkeley: University of California Press, 1964).

Olivier, Bernard Vincent, *The Implementation of China's Nationality Policy in the Northeastern Provinces* (San Francisco: Mellen Research University Press, 1993).

Paine, S.C.M., *Imperial Rivals: China, Russia, and Their Disputed Frontier* (Armonk, NY: M.E. Sharpe, 1996).

————, *The Sino-Japanese War of 1894 to 1895* (New York: Cambridge University Press, 2003).

Parsons, William Barclay, *Report on the Survey and Prospects of a Railway between Hankow and Canton* (New York, 1899).

Patrikeeff, Felix, *Russian Politics in Exile: The Northeast Asian Balance of Power, 1924–1931* (Houndmills: Palgrave Macmillan, 2002).

————, and Shukman, Harold Shukman, *Railways and the Russo-Japanese War: Transporting War* (London: Routledge, 2007).

Peattie, Mark R., *Ishiwara Kanji and Japan's Confrontation with the West* (Princeton: Princeton University Press, 1975).

Pei Jianzhang, *Zhonghua renmin gongheguo waijiaoshi* (The Diplomatic History of the People's Republic of China) (Beijing: the World Knowledge Publishing House, 1994).

Perry, Elizabeth J., *Shanghai on Strike: The Politics of Chinese Labor* (Stanford: Stanford University Press, 1993).

Pomeranz, Kenneth, *The Making of a Hinterland: State, Society, and Economy in Inland North China, 1853–1937* (Berkeley: University of California Press, 1993).

Pratt, Edwin A., *The Rise of Rail-Power in War and Conquest, 1833–1914* (Philadelphia: J.P. Lippincott Co., 1916).

Price, Ernest Batson, *The Russo-Japanese Treaties of 1907–1916* (1933, Reprint; New York: AMS Press, 1971).

Pye, Lucian W., *China: An Introduction*. Third Edition (Boston: Little, Brown and Company, 1984).

Qingdao shubi gummin seibu tetsudobu. *Qingdao shubi gummin seibu tetsudo chosa shiryo,* Vol. 25: JinPu tetsudo chosa hokokusho, Taisho 8 (Qingdao: Qingdao shubi gummin seibu tetsudobu, 1919).

Quested, Rosemary, *The Russo-Chinese Bank* (Birmingham: Department of Russian Language and Literature, University of Birmingham: 1977).

————, *"Matey" Imperialists?: The Tsarist Russians in Manchurian 1895–1917.* (Hong Kong: University of Hong Kong Press, 1982).

Rawski, Thomas, *Economic Growth in Prewar China* (Berkeley: University of California Press, 1989).

Reardon, Lawrence C., *The Reluctant Dragon: Crisis Cycles in Chinese Foreign Economic Policy* (Seattle: University of Washington Press, 2002).

Remer, C.F., (ed.), *Reading in Economics for China* (Shanghai, 1933).

Romanov, B.A., *Russia in Manchuria (1892–1906)*, Susan Wilbur Jones, trans. (Ann Arbor, MI: American Council of Learned Societies, 1952).

Rosen, Roman Romanovich, *Forty Years of Diplomacy*, Vol. 1 (New York: Alfred A. Knopf, 1922).

Rozman, Gilbert, (ed.), *The Modernization of China* (New York, 1981).

Saich, Tony, *The Origins of the First United Front in China: The Role of Sneevliet (Alias Maring),* (Leiden, 1991).

Sanbō honbu [Army General Staff], *Tetsudō ron* (1888), reproduced in *Sanbō honbu tetsudō ronshū,* ed. Noda Masaho, Harada Katsumasa, Aoki Eiichi, Oikawa Yoshinobu (Tokyo: Nihon keizai hyōronsha, 1988).

————, *Man-Kan kōtsū kikan jūbi kansei no kyūmu* (Miyazaki Collection, item 23, [Japan] National Defense Research Institute Library).

————, *Meiji 40 nendo Nihon teikoku rikugun sakusen keikaku* (March, 1907 [Japan] National Defense Research Institute Library).

Seton-Watson, Hugh, *The Russian Empire 1801–1917* (Oxford: The Clarendon Press, 1967).

Shandong dang'anguan, Shandong shehui kexueyuan lishi yanjiusuo (ed.), *Shandong geming lishi dang'an ziliao xuanbian* (Collection of archival materials on the revolutionary history of Shandong), Vol. 1 (1923–28) (Jinan: Shandong renmin chubanshe, 1984–87).

Shandong sheng defang shizhi bianzuan weiyuan hui, *Shandong sheng zhi tieluzhi* (Jinan: Shandong Renmin Chubanshe, 1993).

Shandong sheng zonggonghui, *Shandong gongren yundongshi* (Jinan: Shandong renmin chubanshe, 1988).

Shanghai Jiaotong daxue, *Jiaotong daxue 40 zhou jiniankan* (Memorial Volume for the 40th Anniversary of Jiaotong University) (Shanghai: n.p., 1936).

Sheng Zhihua and Li Danhui, *Research on a number of issues about postwar Sino-Soviet relations* (Beijing: the People's Publishing House, 2006).

Shi Zhe, *Zai lishi juren shenbian* (*Together with the Giant of the history*) (Beijing: the Central Literature Publishing House, 1995, 2nd edition).

Shih, K.T., (ed.), *The Strenuous Decade: China's Nation-Building Efforts, 1927–1937* (New York, 1970).

Shimada Toshihiko, *Kantōgun* (Tokyo: Chūōkōronsha, 1965).

Sladkovskii, M.I., *History of Economic Relations between Russia and China*, M. Roublev, trans. (Jerusalem: Israel Publications for Scientific Translations, 1966).

————, *Istoriia torgovo-ekonomicheshikh otnoshenii narodov Rossii s Kitaem* (The history of trade and economic relations between the peoples of Russia and China) (Moscow: Izdatel'stvo "Nauka," 1974).

Smith, Canfield F., *Vladivostok under Red and White Rule* (Seattle: University of Washington Press, 1975).

SMR, *Honpō seitekkō saku jūritsu to Minami Manshū* (Dairen: SMR, 1924).

Solovev, Iurii Iakovlevich, *Dvadtsat' piat' let moei diplomaticheskoi slyzhboi (1893–1918)* (Twenty-five years of my diplomatic service [1893–1918]) (Moscow: Gosudarstvennoe izdatel'stvo, 1928).

Sovetsko-Kitaiskii konflikt 1929 g.: Sbornik dokumentov (Moscow: 1930).

Sovetsko-kitayskie otnosheniya, 1917–1957, sbornik dokumentov (Soviet-Chinese relations, 1917–1957, collection of documents) (Moscow: Izd-vovo stochnoy literatury, 1959).

Su Chungmin, *Mantie shi* (Beijing: Zhonghua shuqu, 1990).

Sumner, B. H., *Tsardom and Imperialism in the Far East and Middle East, 1880–1914* (1940; reprint, Archon Books, 1968).

Sun, E-tu Zen, *Chinese Railways and British Interests, 1898–1911* (New York: King's Crown Press, 1954).

Suzuki Takashi, *Nihon teikokushugi to Manshū, I* (2 vols., Tokyo: Hanawa shobō, 1992).

Tan, Chester C., *The Boxer Catastrophe* (New York: Columbia University Press, 1967).

Tang Yilu, (ed.), *Zhongguo renmin jiefangjun quanguo jiefang zhanzhengshi* (History of the Chinese People's Liberation Army's war of national liberation), Vol. 1. (Beijing: Junshi kexue chubanshe, 1993).

Tang, Peter S.H., *Russian and Soviet Policy in Manchuria and Outer Mongolia 1911–1930* (Durham, NC: Duke University Press, 1959).

Tedsudosho. Shanhai benjisho (ed.), *Tetsudobu seiritsugo no Shina tetsudo* (China's Railroads Following the Establishment of the Ministry of Railroads) (Shanghai, 1935).

Tetsudōin kantokukyoku, *Mantetsu shisatsu hōkokusho* (1913, No publication data, University of Tokyo Social Science Institute Library).

Tie-dao bu, (comp.), *Tie-dao nian-jian* (The Railway Yearbook) (Nanjing, 1934).

Tiedaobu yewusi laogongke, *Gongren renshu ji gongzi tongji* (n.p., 1931).

Tielu yuekan: JinPu xian (Nanjing, 1932–34).

Tielu zazhi (Nanjing: Guomin zhengfu tiedaobu mishuting yanjiushi, 1935).

Toa Dobunkai, *Shina shobetsu zenshi*, Vol. 4 (Shandong, 1918).

Treadgold, Donald W., *The Great Siberian Migration* (Princeton: Princeton University Press, 1957).

Tsao Lien-en, *The CER: An Analytical Study* (Shanghai, 1930).

Tsunoda Jun, *Manshū mondai to kokubō hōshin* (Tokyo: Hara shobō, 1967).

Tsurumi Yūsuke, *Gotō Shinpei, II* (4 vols., original, 1942, Tokyo: Keisō shobō, 1965).

Van Slyke, Lyman P., (ed.), *Marshall's Mission to China December 1945–January 1947: the Report and Appended Documents* Vol. II, "Appended Documents." (Arlington, VA: University Publications of America, 1976).

Vespa, Amleto, *Secret Agent for Japan: A Handbook to Japanese Imperialism* (London: V. Gollancz Ltd., 1938).

Vilenskii, Vladimir, *Kitaia I Sovietskaia Rossia* (China and Soviet Russia) (Moscow: Moscow: Gos. Izd-vo. 1919).

Vucinich, Wayne S., (ed.), *Russia and Asia,* Hoover Institution Publications 107 (Stanford: Hoover Institution Press, 1972).

Wang Chaoguang, *Zhonghua minguo shi di sanbian di wu juan: cong kangzhan shengli dao neizhan baofa qianhou* (History of the Republic of China, volume 3, part 5: from the victory of the war of resistance to the outbreak of civil war) (Beijing: Zhonghua shuju, 2000).

Wang Dongxin, *WangDongXin RiJi* (Wang Dongxin's Diary) (Beijing: China Social Sciences Publishing House, 1993).

Wang Guizhong, *Zhang Xueliang yu dong-bei tie-lu jian-she* (Zhang Xueliang and Railroad Construction in Manchuria) (Hong Kong, 1996).

Warner, Denis, and Warner, Peggy, *The Tide at Sunrise* (London: Angus and Robertson, 1974).

Weale, B.L. Putnam, *Manchu and Muscovite* (London: Macmillan and Co., Ltd., 1904).

Wei, Henry, *China and Soviet Russia* (Princeton NJ: D. Van Nostrand Company Inc., 1950).

Westad, Odd Arne, *Cold War and Revolution: Soviet-American Rivalry and the Origins of the Chinese Civil War* (New York: Columbia University Press, 1993).

Westwood, J.N., *A History of Russian Railways* (London: George Allen and Unwin, Ltd., 1964).

Whigham, H.J., *Manchuria and Korea,* (London: Isbister and Co., Ltd., 1904).

White, John Albert, *The Diplomacy of the Russo-Japanese War* (Princeton: Princeton University Press, 1964).

Whiting, Allen, *Soviet Policies in China, 1917–1924* (New York, 1954).

Whitson, William W., *The Chinese High Command: A History of Communist Military Politics, 1927–71* (New York: Praeger Publishers, 1973).

Willoughby, W.W., *Foreign Rights and Interests in China* (Baltimore: Johns Hopkins Press, 1920).

Witte, Sergei Iul'evich, *The Memoirs of Count Witte,* Abraham Yarmolinsky, trans. and ed. (Garden City: Doubleday, Page and Co., 1921).

————, *The Memoirs of Count Witte*, Sidney Harcave, trans. and ed. (Armonk, NY: M.E. Sharpe, Inc., 1990).

Wou, Odoric, *Mobilizing the Masses: Building Revolution in Henan* (Stanford: Stanford University Press, 1994).

Wu Xiangxiang and Liu Shaotang, *Lu an shanhou yuebao tekan: tielu* (n.p., 1923).

Xie Xueshi, *Mantie yu zhongguo laogong* (Beijing: Shehui kexue wenxian chubanshe, 2003).

Yamamoto Jirō (ed.), *Terauchi Masatake kankei monjo* (Kyoto: Kyoto joshi daigaku, 1984).

Yang Yonggang, *Zhongguo jindai tielu shi* (The history of modern railroads in China) (Shanghai: Shanghai shudian chubanshe, 1997).

Yonekura, Seiichirō, *The Japanese Iron and Steel Industry* (New York: St. Martin's Press, 1994).

Young, C. Walter, *Japanese Jurisdiction in the South Manchuria Railway Areas* (Baltimore, Johns Hopkins, 1931).

Young, Louise, *Japan's Total Empire: Manchuria and the Culture of Wartime Imperialism* (Berkeley: University of California Press, 1997).

Yu Chengzhi, (ed.), *Xia-an hui-gao* (Ye Gongchuo's Essays) (n.p., 1930).

Zhai Weijia and Cao Hong, (eds.), *Zhongguo xiongshi disi yezhanjun* (China's great armies: the Fourth Field Army) (Beijing: Zhonggong dangshi chubanshe, 2004).

Zhang Ruide [Chang Jui-te], *Ping-Han tielu yu Huabei de jingji fazhan (1905–1937)* (Zhonghua Minguo Taibei Shi Nan'gang: Zhong yang yan jiu yuan jin dai shi yan jiu suo, Minguo 76 [1987]).

————, *Zhongguo jindai tielu shiye guanli de yanjiu: zhengzhi cengmian de fenxi (1876–1937)* (Railroads in Modern China: Political Aspects of Railroad Administration, 1876–1937) (Taibei Shi Nan'gang: Zhongyang yan jiu yuan jin dai shi yan jiu suo, min guo 80 [1991]).

Zhang Runwu and Xue Li, *Tushuo Jinan lao jianzhu* (Jinan: Jinan chubanshe, 2001).

Zhang Yucai, (ed.), *Zhongguo tiedao jianshe shilue (1876–1949)* (A brief history of Chinese railway construction, 1876–1949) (Beijing: Zhongguo tiedao chubanshe, 1997).

Zhang Zanxin, Sun Shufan and Gao Yingjie, (eds.), *Changchun weikunzhan* (The siege of Changchun) (Changchun: Zhonggong Changchun shiwei dangshi yanjiushi, 1999).

Zhanhou diyiqi tiedao jihua (Post-war railroad reconstruction plan, first stage) (n.p., 1947).

Zhi Xia, *Tiedao youjidui* (Shanghai: Shanghai renmin chubanshe, 1977 [1954]).

Zhong-e Guanyu Zhongdonglu zhi Jiaoshe Shilüe (A History of Sino-Russian Negotiations on the Chinese Eastern Railway) (Zhongguo Guomindang Zhongyang Zhixing Weiyuanhui Xuanzhuan Buyin, 1929.11).

Zhonggong zhongyang dangshi ziliao zhengji weiyuanhui, Zhongguo renmin jiefangjun Liaoshen zhanyi jinianguan jianguan weiyuanhui, (ed.), *Liao-Shen juezhan* (The Liao-Shen Campaign), Vol. 1. (Beijing: Renmin chubanshe, 1988).

Zhonggong zhongyang wenxian yanjiushi, zhongyang dang'anguan Dang de wenxian bianjibu, (ed,), *Zhonggong dangshi fengyunlu* (Vivid moments of Chinese Communist Party history) (Beijing: Renmin chubanshe, 1990).

————, Zhonggong Nanjingshi weiyuan hui, (ed.), *Zhou Enlai yi jiu si liu nian tanpan wenxian* (Selected documents from Zhou Enlai's 1946 negotiations) (Beijing: Zhongyang wenxian chubanshe, 1996).

————, *Chen Yun nianpu: 1905–1994* (A chronology of Chen Yun's life: 1904–1994), volume 1 (Beijing: Zhongyang wenxian chubanshe, 2000).

————, Chen Yun yanjiuzu, (ed.), *Chen Yun yanjiu shuping* (Review of research on Chen Yun) (Beijing: Zhongyang wenxian chubanshe, 2004).

Zhong-guo gong-cheng shi xue-hui, (ed.), *San-shi nian lai zhi Zhong-guo gong-cheng* (Chinese Engineering in the Last Thirty Years) (Nanjing, 1946).

Zhongguo renmin jiefangjun disi yezhanjun zhanshi bianxiezu. *Zhongguo renmin jiefangjun disi yezhanjun zhanshi* (Chinese People's Liberation Army Fourth Field Army Battle History) (Beijing: Jiefangjun chubanshe, 1998).

Zhongguo renmin zhengzhi xieshang huiyi quanguo weiyuanhui wenshi ziliao yanjiu weiyuanhui "Liao-Shen zhanyi qinliji" bianshenzu, (ed.), *Liaoshen zhanyi qinliji: yuan Guomindang jiangling de huiyi* (Personal records of the Liao-Shen campaign: memories of former Guomindang generals) (Beijing: Wenshi ziliao chubanshe, 1985).

Zhonghua renmin gongheguo duiwaiguanxi wenjianji,dierji, 1951–1953(Documents of Foreign Relations of the People's Republic of China), Vol. 2, 1951–1953 (Beijing: World Knowledge Publishing House, 1958).

Zhongwai jiuyuezhang huibian (Collection of Old Treaties and agreements between China and foreign countries, Vol. III (Beijing: Sanlian Bookstore, 1962).

Zhongyang dang'anguan, (ed.), *Zhonggong zhongyang wenjian xuanji* (Selected documents of the Chinese Communist Party Central Committee) volume 15 (1945) (Beijing: Zhonggong zhongyang dangxiao chubanshe, 1991).

————, *Zhonggong zhongyang wenjian xuanji* volume 16 (1946–47) (Beijing: Zhonggong zhongyang dangxiao chubanshe, 1992).

Zhu Jianhua and Zhu Xingyi. *Guogong liangdang zhengduo dongbei jishi* (How the Communist and Nationalist parties fought for control of the northeast) (Changchun: Jilin renmin chubanshe, n.d.).

Zhuang Weimin, *Jindai Shandong shichang jingji de bianqian* (Beijing: Zhonghua shuju, 2000).

Index